NOT TALKING UNION

Not Talking Union

An Oral History of North American Mennonites and Labour

JANIS THIESSEN

McGill-Queen's University Press
Montreal & Kingston • London • Chicago

ISBN 978-0-7735-4752-0 (cloth)
ISBN 978-0-7735-4753-7 (paper)
ISBN 978-0-7735-9894-2 (ePDF)
ISBN 978-0-7735-9895-9 (ePUB)

Legal deposit second quarter 2016
Bibliothèque nationale du Québec

Printed in Canada on acid-free paper that is 100% ancient forest free (100% post-consumer recycled), processed chlorine free

This book has been published with the help of a grant from the Canadian Federation for the Humanities and Social Sciences, through the Awards to Scholarly Publications Program, using funds provided by the Social Sciences and Humanities Research Council of Canada. Publication has been supported by a grant from the University of Winnipeg.

McGill-Queen's University Press acknowledges the support of the Canada Council for the Arts for our publishing program. We also acknowledge the financial support of the Government of Canada through the Canada Book Fund for our publishing activities.

Library and Archives Canada Cataloguing in Publication

Thiessen, Janis, 1971–, author
Not talking union: an oral history of North American Mennonites and labour/Janis Thiessen.

Includes bibliographical references and index.
Issued in print and electronic formats.
ISBN 978-0-7735-4752-0 (cloth). – ISBN 978-0-7735-4753-7 (paper). – ISBN 978-0-7735-9894-2 (ePDF). – ISBN 978-0-7735-9895-9 (ePUB)

1. Labor unions – United States – Religious aspects – Mennonites. 2. Labor unions – Canada – Religious aspects – Mennonites. 3. Mennonites – United States – Attitudes. 4. Mennonites – Canada – Attitudes. 5. Labor unions – United States – History. 6. Labor unions – Canada – History. 7. Oral history – United States. 8. Oral history – Canada. I. Title.

BX8128.E36T557 2015 331.880971 C2015-908465-2
C2015-908466-0

This book was typeset by Interscript inc. in 10.5/13 Sabon.

Contents

Tables and Figure

Acknowledgments

This work began as research I conducted while a postdoctoral fellow in the Department of History at the University of Winnipeg. I am grateful to the Social Sciences and Humanities Research Council of Canada for funding, and to my employer at the time – Westgate Mennonite Collegiate – for granting me a leave of absence. Royden Loewen, chair in Mennonite Studies, served as my supervisor and provided much-appreciated advice and friendship – and a new computer. Other University of Winnipeg faculty assisted in crucial ways: Hans Werner provided sunny office space, while Alexander Freund and Nolan Reilly offered advice regarding oral history and loaned me the necessary recording equipment. Following my postdoc, I joined the department, where I now work as an associate professor. Although I miss my former colleagues at Westgate, I am happy to have found a similarly supportive environment at my new workplace.

Several people aided me in finding people to interview. I am grateful to Perry Bush, John D. Roth, Theron Schlabach, Susan Burkholder, Brian Froese, Gordon Matties, Paul Friesen, Wally Kroeker, Ted Koontz, and Geoff Dueck Thiessen. James Urry offered helpful advice during a brief visit to Winnipeg.

People – most of them strangers when we first met – hosted or found hosts for me while I wandered the continent in search of interview participants. Some of them have become good friends, and all offered comfortable rooms, conversation, sightseeing assistance, or interview contacts. My thanks to Marlene Epp and Paul Born, Perry and Elysia Bush, Ken and Becky Horst, David and Betty Giesbrecht, Paul and Ruthanne Wartman, Budi Hartono, Dalton and Beverly Reimer, Sheri Hostetler, and Doug Basinger and John Flickinger.

Historians depend on the skills of archivists, and I am pleased to acknowledge my debt to the following people: Laureen Harder-Gissing (Mennonite Archives of Ontario, Conrad Grebel University College), Susan Mavor (Special Collections, Dana Porter Library, University of Waterloo), Carrie Philips (Archives and Special Collections, Musselman Library, Bluffton University), Rich Preheim (Mennonite Church USA Archives, Goshen, Indiana), the staff at the Mennonite Historical Society of British Columbia (Abbotsford, British Columbia), Kevin Enns-Rempel and Paul Toews (Center for Mennonite Brethren Studies, Fresno, California). I owe much to Rich Preheim in particular, who trusted me with a key to the archives, which allowed me to read documents until the early hours of the morning – what a gift!

I presented versions of the chapters that follow in a number of venues and benefited from the critique of many people. Papers were presented at the Visiting Lecturers Series at the University of Winnipeg's Department of History, and at the conferences of the International Oral History Association (Buenos Aires), Southwest Oral History Association (Los Angeles), the Economic and Business History Society (Columbus), the Canadian Historical Association (Fredericton), and the Oral History Association (Denver). John Lyons (Miami University of Ohio), Clayton Koppes (Oberlin College), Erik Benson (Cornerstone University), and my colleagues Nolan Reilly and Roy Loewen commented on early drafts. Former colleagues Bob Hummelt and Terry Dirks, and my sister Val Paulley also offered helpful advice on specific chapters. I am grateful as well for the helpful critiques offered by anonymous readers for McGill-Queen's University Press; for the support of my editor, Kyla Madden; and for the careful copy-editing of Kate Merriman.

Others provided assistance in important ways. Bruno Dyck provided me with raw data summaries of the 1972 and 1989 Church Membership Profiles (CMP), while Conrad Kanagy provided me with a raw data summary for the 2006 CMP. Jonathan Nathan kindly shared his Bethel College paper with me. The staff at Common Grounds in Bluffton and at Ellice Café in Winnipeg (the latter, sadly, no longer in operation) allowed me to treat their businesses as secondary offices and kept me well supplied with tea and hot chocolate in the process. My University of New Brunswick friends Kirk Niergarth, Allison Ryan, Ben Isitt, and Melissa Moroz opened their homes to me, modelling friendship and hospitality in ways I can only hope to someday match.

In "Stories of Strife," oral historian Katrina Srigley discusses the interviews she conducted with four sisters about their memories of their father during the Depression.[1] Their father had been a motorman with the Toronto Transit Commission, but also worked as a bookie and a bootlegger. His daughters had very different memories of him, influenced in part by their ages at the time that the family home was raided by the police, ending his gambling and alcohol trafficking operations. The oldest sister remembered the family as respectable; the younger ones recalled "poverty and shame."[2] I was reminded of Srigley's interviewees' narratives and counter-narratives when I interviewed Valerie Paulley for this project. Val is my sister, sixteen years older than I. She had volunteered to be interviewed, saying she had stories she wished to share that were of relevance to my study, and I was pleased to take her up on her offer.

During the interview, it was not Val's stories, but her response to a simple factual question that startled me. I asked her to which Mennonite denomination her (our) parents had belonged. It was a question I asked of all the interview participants, and so I asked it of Val, even though I knew the answer. Val's answer was short and direct: "They were Bergthaler."

Bergthaler. Surely not! It was true that our parents had helped establish a Mennonite church in a small town in Manitoba in the 1950s that eventually had become Bergthaler. But they themselves were not "Bergies." How could they be? Our parents had left that church because of its insistence on the use of the German language in an anglophone community and its resistance to the concept of congregational autonomy in decision-making. It had been a disappointing, if not traumatic, experience in many ways, and I had grown up hearing their stories about it. From my perspective, our parents were no more Bergthaler than they were Mennonite Brethren – a church in which they had participated for a few years in another small Manitoba town. The only correct answer to the question of their denominational identity, in my mind, was that they were General Conference (GC) Mennonites. In retrospect, that Val should think otherwise should not have been surprising to me since her childhood coincided with my parents' enthusiastic participation in this Bergthaler congregation. My own came years later, after my parents' break with the Bergthalers, when they had joined a GC church in the city.

I thought of that incident again when I found myself once more at a coffee shop I had frequented when conducting some of the interviews in the United States. Coincidentally, a woman I had interviewed a year earlier was in the shop. We shared a table and talked for a while about my research. "I wonder what sort of awful things I said about the church in my interview," she said. She explained that a year earlier, she had been having a conflict with some congregation members over a decision made in the church. Since then, that conflict had been resolved, and her negative perspective on church community had been transformed.

These two incidents and Srigley's example illustrate that the oral history process can provide only a glimpse of a person's history at a particular time and in a particular context. As oral historian Alan Wong observes, "No two life story interviews with the same person will ever be the same."[3] Written texts provide the same restrictive glimpses, of course, as postmodern theorists have revealed. This book thus cannot be – indeed, *no* book can be – a definitive and exhaustive depiction and analysis of attitudes toward unions and work within a given community. Rather, the individuals with whom I spoke chose to share a limited number of stories, selected in the collaborative context that is the interview process. Reading through my notes of those interviews for common themes, I selected those that offered what I believed to be helpful insights into how and why people in post-1945 North American society had rejected labour unions. Had these interviews been conducted at a different time, or with different people, it is possible that different conversations would have emerged.

And so my final and greatest acknowledgment is of the many people who agreed to be interviewed by me in California, Indiana, Ohio, British Columbia, Manitoba, and Ontario – thank you so much. I learned much from you, in areas not always addressed by this book or, indeed, by academic scholarship. I hope that, although you may disagree with some of my emphases and interpretations in this book, you nonetheless feel that your trust in me was not misplaced.

TALKING UNION

Written by Pete Seeger, Lee Hays, and Millard Lampell

Now, if you want higher wages let me tell you what to do,
You got to talk to the workers in the shop with you,
You got to build you a union, got to make it strong.
But if you all stick together, boys, it won't be long –
You get shorter hours – better working conditions –
Vacations with pay – take your kids to the seashore –

It ain't quite this simple, so I better explain
Just why you got to ride on the union train,
'Cause if you wait for the boss to raise your pay
We'll all be waiting 'til Judgment Day –
We'll all be buried – gone to Heaven –
St. Peter'll be the straw boss then –

Now you know you're underpaid but the boss says you ain't
He speeds up the work 'til you're about to faint.
You may be down and out but you ain't beaten,
You can pass out a leaflet and call a meetin'
Talk it over – speak your mind –
Decide to do something about it –

'Course, the boss may persuade some poor damn fool
To go to your meeting and act like a stool.
But you can always tell a stool, though, that's a fact,
He's got a yellow streak running down his back –
He doesn't have to stool – he'll always get along –
On what he takes out of blind men's cups –

You got a union now and you're sitting pretty.
Put some of the boys on the steering committee.
The boss won't listen when one guy squawks
But he's got to listen when the union talks –
He better – be mighty lonely –
Everybody decided to walk out on him –

Suppose they're working you so hard it's just outrageous
And they're paying you all starvation wages,
You go to the boss and the boss would yell
Before I raise your pay I'd see you all in hell!
Well, he's puffing a big cigar, feeling mighty slick
'Cause he thinks he's got your union licked,
Well, he looks out the window and what does he see
But a thousand pickets, and they all agree –
He's a bastard – unfair – slave driver –
Bet he beats his wife –

Now boys, you've come to the hardest time,
The boss will try to bust your picket line
He'll call out the police, the national guard,
They'll tell you it's a crime to have a union card,
They'll raid your meetings, they'll hit you on the head,
They'll call every one of you a red –
Unpatriotic – Japanese spies – sabotaging national defense –

But out at Ford, here's what they found,
And out at Vultee, here's what they found,
And out at Allis-Chalmers, here's what they found,
And down at Bethlehem, here's what they found,
That if you don't let red-baiting break you up,
And if you don't let stoolpigeons break you up,
If you don't let vigilantes break you up,
And if you don't let race hatred break you up
You'll win – what I mean, take it easy, but take it –

NOT TALKING UNION

Introduction

How does one write a labour history of people who have not been involved in the labour movement in significant numbers and, historically, have opposed union membership? Although Mennonites are typically associated with rural life, they in fact became very involved as workers in specific locations in both traditional Mennonite enclaves in Ohio, Indiana, Ontario, and Manitoba, and places to which they migrated in the twentieth century, such as British Columbia and California. Mennonites in these locales found employment both as field workers for large agri-business operations (for example, the orchards and packing plants of the San Joaquin Valley in California) and as factory hands in manufacturing firms (such as the automotive factories in southern Ontario). The late twentieth-century experiences of North American Mennonites in these settings caused them to confront and reassess their attitudes toward unions. A study of these Mennonites – united by transnational ties of ethnic and religious identity yet shaped, at times, in distinct ways by their differing geographic locations, immigration histories and ethnic origins, denominational ties, and class positions – provides insights into how and why the majority of North American Mennonites have rejected labour unions in the late twentieth and early twenty-first centuries.

The largest Mennonite denominations in North America are the Mennonite Church – formed by the union of the General Conference (GC) and the (Old) Mennonite Church (MC) – and the Mennonite Brethren (MB).[1] These groups have been somewhat divided historically by ethnic origins and migration streams: originally, GCs and MBs were primarily Dutch-Russian in origin, migrating to North America in a number of distinct waves beginning in the late nineteenth century, whereas most MCs were of Swiss-South German origin and migrated in the eighteenth and early nineteenth centuries. In addition, there have been some doctrinal and social differences. GCs long have emphasized congregational autonomy, and have not been as socially conservative as MCs: GCs "were agreed that being Mennonite did not preclude being middle class Americans."[2] Post-1960 changes among MCs included greater congregational autonomy and relaxation of some social restrictions (for example, women were allowed to cut their hair and wear pants, men no longer wore lapel-less coats, and church members were permitted to attend movie theatres). Historically, the MBs have placed between the other two groups in social conservatism and have been more evangelical than either. All three groups emphasize pacifism as a key tenet of the Mennonite faith.[3]

The (Old) Mennonite Church took the most vocal stand against labour union involvement by church members, passing a resolution against union membership in 1937.[4] Bible verses invoked in support of this position included those that were interpreted to mean that one's allegiance to God rather than the union oath of membership was supreme, that Christians should endure suffering rather than press demands for personal justice, and that the coercive and adversarial nature of strikes and collective bargaining were non-pacifist and fundamentally unchristian.[5] The 1937 (Old) Mennonite Church resolution cited one of the most popular biblical passages used by Mennonites to defend their anti-union stance: Christians were to avoid being "unequally yoked together with unbelievers."[6] A second resolution reinforcing this anti-union position was passed in 1941, although mention of potential abuses by employers was also included. Mennonites were to avoid union involvement since "the monopolistic closed shop, the boycott, the picket line and the strike" implied a threat of force. Mennonite employers, meanwhile, were advised to avoid "the lockout, the blacklist, detective agencies, espionage, strike-breakers and munitions." In addition, a new church committee was created to assist members of the (Old) Mennonite Church in negotiating exemption from union membership: the Committee on Industrial Relations (later renamed the Committee on Economic and Social Relations).[7] So few church members adhered to these injunctions, however, that by 1954 the (Old) Mennonite Church softened its views.[8] Noting that unions "serve a useful purpose for the maintenance of justice and a balance of power in a sub-Christian society," Mennonites were free to "cooperate with the union (as ... with the state) in so far as doing so does not conflict with ... Christian testimony."[9]

The General Conference and the Mennonite Brethren churches were less vocal about unions, at least in official pronouncements. The only MB resolution regarding unions was passed in 1969, and it did not forbid church members to be union members. MBs were warned, however, that they should not engage in union-related violence or intimidation.[10] The closest the GCs came to passing a resolution on unions was in 1983, when, together with the (Old) Mennonite Church, they issued a joint statement on "Justice and the Christian Witness." The statement asserts that the issues of justice that face the church vary "by time and place," observing that for "some Mennonites in the 1930s, labor unions were the issue." The statement later notes that demonstrating neighbourly love at times may require "supporting or challenging labor unions."[11] Despite the moderation of Mennonite church leaders' attitudes toward union membership, North American Mennonites remained far less likely than the general population to be union members.[12]

My interest in North American Mennonites' anti-unionism emerged from the research for my first book, *Manufacturing Mennonites,* a study of how Mennonite workers at three Mennonite-owned non-unionized factories responded to redefinitions of their ethno-religious identity by Mennonite intellectuals and employers after 1945 (including failed union drives at two of the factories).[13] Part of a chapter in that book briefly discusses the efforts by some Mennonites in Manitoba in the early 1970s to challenge what they perceived to be the denial of their religious rights by the Manitoba Labour Board (a topic I revisit in greater detail in chapter 5 of this book). I was curious whether there were instances elsewhere in North America of Mennonite labour activism. I was interested, as well, in how and why Mennonites with similar religious beliefs had at times reached opposing positions on union membership; although anti-unionism has been the traditional and prevailing opinion, some Mennonites have been union supporters. Oral history interviews were my research method of choice since they would offer insight into how individuals explained (in the words of Alessandro Portelli) "not just what [they] did, but what they wanted to do, what they believed they were doing, and what they now think they did."[14]

Readers familiar with the North American Mennonite community will recognize my last name as an ethnically Mennonite one. I was born into a Dutch-Russian Mennonite family whose ancestors arrived in Manitoba in the 1870s.[15] I was baptized into a General Conference

(GC) Mennonite church, have taught Mennonite history at the secondary and post-secondary levels, and have spent much of my career working for and with Mennonites. As I discuss later in this book, my common identity with interview participants for this project was both a help and a hindrance. A shared ethno-religious identity could, at times, contribute to establishing a sense of rapport between us. But in other instances, I was the "wrong kind" of Mennonite: GC rather than MB (Mennonite Brethren), Canadian rather than American, of Dutch-Russian heritage rather than Swiss. Thus I was both an insider and an outsider.

This book is an experiment in a different kind of labour history, one that examines the history of people who (for the most part) were not labour activists and investigates not the story of union members or unionized workplaces but of people's historically constructed attitudes toward unions. Additionally, this book is a contribution to growing scholarly efforts to bring labour historians and historians of religion into conversation; it does so in part through the use of oral history. Finally, this work is an internalist history in that it attempts to understand a particular religious group on its own terms and from its own perspective(s).

The research is grounded in oral history interviews, newspaper accounts, and archival documents. Oral history helps avoid some of the pitfalls of determinism associated with internalist history, which, as economist Kevin Hoover observes, the "tide of history is clearly against ... Historians now prefer a history in which the wider social context – the interpretive communities that give meaning to mere chronologies – are given center stage."[16] Like Hoover, however, I argue for the value of this unpopular approach. Whereas externalist history is concerned "with the relation of beliefs to society," cultural historian Peter Burke explains that an "'internalist' history of mentalities" is concerned instead with "the relation of beliefs to one another."[17] I am interested here in how a particular group of people integrated their religious beliefs with their beliefs about labour unions, not with how members of that group interacted with or were perceived by outsiders. This study nonetheless avoids the Whiggish approach to history into which internalist perspectives are often lumped,[18] in that an effort is made to understand religious beliefs as expressions of economic interests and social power.

I interviewed members of three Mennonite groups – the GCs, MBs, and MCs. I chose these three because they were the largest

Mennonite denominations, because I was interested in examining the experiences of the most assimilated of the various Mennonite groups, and because they have received less scholarly attention than some other Mennonite groups. Royden Loewen, for example, has done excellent work examining the histories – including the labour histories – of rural and more socially conservative Mennonites such as the Evangelical Mennonites (or Kleine Gemeinde).[19] Another, more important, reason I chose the groups of mainstream Mennonites was because they were – by virtue of their more urban locations – more likely to be personally familiar with unions. As those perhaps most confronted with the challenges of postwar capitalism, their stories were more likely to shed light on the question of how people with a history of "labour quietism" – that is, a reluctance to become involved in the labour movement – navigated late twentieth-century capitalism. Their stories would provide insight into why so many working North Americans – Mennonite or otherwise – are not union supporters,[20] and how people in general negotiate tensions between their moral commitments and the demands of their employment. Unlike the Almanac Singers in their classic folk song, North American Mennonites, by and large, were not "talking union."[21]

While my initial research objective was to document instances of Mennonite involvement in unions and the labour movement, the focus of the project changed over the course of the interviews I conducted. Alessandro Portelli notes that oral history interviews "are always the result of a relationship, of a *shared project* in which both the interviewer and the interviewee are involved together, if not necessarily in harmony."[22] It is in this sense that I shared authority with the interviewees: their discussion of their thoughts and personal experiences shifted the emphasis of my research from the recovery of specific historical events of collective action to an examination of interviewees' religious beliefs and attitudes toward work and unions.[23]

Oral historian Linda Shopes asks how interviewer-interviewee relationships "inflect the content of the interviews, the questions asked, the answers given?"[24] She states that authors need to analyse "the various ways what happens within the interview are connected to relationships and structures external to it."[25] In my case, the relationships and external structures included my identity as a Mennonite and the fact that the majority of the interviews were conducted in 2009 and 2010, after the global financial crisis that began in late 2007 with the bursting of the housing bubble and the defaulting of subprime mortgages in the United States (followed by government bailouts of banking and industry) – but before the Occupy Movement.[26] Thus the explanations by some interview participants of their attitudes toward unions were shaped in part by the then current popular blame of "excessive union demands" for the economic failure.[27] As well, the interviews reflect the assumptions many of the interviewees made in defining unions as urban industrial, rather than rural agricultural, entities. Union organization and support often were seen as the consequence of "outside" agitators rather than organic responses of workers themselves. Thus unions, including agricultural labour groups such as the United Farm Workers with its predominantly nonwhite membership, were cast as the other by definition.

The ability of interview participants to shape the direction of this research project was made possible in part by my choice of interview process. I used the four-stage life history method proposed by oral historian Alexander von Plato, which allows the interview participant to direct the conversation to a great degree. I had anticipated that interviewees would discuss specific examples of labour activism (union membership, strike participation, labour legislation campaigns). Very few did so. Instead, most spoke of their individual theological commitments and their personal work experiences. As Portelli reminds us, "The first requirement … is that the researcher 'accept' the informant, and give priority to what she or he wishes to tell, rather than what the researcher wants to hear."[28] I had set out to find stories of collective action: what I heard were stories of individual negotiation.

Von Plato's life history method involves four distinct stages.[29] In the first stage, interviewees were asked to "tell me the story of your life" and were given as much time as they wished to reply. No prompts or questions were used during this stage, allowing participants to craft a life narrative of their choosing. When interviewees signalled that they were finished telling their story, stage two involved asking questions for clarification of the story just presented. If not already addressed in the life story, participants were asked how their parents shared their religious beliefs and in what ways they discussed labour issues with them as children.

In the third stage, the questions of specific interest to the research project were asked. This portion of the interview was conducted as conversationally as possible – given the presence of a comparative stranger hastily writing notes lest the digital recorder fail to function! Questions included variations on the following: How have you experienced spirituality, or faith, or God in your life? What did these experiences mean to you? What does being Mennonite mean to you in the workplace? How do you share your beliefs about religion and work with your children? As well, participants were asked to explain how their religious beliefs and their perspectives on labour issues had changed over time, if indeed they had. A number of unscripted questions often were asked at this stage, inspired by the interview participant's discussion of unanticipated topics.

The fourth and final stage of the interview – which von Plato terms the optional "conflict phase" – was conducted on almost all occasions. This stage allowed me to question the participant's presentation of their story, to draw comparisons to other interviews or to written sources and ask the participant's perspective on perceived inconsistencies, or to challenge the interviewee's interpretation of events.[30] Often I would introduce this phase by stating, "Some people might say" and then describing a conflicting perspective, before asking, "How would you reply?" The specifics of this question were very much determined by the content and tone of our earlier conversation.

Six urban centres were the geographic focus of the project: three each in Canada and the United States. These were Winnipeg, Manitoba; Kitchener-Waterloo, Ontario; Abbotsford, British Columbia; Bluffton, Ohio; Goshen, Indiana; and Fresno-Reedley, California. I conducted 115 interviews in these locations. Interview participants were solicited through a variety of means; snowball sampling was critical. I obtained initial contacts through fellow historian Perry Bush in Ohio and through postings about the project on Facebook. I also placed advertisements in a variety of local, university, and student newspapers.[31] Notices were placed in North American Mennonite periodicals and with various Mennonite institutions.[32] These efforts were not nearly as successful in soliciting participants as was simple word-of-mouth, however. With the exception of Ohio, I arrived in each location with only a couple of interviews pre-arranged, and made further contacts by cold-calling people whose names I obtained from interview participants and from people I met while researching and living in the community. The majority of those I interviewed were of ethnic Mennonite background, and a few were converts to the Mennonite faith from other Christian denominations. All interviewees were white; my efforts to interview Hispanic Mennonites (discussed in chapter 4) were unsuccessful.

Interviews were usually conducted in participants' homes, although occasionally we met at their workplaces or in restaurants and coffee shops. With the exception of those in California (discussed in detail in later chapters), the overwhelming majority of people I contacted accepted my request for an interview. Interviews lasted from one to two hours. All interviews used in this project were recorded in digital audio with the participants' approval, and will be deposited at the Mennonite Heritage Centre Archives in Winnipeg.

Interviewees were asked whether they preferred to remain anonymous or use their real names. I began interviews by reviewing the consent form. In some cases, people preferred to sign the consent form only after the interview, after they had reflected on what they had said and how they wanted that material to be handled. On two occasions, people agreed to participate in an interview but afterward declined to sign a consent form. In the first instance, the person was interested in the project but expressed doubts about whether he was a suitable subject for the study, since he no longer identified as a Mennonite. In the second instance, the person shared stories of his family that were more personal than he had anticipated and therefore he did not want a record of our conversation retained. Of course, these two people's stories were not used in the writing of this book. Two others requested that the recorded interview be destroyed rather than archived; I chose not to use their stories either, since the archival deposit of interviews is part of best practices in oral history.[33] Three senior citizens heard of my work and requested the opportunity to record the story of their migration to Canada; their stories will be archived as they requested but are not relevant to this study and so are not included. Of the remaining 108 people I interviewed, fourteen anonymous participants are not listed in the bibliography and are identified in the chapters that follow by pseudonymous first names. In the final chapter on conflicts in Mennonite workplaces, I also have chosen to use pseudonyms for the four people discussed, despite some individuals' consent to use their real names, out of respect for the delicacy of what they chose to share with me.

This study is qualitative rather than quantitative in nature. Some readers nonetheless may be interested in the question of the extent to which my interview sample is representative – a question that is not readily answered. A comparison of the occupational categories of my interview participants with those who participated in the Church Membership Profiles (CMP) conducted by five North American

Table 1.1 North American Mennonite occupations of participants in Thiessen interviews of 2009–14 and in Church Membership Profiles of 1972 and 1989.

Occupational category	*Thiessen life histories*	*1972 CMP*	*1989 CMP*
Workers[1]	15%	22%	25%
Academics	26%	na	na
Business people	17%	5%	9%
Professionals	35%	16%	28%
Pastors	7%	na	na

Sources: J. Howard Kauffman and Leo Driedger, *The Mennonite Mosaic: Identity and Modernization,* with a foreword by Donald B. Kraybill (Scottdale, PA: Herald Press, 1991), 38 Table 1–3.

1 I have combined the following five occupational categories listed by Kauffman and Driedger: sales/clerical workers, craftspeople, machine operators, service workers, and laborers.

Mennonite denominations[34] in 1972 and 1989 is summarized in Table 1.1 The CMP for 2006 is not included in this table, for reasons discussed later.

Direct comparison of these statistics is problematic for a couple of reasons. The CMP data includes agriculturalists in their total sample, whereas I deliberately interviewed few farmers since I was interested in interviewing people in urban occupations that had the potential to be unionized.[35] Most significantly, the construction of categories itself is a contrived exercise. Slotting interview participants into occupational categories is challenging: many had jobs that crossed boundaries, or had worked in a variety of fields over the course of their careers. And the categories I have created do not easily equate to those used in the CMPs – nor are the categories used in the CMPs consistent from one study to the next, particularly for the 2006 CMP.

The CMP was altered significantly in 2006, making comparisons with earlier years difficult, if not impossible. Only Mennonite Church (combined GC and MC) members in the United States were surveyed in 2006; no Canadians or Mennonite Brethren were included. (The Mennonite Brethren were one of the groups I included in my interviews who have a longer history of non-agricultural employment.) The 2006 CMP eliminated the job categories of "housewife/husband," "student," and, most significantly, "business owner." Business owners completing the 2006 survey had to define themselves not by their occupation but by the nature of the business they conducted. Thus, the owner of a machine shop and the machinists who worked there were not differentiated in the 2006 CMP but were listed in the same category – completely obscuring class differences. North American Mennonites have been "disproportionately concentrated in white collar jobs,"[36] partly as a result of early twentieth-century Mennonite religious authorities' emphasis on the "helping professions" (teaching, preaching, healing) as preferred occupations and their preaching that Mennonites should avoid unionized workplaces.[37]

Just under one-third of interview participants were or had been members of unions or professional associations (with numbers divided equally between these two groups). The number of those in professional associations is roughly equivalent to that estimated for the North American Mennonite population as a whole, whereas the number of those in unions is approximately triple the North American Mennonite average (statistics which are discussed in greater detail in chapter 2). These interviews thus provide a useful window into Mennonite attitudes toward and involvement in unions.

As an atypical labour history, this book suggests one way in which to study the labour history of non-unionized people who continue to be largely ignored by labour historians. Despite the shift in labour historiography from institutional history (unions) to the history of the working class,[38] the stories of large groups of working North Americans are under-represented: those who are not unionized and those who are white collar workers. Studies of labour conflict have tended to focus on strikes. This study reveals that labour conflict can be more inward-focused though no less dramatic, as when North American Mennonites debated their response to the Farm Workers movement, or when Mennonites working for Mennonite church-related institutions faced challenges. As blue collar manufacturing jobs in North America since the late twentieth century have been replaced not only by jobs in the service industry but by white collar jobs in the knowledge industry, new ways of writing labour history will be increasingly important. The usefulness of oral history is apparent here: with limited union involvement (and thus no union records as research material), life history interviews provide insight into how and why non-unionized people (an increasing majority of workers) responded to not only their own working conditions but the working conditions of those around them.

As an atypical religious history, this book addresses the linkages among religious beliefs, vocation, and the workplace. Lived religion is not only the way in which religious laypeople interpret and make use of religious rites, symbols, and places – although this has been the focus of most studies of lived religion. Lived religion is, more broadly, the ways in which people connect their religious beliefs to their daily lives. Mennonites are a religious group that historically has not valued iconography, liturgy, or pilgrimages – popular sites of examination for scholars of lived religion. Mennonite theology has emphasized, however, the connection between religious commitment and employment. In an urban environment, occupational choices and union membership have been important foci for Mennonite religious authorities. And as rural people employed in agriculture for much of their history, Mennonites have encountered labour conflict as both farm managers and farm workers. Thus a lived religion approach to this group necessitates examining how Mennonite laity viewed the connection between religion and work. Again, oral history is a useful methodology for investigation here.

Religion, for all the attention it currently receives in both Canada and the United States, has had little impact on the fields of North American labour and working-class history.[39] Religious historian Jon Butler argues that scholars "need to know more about relationships among religion, class, and race."[40] What few integrative studies exist tend to focus on the nineteenth-century period of industrialization.[41] Little progress seems to have been made since Max Weber's oft-cited (and oft-debated) discussion of the connection between religion and capitalism.[42] Religion and gender historian Lynne Marks suggests that leftist labour historians have been shaped by "a more materialist focus and by a personal secularism, often based in deep-seated hostility to religion (linked in some cases to troubling childhood memories of religious patriarchy, misogyny, and oppression)."[43] Male historians, she asserts, may ignore religion because "it is associated with the feminine and might be seen to taint rational working-class heroes with hysteria and irrationalism."[44]

Early labour history focused on labour institutions (trade unions, workers' fraternal organizations), the "great men" of the labour movement (union presidents, strike leaders), and the labour process as seen from the shop floor.[45] Religion made an appearance in these histories in limited ways: the influence of religious beliefs such as the social gospel on labour radicalism, for example, or examination of the paternalism of particular employers.[46] Religion thus was depicted as (at best) a motivating factor in the drive for workplace justice that was insufficient in and of itself in achieving social transformation, or (at worst) a negative force responsible for employer abuses of their employees. Even when the shift was made from institutional and biographical labour history to the social history of the working class, this limited engagement with religion did not change markedly.[47]

In a similar fashion, religious history has ignored class.[48] The historiography of religious history parallels that of labour history. Earlier religious histories told the stories of denominations and religious leaders.[49] Later social histories of religion have focused on the interaction of religion and culture and on what is termed "lived religion."[50] Those studying the Mennonite experience, unfortunately, have written very little about Mennonites and labour unions, whether from a theoretical or historical perspective.[51]

In the period after 1945, Mennonite community leaders exhibited concern regarding North American Mennonite involvement in urban and industrial labour. The degree and nature of concern did not differ significantly across geographic contexts. For example, the leaders of Mennonite Central Committee (MCC) Manitoba were asked by their constituency in the early 1970s to assist Manitoban Mennonites who were seeking exemption from union membership. These Mennonites believed that union membership was incompatible with their religious beliefs. Further, they thought the newly elected New Democratic Party government and the Manitoba Labour Board were interpreting provincial labour legislation in a manner biased against Mennonites, and wanted assistance in their struggle against union membership. MCC Manitoba actively supported them in this struggle.[52] Three provinces away, MCC British Columbia organized a series of seminars in the 1950s and 1960s which asserted that Mennonites should be debating the question "*How* can a Christian be a union member?" rather than "*Should* a Christian be a union member?" The seminars, however, spent as much time debating the latter question as the former, and the committee members themselves viewed unions as "a necessary evil" and "definitely, in some of their methods, not Christian."[53] In the United States, Mennonite leaders viewed unions with similar suspicion. MCC US investigated the origins of the United Farm Workers strikes in California in the 1960s. Partly because Mennonites were involved on both sides, as both migrant pickers and resident growers, MCC US was unable to recommend a definitive "Mennonite position" on the issue, and refused to side with either group.[54]

The North American Mennonite response to labour unions began with the (Old) Mennonite Church and leader Guy Hershberger at a time when Mennonites were beginning to urbanize. The rural-to-urban shift began in the northeastern United States in the 1940s before spreading to Mennonites in Canada and other parts of the USA a few decades later. While there was not quite the same degree of anti-union activism by General Conference Mennonite and Mennonite Brethren churches as by the (Old) Mennonite Church, a similar tradition of anti-unionism nonetheless emerged. This similarity arose because religious training and theological discourse were trans-denominational and because of the rural origins of North American Mennonites and the anti-communism of Russian Mennonites (who equated unions with urban worldliness and Godless socialism).

This book examines Mennonite attitudes and responses toward labour unions over six chapters. The first two chapters set the stage by examining Mennonites' religious beliefs and their historical and contemporary attitudes toward unions. Chapter 1 reveals the diversity and individualism of religious narratives within the North American Mennonite community, which limits their ability to reach consensus on questions of religion. Chapter 2 investigates Mennonites' attitudes toward unions and determines that, while some profess that their stance stems from their religious convictions, for the past sixty years there has not been unity in the Mennonite community on labour issues. Their views of unions are diverse, in part because of their individuated narratives of faith. The next three chapters then explore specific collective Mennonite experiences with unions in the United States and Canada. Two chapters focus on the particular case of Cesar Chavez and the United Farm Workers (UFW) strikes in California in the 1960s. Chapter 3 examines various Mennonites' reactions to the UFW and reveals that there was little agreement among Mennonites as to how their religious beliefs should shape their response to this class conflict. Chapter 4 examines the conflicted nature of Mennonite memory of these events, revealing that contemporary Mennonite reticence regarding this historical event is a symptom of class conflict within the community. Chapter 5 investigates the experiences of Manitoban Mennonites as they took advantage of an amendment to the Labour Relations Act that allowed exemption from union membership on grounds of conscience. A discussion of Mennonites working for Mennonite church-affiliated institutions in chapter 6, the final chapter, shows that Mennonites' integration of their work lives and religious beliefs has not been simple, even in environments seemingly tailor-made for such integration. Some Mennonites who sought non-unionized Mennonite employers in order to avoid the conflicts between religion and labour discussed in earlier chapters instead found it was a challenge to integrate work and religiosity in these settings.

Sociologist N.J. Demerath reminds us that "charting the sacred involves an exploration of inner space that is every bit as challenging as the astronomer's exploration of a continually expanding outer space."[55] The following stories of North American Mennonites' religious attitudes toward unions illustrate the complexity of that inner space. I hope that these stories will encourage further scholarly exploration of work and faith, and the spaces between them.

1

"I tell you these things because it cast my view of God"

Narratives of Religious Belief

At a farmers' market in the Midwestern United States early one Saturday morning, a young Everett Thomas publicly hugged his father, told him that he loved him, and commented that he found it hard to love his mother, a woman who was both verbally and physically abusive.[1] Recounting the story to me decades later, Thomas explained, "I tell you these things because it cast my view of God." He went on to describe his father's qualities of grace, love, and acceptance, and contrasted them with his mother's distant coldness and emotional estrangement from her children. Observing that many men have "father issues," Thomas noted that he was "given a gift that many men were not": he is able to think of God positively in conjunction with his father's qualities. His father was "a person people wanted to be around," and as such is the "foundation for my theology."

Thomas then related an incident from his childhood that shaped his and his family's lives for years afterward. His brother, alone in the family's butcher shop, attempted to imitate his older brothers' work. He turned the meat grinder on and off, but not before pinching his fingers in the machine. His screams brought both the family dog and his mother running to the shop. In her panic, she accidentally turned the machine on, and "it took his [brother's] hand." The incident affected the children's perception of their mother, although it was many years before they were able to discuss it openly in their family. The "hardest thing" about Thomas's childhood, he said, was trying to sleep at night, hearing his brother crying with phantom pain, and not knowing how to respond. This early experience of suffering was so powerful that Thomas said he made efforts to close himself off emotionally and thus inure himself from further anguish.

He assuaged the emotional pain of his childhood through overachievement in leadership activities in school, university, work, politics, and the church. Even as a middle-aged man, the legacy of this early experience persists in that "this strength, this coping mechanism for the pain in my life, has carried me through life and it has a shadow side that I need to be careful about."

James Yoder's Midwest American world and his perception of it were changed radically at age four, when one of his brothers accidentally drowned.[2] The death was very difficult for the entire family, and each member handled their pain differently. Yoder remembers being confused and unable to understand what was going on. As an adult, he realizes that he probably suffered from depression as a child, as did his father, but the family "carried on" nonetheless and "the weight lifted over time." When his youngest brother was killed in a bicycle accident a few years after the drowning, Yoder understood that he had not done anything wrong to cause this event. With the "magical thinking" of a four-year-old, he had thought that he could influence such outcomes, but as a school-aged child, he realized these circumstances were beyond his control. These life experiences "set the path" that he would follow in his work life: Yoder always thought he would become a social worker in order to assist others who were hurting in various ways.

While the losses of his siblings were undoubtedly painful, it was not their recollection that triggered Yoder's unexpected weeping a little later in the interview. Tears are not uncommon during life history interviews – whether those of the interview participant or the interviewer – because the willingness to make one's self emotionally vulnerable to another person can be a profoundly moving experience. The suddenness and strength of the lament in this instance, however, were surprising, particularly since the interview had moved to discussion of less obviously tragic topics. I turned off the audio recorder while we both regained our composure, and continued the recorded interview when Yoder was ready. He explained what had prompted his expression of grief. As a child, his parents had been very concerned that he should become a Christian. At age nine, his mother told him that she had prayed to God that, if he were not to become a Christian at some point in his life, God would allow him to die in his youth. The conversation, he said, had terrified him. As an adult, Yoder agreed with his parents that religious commitment is very important, but he observed that he "understands faith differently" and does not "know how to reconcile [his] brothers' deaths" with his parents' prayers. He trusts that "God is bigger than religious beliefs." He "appreciates mystery," in that he accepts that he does not know everything about faith and never will; "God knows the questions and enjoys mystery."

Both Thomas and Yoder had tragedies befall their siblings. Both men had mothers whose behaviour resulted in their questioning of their religious beliefs. Thomas turned to his father as a model of forgiveness and gentleness, and as an image of God. Yoder instead turned to a more expansive understanding of God, one shaped in part by his encounters with Quakerism and Buddhism, and one that emphasized God, in his words, as "inclusive and understanding and compassionate." For these men, it was life experiences – not intellectual encounters with the pronouncements of theological leaders or religious practices such as church attendance – that prompted the (re)construction of their religious belief system.

In the late twentieth century, Mennonite religious understandings were individualized. The migration from rural to urban environs after the Second World War resulted in a diasporic community that embraced "middle-class values, evangelical faith, and a symbolic ethnicity."[3] In the postmodern world, urban Mennonites found themselves part of a diverse group of communities centred on ethnicity, religion, work, and other identities. Where conservative Mennonites might have difficulty articulating their religious beliefs (in part, because salvation for them was not a singular event but a life-long journey), the Mennonites[4] I interviewed used a limited number of narrative forms to describe their religious understandings. These narrative forms are revelatory not only of the nature of contemporary Mennonite belief but of the increasing importance of individualism rather than church authority. One consequence of these individualized approaches to religious understanding is that Mennonite responses to unions were similarly fragmented and based on personal and familial experience rather than national identity, gender, or denominational membership.

Thomas's and Yoder's religious narratives, tied to their emotional childhood experiences of tragedy, were difficult to relate (and, at times, difficult to hear). Anthropologist Michael Harkin observes that Western cultures' emotional detachment and emphasis on rationality are "conditioned by our professional avoidance of unpleasant realities."[5] He notes that the reluctance of historians to embrace and investigate emotions "whether from fear of colleagues' censure for being too subjective or from an unwillingness to face all those tears, continues to deform ethnohistorical research and writing."[6] At the other extreme, scholars willing to engage emotionally may run the risk of silencing the interview participant's voice. Citing trauma scholars Dori Laub and Shoshana Felman, oral historian Mark Klempner warns, "By a display of emotion, the one who asks the questions is able to escape the uncomfortable experience of having to listen to the answers."[7] It is not only trauma scholars who face these challenges, but all oral historians.

American interview participants, I found, tended to share lengthier and more detailed stories in response to my opening request: "Please tell me the story of your life." They were more likely to delve into their emotional and intellectual responses to the events they described. Canadian interviewees, by contrast, tended to tell their life story almost as a job resumé: birth, baptism, schooling, marriage, children, occupations – dates and locations and events, offered more as a list than a narrative. They shared emotions often only after further questioning. Are these differences simply an artifact of these particular interviews, or are they reflective of national differences? In Ohio, for example, the town I visited was a small and close-knit community where everyone seemed to know everyone else. People told me that word went around quickly about my interview process, and so people were preparing for their interviews by discussing their stories with those who had already been interviewed. Thus they were prepared to offer lengthy responses to my opening question. Whatever the explanation, the narratives of religious belief shared by Americans were often in response to my open-ended request. Canadians' narratives of religious belief often emerged from more direct questions about their spirituality or their parents' religious teaching.

Oral history in general, and the life history approach in particular, are useful means for exploring what shapes individuals' religious understandings and how, and for investigating the comparative importance of significant life experiences in the shaping of religious identity versus the role played by doctrine and religious institutions. Many interview participants, when asked how their parents shared their faith with them or how they had experienced God or spirituality in their lives, listed family devotional practices, prayer before meals, church and Sunday school attendance, and Bible college classes in response.

They rarely elaborated on these activities, however. Instead, their most detailed stories regarding their religious beliefs involved specific life experiences that had emotional meaning for them. Religious understandings were shaped most profoundly by these individual and emotional experiences – some of which were not obviously religious incidents – rather than by collective and intellectual engagements with religious organizations or theology.

During the course of our conversations, I asked interview participants how their parents shared their faith with them, how they themselves experienced spirituality or faith or God in their lives, how they connected their work lives with their religious beliefs, and if their religious beliefs had changed over time. These questions were deliberately open-ended and attempted to avoid narrow religious language (regarding conversion experiences, for example) that may have limited the responses. Some – mostly Americans and particularly those in Ohio, as I've noted – did not wait for these questions to be asked, and instead addressed their faith experience in response to the opening question of the interview: "Please tell me the story of your life." Studying their responses, five types of religious narrative emerge: death narratives, problem narratives, affective narratives, countercultural narratives, and progress narratives.

West coast Canadian Ed Penner had been invited by his church's adult Sunday school class to deliver his "testimony" and decided that reading the text he had prepared for this occasion would be his response to my invitation to tell me his life story.[8] He began with the story of his parents' escape from Russia after the Revolution, and then detailed his own experiences. His mother died of a heart attack at age 64, a loss that was difficult for him. Shortly thereafter, he was injured in a serious car accident, a mere eight months before he graduated from dental college. These events made him angry with God, he said, because his future as a dentist was "in jeopardy" due to his injuries. He commented that "the Jacob in me was not impressed" – by which he meant that his acquisitive nature (which had prompted his study of dentistry) was thwarted. This reference was one of many parallels that Penner drew between his life and that of Jacob as described in the biblical book of Genesis. Another significant event in his life, he said, was his wife's postpartum hemorrhage that brought her close to death. In these circumstances, Penner felt like he was "wrestling with God" – again, much as Jacob had done with the angel in the Old Testament story. His wife's brush with death also reminded him of his grandfather's wife, who had left eight children when she died in 1916. He thought as well of the death of Rachel, Jacob's wife, who died in childbirth (Genesis 35). Penner's wife's life "was spared," however, and for him, it was a "pivotal" moment. The focus of his life changed, he said, from the pursuit of wealth to voluntary service to others.

The "most painful loss" in Penner's life was that of his daughter, who was killed in a car accident at age eighteen. He was on a hiking trip with fellow church members and woke from sleep. The night before, he had agreed to plan a devotional message for the group, and "the Lord had given [him] verses from Psalm 23." He talked with his travel companions about "the value of valley experiences," referencing the "valley of the shadow of death" in Psalm 23, and then came home to receive the news about his daughter. Her death, he learned, had occurred at the same time as he prepared his devotional message. She had left "a legacy of journals" which was an "incredible comfort" to him through her discussion of love, faithfulness, peace, beauty, and "God's glory." He said that "her life had drawn many young people to receive Christ as their saviour." In the aftermath of her death, "God's Holy Spirit was like a feather comforter to [him]." His family and church helped him "through that most difficult valley."

Midwest American Linda Houshower described the role played in her religious understanding by her experience with death as a nurse.[9] While many people are squeamish about health problems, she "actually value[s] the occasions when [she] was with somebody when they died." She recalled her first experience of the death of a patient. "It was very good. It was sort of special. Those things stick with you. It was kind of like a gift." This patient, an older lady in intensive care with a do not resuscitate order, suddenly went into rapid and irreversible decline while her family was away. "And she was *singing*. She was singing a hymn." Houshower recognized the song and joined in. "And she just kind of faded out. And I could see – it was kind of these two things: I could see the monitor above her head, knowing what her heart was doing, knowing that she was dying right then, but I was standing with her and it was very peaceful. Very wonderful." She informed the family, who said the hymn had been the woman's favourite and that they were comforted that Houshower had sung it with her. Other deaths "weren't so nice," but this – her first patient death – had been "a real gift. A spiritual gift."

Later in the conversation, Houshower described the deaths of her own father and stepfather. Her father died from cancer at age 80. A month before his death, he was hospitalized and the staff feared the end was near. The family gathered in his hospital room to pray. "And it just was real clear. We were all calm. It was just a real clear sense of God being with us." She was with her father on the day he died. "He waited for me. It was like one of those stories like people have ... I walk in and say, 'Hi, Dad.' And he stops breathing ... And that was it. That was it. He waited for me. Wow. You just kind of wonder, where did that come from and how can they do that? ... There are things that we can't see, we don't know how it works, but they happen."[10] Her mother remarried, and it was this man's death that was, Houshower said, "the other amazing – really amazing – time with someone who died." While her stepfather waited for aneurysm surgery, "we had this time. It was like this bubble, again, around us, of grace. Everything was really calm." Her stepfather gave final messages to his children, and then the family sang together. Just before his surgery, he started singing and recited the Lord's Prayer. "He went off just having sung, having said the Lord's Prayer, smiling, just serene and calm. And that was it. So it was still like having another gift. Missing him. And God's love and grace and being with us." Houshower commented that she is not a religious "proselytizer," but "feel[s] strongly" about such experiences. She declared that "probably, it's true" that, having experienced life's vicissitudes, as people age, they "feel more clearly the presence [of God]." She observed that she has no ability to understand theology, unlike her husband, but can "do the other part." As for detailed theological arguments, "Oh, give me a break! I can't do it. I don't know. And it doesn't really matter to me. And really, most of the time, hey, you know, I won't understand most of that but I can certainly feel that His presence is there."

Narratives of religious belief that incorporate discussions of death are not unusual. One of the key functions of religious belief is to mediate one's understanding of the end of life and the existential crises that are associated with mortality. Religion scholar Wayne Proudfoot and psychology professor Phillip Shaver note that "religion functions as a cognitive system to reduce anxieties over problems of interpretability raised by 'boundary situations' – anomalous experiences and events that bring people face to face with the limits of their worlds, e.g., birth, death, inexplicable suffering, or the calling into question of the moral code of a culture."[11] Religious belief thus has a therapeutic effect, allowing one to come to terms with the loss of loved ones as well as with one's own eventual demise.

These two individuals' stories illustrate the range of responses possible within the "death narrative" framework. Ed Penner's religious narrative is a formal religious testimony. He not only cites the Bible but makes explicit connections between his life and the words of scripture and deliberately parallels his life story with that of the Old Testament's Jacob. Religious belief is presented as more than a means of coping with the tragedy of death. Sudden deaths and serious health problems are, in light of his faith and that of his daughter as revealed after her death in her journals, the triggers that cause him to re-evaluate his life ambitions, directing them away from a purely monetary focus. Houshower's religious narrative reveals that she privileges religious experience over religious knowledge. She is not interested in theological arguments about salvation and life after death. In fact, Houshower concluded her interview by discussing her doubts that non-Christians will not enter heaven or that Christianity is the only "true" religion. The narrative structure she presented suggests that her religious belief is grounded not in theories of the atonement (for example), but in her bodily experiences of serenity at the deathbed and the mysterious timings involved in saying goodbye to the dying. For her, religion is not a set of propositions to which to agree or a dogma to which to conform, but an emotional encounter with the unknown.

As a child, Fred[12] attended church, Sunday school, and evangelical crusades. He has vivid memories of Barry Moore crusades, although what he "remember[s] most dramatically" is "a lot of guilt" associated with them. In 1970, as a pre-teen, he responded to an altar call at one of these crusades. His uncle, who was serving as a crusade counsellor "assured [him] of [his] faith," an experience that was "somewhat traumatic." The fire-and-brimstone preaching of these crusades had a "pronounced impact" on him for years to come. As a young person, Fred was convinced that faith is important, but he was "riddled with a great deal of anxiety and lack of assurance." He was baptized at age fourteen or fifteen because he thought "it was the right thing to do." Even as he participated in baptism classes and preparation, he experienced "a lack of assurance" and asked himself if he was "ready" and if his conversion was "authentic." He continued to experience "guilt and uneasiness." His mother, whom he described as sensitive and nurturing, was aware of his anxiety and tried to help him "understand the grace of God" and that he "didn't have to prove worth" to be baptized.

Fred's doubts and fears persisted through young adulthood. Later in life, he learned that he suffered from depression and anxiety and obsessive-compulsive disorder. This diagnosis helped him come to terms with how his "mind sometimes messed with [his] thoughts and worries" and "how anxiety built up." He came to realize that he had "unhealthy mind processes" and not a lack of faith. In his mid-40s, he was so anxious and frustrated with his job that he took a year of medical leave to address these issues, in part by seeing a Christian psychologist. He "abstained from going to church" for a time because he had so much anxiety and guilt that he found attendance to be "counterproductive." He emphasized that, in doing so, he was "not abandoning faith" but that he had "so much anxiety" that he "felt [he] needed to be away from that environment." He continued to read the Bible, but did so more selectively, following a counsellor's urging him to find "passages of comfort and encouragement." Doing so "helped [him] to break out of some of the rigidity" and the "sense of breaking rules, disappointing God, or grieving the Holy Spirit." The part of church tradition that gave him "particular anxiety" was communion (also known as the eucharist), "the whole idea of 'Consider whether there is any sin in your life and partake [of the eucharistic elements] accordingly, and make sure that everything [in your life] is clean and that you don't have anything against anybody.' And I tended to perseverate on whether, is it really true that everything is okay? Probably not. Probably there is something wrong, right? And then at the same time thinking, 'Well, if I don't take communion, what is that going to look like?'"[13] Looking back, he now finds his struggles with communion "a little bit humorous."

Like Fred, Marianne Coleman has struggled with family and mental health challenges.[14] She dated a "very nice" graduate student at university, and accepted his marriage proposal because, she said, she did not want to hurt his feelings. The couple moved from Canada to the United States so that he could pursue job opportunities. Coleman's aspiration, at the time, was to have children and "raise happy human beings." Coleman's first child, she said, "was pretty normal, but he seemed to [her] at the time, really fussy and impossible to satisfy or please." The baby's short sleeps "drove [her] crazy." She had little idea that she could seek out emotional support. She was "so determined to do everything perfectly that [she] never gave [her] self a break," and what turned out to be "lifelong chronic depression just kept getting a little worse and a little worse ... I didn't know how to help myself, I guess."

After giving birth to her second child and meeting regularly with a psychiatric social worker, Coleman saw that "being able to acknowledge and express [her] feelings to another human being" was necessary for health. She discovered that "life and a feeling of selfhood were based on saying what you felt." She realized she had never done that with her husband. Her depression returned, and "the idea took root that the only way [she] could continue to develop as a human being was not to be married" to her husband. That, however, seemed "too horrible to contemplate." After she was twice hospitalized in a psychiatric ward, the couple amicably separated.

After thirty years away, Coleman returned to Canada for a family reunion. "It was nice to see cedar trees. It was nice to see sparkling gravel made from granite. In Ithaca [New York], everything was shale and slate." She was inspired to move back home, and was encouraged to do so by her mother and sister. She returned, but the onset of menopause triggered clinical depression. Her recovery from that depression coincided with her attendance at her mother's Mennonite church, where she was stirred by the church's "vibrancy" and the four-part harmony congregational singing. She observed, "The time of recovery from a serious depression is so wonderful, that you feel like saying 'yes' to everything." The church minister asked her if she wanted to be baptized and "so I said yes, because I couldn't think of why I would say no." Since then, she has wondered why she returned to Canada after thirty years away: "Did none of that mean anything? ... The person who I became in those intervening years is the person I don't want to go away, the person that I want to be." She thinks she should renounce her church membership because she is

> not interested in being an active part of a Mennonite church, which is a strange thing for the eldest daughter of [Canadian Mennonite historian and church leader] Frank Epp to say.[15] But that might be another piece of the puzzle, that now, I'm finally grown up enough that I think it will be quite alright for me to say to my mother, "You know, Mom, I'm dropping my membership with Rockway [Mennonite Church]. It's my decision. And

> that's okay." [laughs] I don't know when I'll do it. I don't feel any urgency about doing it. But maybe that's why I came back here [to Canada], so I could not run away to be the person who I thought I was, but I could do that, I could be the person who I've become, here, and still be able to love my mother.[16]

In these problem narratives, religious belief is presented as a means of coping with personal or family difficulties. Like death narratives, problem narratives can demonstrate the therapeutic effects of religious understanding, but they need not be limited to such a role. The first example illustrates this complexity, as the narrator describes the intersection between his religious identity and his mental health issues. In the second, the narrator's struggles with religious identity aggravated rather than alleviated some of her personal difficulties.

Religious belief is often viewed as a means of coping with challenges in one's life. With Fred, the reverse appears to be the case. His understanding of his mental health issues was what allowed him to reassess his religious experiences with conversion and communion. He was able to reconsider his feelings of religious guilt and spiritual inadequacy and place them in a new bodily context that subsequently liberated his religious perspective. Coleman has fought to establish an identity independent from that of her father, her husband, and her ethno-religious community. These efforts to gain independence influenced – and continue to influence – her marriage, her health, her national identity, her relationship with her mother, and her church membership. Her religious belief did not so much sustain her through times of crisis as exacerbate tensions within her life.

West coast Canadian Marlyce Friesen experiences spirituality "often in a very surprising way. And it's not something you can set out to plan, that now you're going to be spiritual."[17] She gave an example: strolling in Prague at dusk, she and her husband "heard music coming from a dark doorway." It was music from a Catholic mass. The church was crowded with local people, old and young, and there was "a marvellous orchestra playing the mass. It was incredible." During the passing of the peace,

> this local gentleman grabbed my hand ... And he had very rough, rough hands. He was a labourer; you could tell he worked very, very hard. But, you know, when our eyes met – and here we

> were, different country, different forms of Christianity, but our souls kind of communicated in that instant. And how do you plan that kind of thing? I don't know. You don't. But when it happens, it's joy. It's pure joy. I think, basically, God has set us out to live our life, and as we are walking that path, experiences meet us. And it's how we respond to those experiences that we really meet God through our fellow people and through what we can do through their lives. And I think that's really how I would describe experiencing spirituality.

Dave Klassen, also from Canada's west coast, has had a variety of conversion experiences, each of them tied to strong emotions.[18] The first time he "committed [his] life to the Lord" was when he was eight years old, on 11 November 1961. Doing so was "not really [his] own decision" but was more to "please [his] parents." When he was nineteen, he had what he described as a more "sincere" conversion experience when he attended an evangelism crusade led by Rudy Boschman.[19] And at age thirty-one, he and his wife went on a church retreat for young married couples at Columbia Bible Camp. The speakers at the retreat were "very charismatic, filled with the Holy Spirit." Of some thirty couples in attendance, "about half of us were baptized in the Holy Spirit that weekend and our lives have never been the same since then." The experience was difficult, he said, because "baptism in the Holy Spirit" was something the Mennonite church "shied away from quite a bit." Klassen and the others "had been renewed in a sense that the church didn't know what to do with it." The group began holding worship services on Friday nights and mid-week. "We experienced God in a new way, where He touched our hearts and our lives with such tenderness but yet such depth, that the church felt that this was kind of a wildfire." He took some comfort in the fact that such experiences were "not the first or last" such incidents in Mennonite history. The experience has "never left" him and his wife. "We have been touched by the Holy Spirit in a powerful way, that we know, deep within our hearts, that this is the essence of who we are. We live our lives with passion. Our hearts are full of joy for the Lord." He still reflects on that experience twenty-six years later and "speak[s] of it with fond, fond embracing. And [we] have not walked away from that even though we came back to the Mennonite church. We have not been ashamed to say that we lean towards the charismatic persuasion, I guess, to some degree. God has blessed us richly in this walk, and we wouldn't trade it for anything."

At the end of his interview, Klassen volunteered a summary statement. He said he was very thankful for the foundation he had been given by being born into a Mennonite family and raised in a Mennonite culture. This foundation, he said, was a stable grounding for life. The values he holds, and the choices he makes, are a consequence of his ability to "stand on the shoulders" of many generations of Mennonite forefathers. He recalled, with considerable emotion, having read his great-great-grandfather's memoirs and heard stories from his parents that this ancestor had prayed for every generation that would follow him.

> I am a recipient of those prayers. I stand on the shoulders of our forefathers, who paid a much greater price than we, many, many times, acknowledge or understand or have been willing to recognize. And I am so thankful for that heritage – and now I am talking about the *spiritual* heritage that I have received through them ... By God's grace and through prayers, we will continue to pass this on for generations, as long as the Lord tarries. We pray for the generations that would follow us, that they would remain strong in their beliefs, and strong in their faith, and that they would continue to walk in God's ways, and be grounded – grounded in the truth of Christ. Have a Godly understanding of who they are, what they are called to become, and to walk with confidence into the future, not with fear. Confidence that God will see us through until the day He calls us home.[20]

West coast Canadian Erwin Cornelsen offers a religious narrative that could be described as miraculous. Cornelsen was born in 1919 in West Prussia.[21] He explained that he had the opportunity to attend university for free if he served twelve years in the military, so he joined the German air force shortly before the Second World War. He said he felt "very fortunate" to be able to serve in a noncombatant unit. "That was where I met Jesus Christ in reality. I was a young soldier in the big city of Hamburg, a harbour city, and I was out to explore the big city, coming from the country [laughs]." He was about to enter a bordello, "to see what's going on there," when he noticed a black sailor. "With very, very deep concern, he looked at me. Almost with tears in his eyes, he looked at me. And he said,

'Nicht gut, nicht gut, nicht gut' [not good, not good, not good]." Cornelsen turned away from the brothel, and saw a huge building with a sign on it that read, "Jesus is alive." He then recalled all the religious training he had learned at home, he said. The building was an Evangelical Free Church. "So my past became very much alive, very real, and I noticed, yes, nicht gut, nicht gut." He was left, he said, with a "clear decision: to follow Christ or Hitler." After the war and following his release from a prisoner-of-war camp, Cornelsen and his wife left Germany for Canada. Their church congregation in Germany sang a gospel song as a farewell. When they arrived in Canada, a Mennonite church minister greeted them with the same song. "So I said, on one side of the ocean, that farewell, and here on this side of the ocean, the welcome. That's how God has been leading us."

Affective narratives are those that define an uncommon or distinctive bodily experience of strong feeling (joy and awe, for example) as a spiritual encounter. They were comparatively rare among the interview participants. Extreme examples of such affective narratives characterize the individual's religious experience in miraculous terms: coincidences or unanticipated occurrences are presented as evidence of God's guidance in one's life. Whether the individual understood the unfolding of circumstances at the time as the result of divine influence or not is unimportant. In one variation of the miracle narrative, in fact, the individual's inability to perceive the "hand of God" in their circumstances at the time is further evidence of their "miraculous" nature. There are (at least) two possible reasons why affective narratives were uncommon among those interviewed for this project. First, urban or liberal Mennonites may be hesitant to speak of miracles because of reluctance to identify with charismatic religion, as Klassen's narrative suggests, or because many ethnic Mennonites have cultural values that privilege emotional restraint. Second, almost none of those I interviewed were first-generation immigrants to North America. Those with a migration history touched by violence and hardship may be more likely to structure their religious narratives as stories of the serendipitous and salvific acts of a divine being.[22]

Friesen's encounter with a Czech labourer during a Catholic mass reveals her belief that spirituality is experienced in the body, in emotions, and is not under intellectual control. Klassen's baptism in the Holy Spirit is a similar bodily encounter with spirituality. His emotionally evocative descriptions of the experience are a counterpoint to the traditional depiction of male spirituality as emphasizing dispassionate theology over sensitive emotional expression. Even his summation, although full of rhetoric about religious ancestors and history, is subtly shaped by this emotional understanding of spirituality. He delivered these words extemporaneously, with passion and sincerity, and with tears in his eyes. These emotions, even more than his words, were seemingly the core of the message he wanted to convey in his interview.

Cornelsen encountered the miraculous through a German-speaking foreign sailor, through a church sign, and through the continuity of a transnational religious community. If the sailor had not been visibly different by virtue of his skin colour, or if he had not been able to communicate clearly (and emotionally) in German, Cornelsen may not have taken notice and thus not been forced to re-examine his participation in Hitler's military. If the church's sign had not spoken of the historical Christ as present in the here-and-now, Cornelsen may not have recalled the moral teachings from his childhood and made the connection to his contemporary circumstances. For Cornelsen, the significance of these events was confirmed by the serendipitous singing of the same hymn on both sides of the Atlantic Ocean. The decision he made in Hamburg – against Hitler and for Christ – led to his recommitment to a church community in Germany, one that was part of a broader transnational religious community, as he discovered (again, in a miraculous way) on migration to Canada.

Midwest American Allan Dueck recalled that when he was a child, Sunday lunch often included discussion of faith issues because his father liked to debate such topics.[23] Dueck commented that what tied his childhood to his later studies in seminary was his father's experience as a conscientious objector during the Second World War. Nothing else was "as impressive or strong or clear," and he declared that he was proud of his father for taking this stance. During the war, his father performed alternative service as a cook in a logging camp populated with conscientious objectors. Dueck grew up eating breakfasts of flapjacks made from the recipe his father had used, and heard many stories from him about his experiences. Dueck's most vivid childhood memory – "besides chicken butchering" – was reading the *Martyrs' Mirror,* with its "emphasis on faithfulness and obedience." These threads, he said, "carried through to adulthood." From the time he "committed his life to Christ" in his twenties until today, Dueck said he has "never questioned" the "peace position." The teaching that it was "anathema to be violent" was influential and remained with him.

Roger Miller, also an American Midwesterner, served as a conscientious objector during the Vietnam War, a decision that was shaped in part by his childhood experiences.[24] He moved as a child to Mississippi in 1962; his parents had bought a 1600- acre plantation where thirty families lived and sharecropped. He said he arrived not knowing anything about life in Mississippi, totally unaware of the emergent civil rights movement. He made friends of two boys and went fishing with them. When he was unable to reconnect with them later, he was "devastated" to learn that their father had traded them to an uncle for two cows and a pig. Miller asked if he could buy his friends back, but was told that their uncle needed them to work his farm.

Miller recalled that his father, a small business owner, was approached one day by a man asking for employment. The man told Miller's father that he would have to speak with the owner of the plantation where he lived and pay his debt before he could be hired. The man, Miller recalled, did not know how much he owed the plantation owner. When Miller's father asked the owner about the debt, he was asked, "How much do you think it might be? Maybe ten thousand dollars?" Miller's father was surprised by the question, and said he was unable to pay such a large amount. When the owner said the debt "might be" only $5,000, he realized that they were negotiating for the sale of the man. In the end, he gave the plantation owner $2,500, and received a receipt for the *man* – not the *debt* – that noted that he had paid in cash.

Miller shared one final story of his childhood in Mississippi: his memory of the assassination of President Kennedy. Saddened by the event, he went in tears to the office of his elementary school for more information, and found the staff cheering. The students were given the afternoon off and went to play in celebration. Miller was troubled by this behaviour and spoke with his father who, he said, "explained the regional differences." It was Miller's "first real political discussion." His father, he commented, was "good at understanding intricacies" and spoke of the event in the context of the family's religious beliefs – specifically, that "Mennonites didn't believe killing is proper in any event." These circumstances, he said, were his "first introduction to conscientious objection."

Countercultural narratives attempt to establish the narrator's personal religious experience as different from the norm – a difference that is not merely coincidental but is central to the meaning of the religious experience. Dueck connected the martyrdom of his theological ancestors to his father's experience as a conscientious objector to war and to his own studies in seminary. He linked the execution of sixteenth-century Anabaptists to his post-secondary education in order to emphasize the significance of pacifism in his religious understanding. In doing so, he implied that this belief was, in his opinion, worth dying for. In joining his father's experience in alternative service to his own religious beliefs, he highlighted the countercultural nature of his commitments. Similarly, Miller's stories of his childhood encounters with racism in the southern United States serve to highlight his presentation of his family's religious values as atypical.

Central Canadian Brian Hunsberger noted that, as a teen, he had been immersed in a fundamentalist church culture that did not reflect his own understanding of religion.[25] He observed that the "appeal of fundamentalist religion" is that it provides clarity and the absence of complexity, but stated that he himself had "never been of that persuasion." He recalled a church discussion as a teenager in which he suggested that the story of the biblical prophet Jonah was perhaps allegorical rather than literal. He was told by a fellow young adult that if he "didn't believe Jonah was swallowed by a whale, [then he] didn't believe anything." He began to take "more critical views" of religious doctrine and to "be less accepting of the party line." His university education, which included courses in world religions and the required reading of *The Secular City* by Harvey Cox,[26] "opened [his] mind a little bit to other perspectives on religion." A tutorial leader at university introduced him to Christian-Marxist dialogue and helped shape his religious views, which led to "some separation" from part of his traditional Mennonite upbringing. This partial separation, Hunsberger commented, was not "hostile" or "resentful" but rather involved questioning if he "could really buy enough of the package to remain connected" to Mennonitism. He encountered "broadmindedness" among some Mennonite church members and experienced their acceptance, both of which he described as "unanticipated." As a consequence, he was "brought back to regular church participation" although he still feels "a little bit on the fringe." While he continues to question aspects of theology, he said, he appreciates the values espoused by the church and the friendships he finds in his church community.

Barb Draper, also from central Canada, was raised in a conservative religious community where "you don't have to talk about things, because the boundaries and the expectations are very clear and known."[27] She had many questions as a child, she said, but did not voice them. She found employment as a teacher at a Mennonite high school because "there weren't any other options," although she now feels that "God led me to go there." She expected the school to be a "conservative, evangelical" workplace, but found instead that "it was so freeing." Her fellow faculty members' approaches to religion were "much more nuanced" and allowed her to ask questions "without fearing the answers." She discovered there "an experiential kind of Christianity" that de-emphasized "strict rules. It's recognizing that life is full of shades of grey, and it's not black and white, and that you can find truth in the dark grey as well as the black." Her work experience at this school was "foundational" for her, in that it taught her "what it means to be Mennonite, and that it's not boxed, and it's not evangelical, and it's not ... yeah, it's not in a box."

As a child, Harold's parents read Bible stories to him regularly.[28] After supper, the family would gather to sing, read the Bible and often a religious devotional book, and pray. He was raised with an evangelical theology that emphasized the necessity of a crisis conversion experience: "recognize that you're a sinner and in need of God's grace, and you need to come and accept Jesus into your life, and be converted." As a young person, he had multiple conversion experiences "to make sure that I was in, you know? [laughs] Looking back on it, it seems sort of silly, and yet I think there is something about the passion of that which I don't entirely discount." Over time, discipleship (that is, patterning one's life after that of Christ) became more important to him. For a time as a teenager, Harold's religious expression was more charismatic, "where one encounters the Spirit more directly with emotion and openness to direct interventions of God." As a young adult, his religious expression gradually shifted to one that was "more contemplative." He discovered Catholic writers, including Thomas Merton and Henri Nouwen. He "fell in love with liturgy" and his personal Bible reading shifted from "a Bible study orientation to kind of a *lectio divina*, a kind of prayerful experience of scripture, and finding meaning in liturgy and ritual and symbol." Harold concluded that, over the years, he has become "much more comfortable with mystery" and is "not as categorical on some things" as he once was.

These progress narratives characterize an individual's religious experience as a journey from limited or inadequate theological understandings to understandings that are more enlightened or more valid. As scholars Robert Wuthnow and Wade Clark Roof have shown, many North American Christians describe their religious understandings using a journey or growth model,[29] as did many of the Mennonites I interviewed. Hunsberger was one of the few interview participants who discussed in detail the importance of books, post-secondary education, and church attendance in shaping his religious views. These all played a role in contributing to his increasing willingness to question religious authority. Draper was raised in an environment in which religion was "always-already" and in which religious understanding was primarily about cultural and moral boundaries established by her parents and the Mennonite community. Using the metaphor of a box, she explained how her work experience expanded her religious world view to the point that she no longer acknowledges such limited boundaries. Harold described a variety of religious understandings during the course of his life, from traditional crisis conversion experiences through religious charisma to liturgy and mysticism. His story reveals the inherent danger of religious narratives of progress, which can be dismissive of earlier religious understandings. While Harold acknowledged that his religious views had changed over time, he refused to describe his religious trajectory as "progress," because doing so would deny the emotional truth of his previous experiences.

Stories, Robert Wuthnow reminds us, are "the main vehicles by which the sacred is communicated and transformed."[30] Telling stories is "a way of reconstructing ourselves ... A story provides us with an account of how we arrived here, where we were before, and what the differences are."[31] As was the case with the religious "small group" movement Wuthnow studied, the Mennonites in this study told certain stories about themselves and their religious experience, and the content and form of their stories were equally revealing. The narratives shared within the context of the small groups Wuthnow studied all tended to have "happy endings."[32] However, in the privacy of the oral history interview, which at times felt almost confessional, participants were not bound by the collective religious expectations of their co-religionists. Accordingly, unlike Wuthnow's findings, not all of the religious narratives shared by the Mennonites I interviewed were triumphalist.

Sociologist Nancy Ammerman argues for the usefulness of narrative analysis in the study of religion.[33] Religious stories, she declares, are "contingent accounts of how life proceeds" and thus are capable of taking many different forms.[34] It is important, then, that scholars not judge people's religiosity and refrain from assuming "that people who choose or who mix and match are inherently 'less' religious than those whose lives are shaped by a single religious trajectory in a homogeneous religious community."[35]

The interview participants discussed here used five narrative structures. Affective narratives were less common, perhaps because charismatic religion, emotional display, and engagement with the arts have been undervalued in the North American Mennonite community historically. Progress narratives were in abundance in part because, during interviews, my question asking how their religious belief or understanding had changed over time invited such a narrative (although there were some narrators who stated that their faith had remained unchanged). As well, progress narratives may have been popular because crisis conversion is not as common an understanding among Mennonites. Although some of the narrators had been affected by the evangelical revival movements of mid-twentieth century North America, many of these worked through the psychological and emotional repercussions of fire-and-brimstone salvation stories to embrace faith-as-a-journey narratives instead. Countercultural narratives were similarly widespread among interview participants, probably as a consequence of the collective memory of Mennonites as a persecuted people (particularly in sixteenth- and seventeenth-century Europe).

Narratives regarding death and adversity, while not uncommon among religious people, were given some unexpected nuances here. Death narratives were more than attempts to cope with an inevitable telos. Narrators used them to explain their decisions to change their life goals, to find positive value in serious illness, and to assert the authority of emotion over intellect. Problem narratives were likewise boundless, not merely depicting religion as a coping mechanism. Such narratives allowed interview participants to view problems as triggers for religious re-evaluation or as motivators for personal agency. And in some cases, the problem narrative was presented without resolution.

These varieties of religious narrative demonstrate that religious understandings are complex, are shaped by both individual and collective experience, and are revealed in stories. "We tell stories not so much to illustrate as to affirm who we are and what gives identity, purpose, and meaning to our existence ... Narrative is motivated by a search for meaning; when people tell stories, essentially they bring order and direction to their lives."[36] One of the most important conclusions that may be derived from these stories of religious belief is that scholars cannot understand how and why people believe as they do by simply studying church doctrine or theological texts. As religion scholar Wade Clark Roof observes, "Talking with adults about their religious upbringing has convinced me that spirituality is much more deeply rooted in our personal histories, in our families and congregations, than in anything else. If we are to understand it, one way of doing so is by paying close attention to these life histories."[37] A "lived religion" approach that focuses on those in the pew rather than those behind the pulpit must be combined with an oral history approach that allows participants to craft personal religious meanings, and with discourse analysis that is attentive to the meanings contained by the narrative structures of the life stories so obtained.[38] To rephrase oral historian Alessandro Portelli's well-known dictum, such a method reveals "not just what people believed, but what they wanted to believe, what they thought they believed, and what they now think they believed."[39]

Mennonites expressed their connection to the divine through individual experiences rather than doctrinal statements. Although the experiences were unique, their use of a limited number of narrative forms to describe them and express their meaning allowed them to identify as part of a larger community. With an individualized understanding of their relationship to God, and without a central authority to determine their response to labour unions, it is perhaps not surprising that Mennonites in the late twentieth century were unable to reach agreement on what their religious response to labour conflicts should be. In an environment in which such varied (and even contradictory) narratives testified nonetheless to a shared religious commitment, how could one expect uniformity of opinion on other matters? Competing individualist responses to questions about the integration of religion and labour were unavoidable. The narrative forms of religious belief discussed here, then, reveal the significance of individualism in modern Mennonite belief. Such individualized approaches to religious understanding meant that North American Mennonites did not have a cohesive theological response to contemporary issues – including labour unions. Instead, as will be seen, their attitudes to unions were similarly fragmented and based on personal and familial experience, rather than national identity, gender, or denominational membership.

2

"Not part of the landscape"

Attitudes toward Unions

Led by the (Old) Mennonite Church in the northeastern United States, most North American Mennonite church leadership bodies adopted a strong anti-union position in the first half of the twentieth century.[1] "In most places Mennonite leaders urged their people to avoid labor unions, which they saw as potentially violent and competing with the church for members' loyalty."[2] By the 1960s, these strictures against union involvement by church members had largely disappeared, in part due to the difficulty of enforcing them among an increasingly individualist laity. Nonetheless, the legacy of this religious teaching – but even more so, the farm and small business background of most Mennonites in the mid-twentieth century – persisted in the continued refusal of most Mennonites to join unions.

Many of the comments of the Mennonites I interviewed reflect their definition of unions as urban industrial organizations, although farm labour organizations did exist in rural settings. (Two such are the United Farm Workers and the Farm Labor Organizing Committee, discussed in chapters 3 and 4). Rural Mennonites encountered labour conflict as both farm managers and farm workers, unsurprisingly. Such conflict, however, tended not to shape the assumptions they held that unions were primarily expressions of urban industrial organization. Unions were seen as "outside" influences rather than organizations that emerged from and responded to the demands of their rank-and-file members.

In the last half of the twentieth century, then, unions were not a regular part of either the daily familial or religious discourse of Mennonites – they were simply, in the words of one interviewee, "not part of the landscape."[3] Thus, Mennonites absorbed the anti-union ethos of the farm and small business communities of which they were a part. A further influence on Mennonites' attitudes at the time I conducted these interviews was the broader North American society's popular criticism of union greed – a criticism that escalated with the automotive industry crisis of 2008–10.

Mennonite disinterest in labour unions is part of a broader North American anti-union sentiment that has received some scholarly attention of late. Historian Lawrence Richards argues that it was not just employer resistance, labour legislation, and de-industrialization that brought about the decline of union membership in the United States in the late twentieth century, but the existence of an anti-union culture. The Red scare, union bureaucratization, and an improved standard of living all contributed to postwar disinterest in unions; as well, unions competed with the "ideal of individualism, of getting ahead on one's own."[4] Richards' analysis has been critiqued for relying on popular media as representative of people's beliefs;[5] in this chapter, I rely instead on the oral history interviews I conducted. Sociologist Seymour Martin Lipset and economist Noah Meltz note that, although American attitudes toward unions are more negative, Americans are more likely than Canadians to join unions. They argue that Canada's combined history of social democracy and European conservative heritage – and, as Richards argues, American values of laissez-faire individualism – are the explanation.[6] Within the Mennonite community, unions competed with religious leaders and the church as a form of alternative counter-cultural collective identity and authority.

For the Mennonites I interviewed, this greater social context, together with their parents' and their own experiences with unions, were far more significant in shaping their attitudes than was the limited religious teaching on unions that they received in church. Few of those interviewed articulated a religious explanation for their views, outlining the extension of religious tenets to the labour sphere. For half of the participants, unions were so irrelevant to their lives and beliefs that they had nothing at all to say about them. And unlike Lipset and Meltz, I did not find that the views on unions these interview participants expressed were differentiated by nationality – nor by the particular denomination of Mennonitism to which they belonged. I conducted interviews with workers, pastors, business owners and managers, professionals, and academics in three US states and three Canadian provinces. The views of these Mennonites were differentiated by their class position to some extent. Far more significant, however, were personal work experiences and parental attitudes.

Union membership among Mennonites in the late twentieth century was far lower than among the general population. Surveys of North American Mennonite church members reveal that only 5 percent were union members in 1972, and 6 percent in 1989.[7] An additional 11 percent in 1972 and 18 percent in 1989 were members of professional or academic societies, some of which (such as teachers' associations) should be considered labour unions.[8] Even including these latter percentages, Mennonite union membership fell considerably short of average membership rates in Canada and the United States. In Canada, union density (the ratio of unionized workers to paid workers) has remained fairly constant since the Second World War, at about 30 percent.[9] In the United States, union density has been in steady decline since the 1950s, dropping from 34 percent to 12 percent.[10]

Lipset argues that the difference in union density in the two countries can be explained by their differences in values: Canada as a nation is "more statist, group oriented, communitarian, less individualistic, and, ironically, more social democratic."[11] Other scholars criticize Lipset's explanation of the differences in union membership between the two nations,[12] since surveys suggest that nationality is not a significant factor in shaping public attitudes toward unions. South of the border, a review of statistical surveys by political scientists Costas Panagopoulos and Peter Francia reveals that the attitudes toward unions of most people in the United States have been "generally favorable since the mid-1990s."[13] Although more Americans were union members in the 1950s, a slightly higher percentage in 2005 than in the 1950s was sympathetic to unions involved in labour disputes.[14] Approval of unions in the United States has remained fairly stable since the 1940s (see Table 2.1).[15]

Scholars have attempted to determine whether union support is differentiated within the population. Political scientists Matthew Mendelsohn and Richard Nadeau examined the 1988 Canadian Election Study data and found that, while the majority of Canadians have positive attitudes toward unions, such support is divided along religious lines. A strong majority of 63 percent of Canadian Catholics support unions, whereas only 53 percent of Canadian Protestants do so.[16] Ignoring religion, sociologist Tracy Chang, using data from the 1991 US General Social Survey, concludes that personal experience of economic hardship has a greater influence on attitudes to unions than does gender, race, or class.[17] Panagopoulos and Francia suggest

Table 2.1 Gallup Poll data on attitudes toward labour unions in the United States.

Decade	*Average approval rating (%)*
1940–1948	65
1951–1959	71
1961–1967	67
1972–1979	61
1981–1986	57
1991–1997	60
2001–2005	60

Source: Calculated using data provided in Costas Panagopoulos and Peter L. Francia, "The Polls – Trends: Labor Unions in the United States," *Public Opinion Quarterly* 72 no. 1 (2008): 139 Table 4.

that the media is also a strong influence in shaping these attitudes. They observe that polls that coincide with well-publicized negative news about unions' roles in contemporaneous labour disputes result (perhaps not surprisingly) in less sympathetic views of unions.[18] This observation may explain the responses of some Mennonites in this study, since many of the interviews were conducted not long after bailouts by both the Canadian and the US federal governments of the automotive industry, whose failure many in the media at the time blamed on the autoworkers unions.[19]

Several interview participants referenced government rescue of the big three automakers as evidence of the inherent greed of organized labour. One professional explained that unions had been "indispensable" in addressing the abuses of industrial capitalism in the past, including child labour, unregulated working conditions and hours, and the mining industry. Modern unions, however, were "too powerful," as when "General Motors employees with seniority earn seventy dollars an hour." Such wages, together with autoworkers' pensions, had "bankrupted the industry."[20] Nor was union greed limited to the United Auto Workers and Canadian Auto Workers. "Local companies [in other industries] shut down because union demands are unbearable."[21] A business owner concurred, commenting that the auto industry's problems were due to "union refusal to make concessions" and unions' desire to make "money for nothing, holding companies hostage."[22] An academic declared that unions had "succeeded to such a degree" that they were "just as selfish and ruthless" as any

Table 2.2 Responses to the statement: "A church member should not join a union even if getting or holding a job depends on union membership."

Response	*1972*	*1989*
strongly agree	na	2%
agree	18%	12%
undecided	38%	32%
disagree	44%	45%
strongly disagree	na	9%

Source: Raw data of 1972 and 1989 Church Membership Profiles, provided by Bruno Dyck, Asper School of Business, University of Manitoba. This raw data is more detailed than the summarized results published in *Anabaptists Four Centuries Later* and *The Mennonite Mosaic*. J. Howard Kauffman and Leland Harder. *Anabaptists Four Centuries Later: A Profile of Five Mennonite and Brethren in Christ Denominations* (Scottdale, PA: Herald Press, 1975); J. Howard Kauffman, and Leo Driedger, *The Mennonite Mosaic: Identity and Modernization,* with a foreword by Donald B. Kraybill (Scottdale, PA and Waterloo, ON: Herald Press, 1991).

employer, "even to the point of self destruction in the auto industry."[23] A business manager observed that the economic downturn that began in 2008 had led to "bad friction," and that part of the problem was the "unsustainable costs" of organized labour.[24] A farmer agreed, noting that unions had "probably contributed to the economic downfall." Unions were no longer a positive influence; instead, they protected "those who don't want to work."[25] Another business owner recalled how "upset" he was when watching Canadian Auto Workers president Basil E. "Buzz" Hargrove on television. He believed Hargrove "did much damage and abused the system," and he had "neither time nor respect" for that.[26] A professional noted that labour unions in Canada created their own problems by being too demanding. He declared that collective agreements and pensions that were too rich were at least partly to blame for the collapse of General Motors.[27] Another professional stated bluntly, "Auto workers killed the industry."[28]

Notwithstanding such vehemence against unionized auto workers, among North American Mennonites historical *attitudes toward unions* may not have been markedly different from those of the general population, although union *membership rates* have been. Less than 20 percent of Mennonites had religious objections to union membership in the late twentieth century (see Table 2.2), and their attitudes varied according to their class position.[29] Economist Roy Vogt's examination of the 1972 church membership survey data reveals that Mennonite professionals had the least negative views of organized labour (with only 16 percent holding strong negative attitudes toward unions), while farmers were most negative (30 percent with strong negative attitudes). The percentages for Mennonite business people and blue-collar workers were 21 percent and 25 percent respectively.[30]

Missing from these sociological studies is an analysis of *why* people hold the opinions they do. The earlier interest of labour historians in explaining why the working class failed to organize in any lasting and significant manner in either Canada or the United States has been replaced with an almost complete avoidance of discussion of workers' motivations.[31] Labour historians Leon Fink and Alan Dawley were instrumental in turning the debate away from the question of why workers had failed to act in accordance with leftist political theory.[32] Historian Elizabeth Faue notes that these and other labour historians' redirection of attention – from the focus of John R. Commons and the "Wisconsin School" on institutions to the study of under-represented groups, gender differences, and the labour process itself – has resulted in the neglect of "little researched and difficult dimensions of class identity or the subjective meaning of these experiences."[33]

This critique should not be interpreted as a dismissal of the significance of labour historians' incorporation of culture, race and ethnicity, gender, and religion into their work in the last few decades. Contributions by scholars in both the United States and Canada have transformed the historical study of work and workers.[34] Nonetheless, much work remains to be done, particularly with respect to the integration of religious studies and labour history.[35] E.P. Thompson's brilliant discussion of the relationships between Methodism and the English working class is an oft-cited classic, and Herbert Gutman has made a similar (although much less extensive) effort with his discussion of Protestantism and American workers.[36] In Canada, Lynne Marks's integration of religion and labour history was met with some vituperation.[37] While some historians acknowledge the importance of identity creation, values formation, and narrative in understanding labour history,[38] few seriously examine the role that religion plays in these formative processes.

Labour historians Elizabeth Faue and Lucy Taksa have argued that different methodological approaches are needed if scholars are to better understand the historical creation of identities and formation of values. Biographies and family stories allow historians to uncover the diversity and malleability of class identity.[39] Oral history reveals the significance of the private sphere in labour history and uncovers individuals' understandings of class.[40] This study of North American Mennonites' attitudes and beliefs regarding unions, therefore, contributes to the literature by exploring how and why individuals construct narratives that weave together their religious understandings with their work experiences.

As the twentieth century opened, North American Mennonite churches made efforts to direct Mennonites' work experiences. Beginning in the 1930s, Mennonite church conferences issued statements warning against the compromise of Christian principles that union membership would entail. Union membership was rejected in part because the threat of strike action was considered an exercise of force (coercion) on the part of labour. The 1937 (Old) Mennonite Church resolution against union membership referenced the Bible verses that were typically used by Mennonites to defend their position against organized labor: "Be ye not unequally yoked together with unbelievers: for what fellowship hath righteousness with unrighteousness? and what communion hath light with darkness? And what concord hath Christ with Belial? or what part hath he that believeth with an infidel? And what agreement hath the temple of God with idols? for ye are the temple of the living God; as God hath said, I will dwell in them, and walk in them; and I will be their God, and they shall be my people."[41] The 1937 statement was one in a series of condemnations of union membership by various Mennonite denominations.[42]

After the Second World War, these Mennonite churches slowly began to withdraw their objections to organized labour. The (Old) Mennonite Church's Committee on Economic and Social Relations (formerly the Committee on Industrial Relations) acknowledged in 1954 that unions "serve a useful purpose for the maintenance of justice and a balance of power in a sub-Christian society." Mennonites were free to "cooperate with the union (as ... with the state) in so far as doing so does not conflict with ... Christian testimony."[43] Similarly, the Mennonite Brethren Church decided in 1969 not to forbid union membership. Mennonites were warned, however, that they should not engage in union-related violence or intimidation – presumably striking and picketing could be defined to be included in this restriction.[44] Prejudice against unions had not completely disappeared: the original motion had included the phrase "nor should we judge or condemn those who are members of unions." This wording was removed when the motion was amended.

The fact that Mennonite churches by the 1970s no longer forbade their members from joining and participating in unions did not end church leaders' efforts to assist fellow Mennonites in avoiding such membership. The (Old) Mennonite Church's Committee on Industrial Relations, under the direction of Guy F. Hershberger, had been active in making arrangements with eastern United States labour unions and employers that allowed Mennonites to plead conscientious objection to union membership and pay the equivalent of union dues to charity.[45] The absorption of this committee into the (Old) Mennonite Church's Committee on Peace and Social Concerns, together with the onset of the Second World War and then the Vietnam War, meant that Mennonites' conscientious objection focus shifted from unions to the military. Nonetheless, Mennonite church leadership continued to provide assistance to individual Mennonites who objected to union membership. In July 1974, the (Old) Mennonite Board of Congregational Ministries held an ad hoc meeting at Goshen College to discuss the California migrant labour situation. Meeting participant Darrel Kaufman "asked that the church spell out what we believe concerning labor unions."[46] Kaufman was a Teamster Union member, but objected to corruption in that union. He asked the meeting how Mennonites could be union members "in light of our peace position. He felt he may need to turn in his union card." The economic consequences for him could be serious, as doing so would "jeopardize his job and may mean selling his business." A discussion followed as to "how the church can support Darrel and other persons when they need to make costly decisions."[47]

Jim Troyer, a former school guidance counsellor in Michigan, was one of the few Mennonites I interviewed who provided a detailed theological rationale for his anti-union stance and who described having to make just such a costly decision.[48] In the 1970s, he refused either to join the Michigan Teachers Association (MTA) or to participate in a work stoppage the union had called. One of his objections to paying dues to the MTA was that some of the money was used to purchase alcohol for teacher parties or for general meetings. Because he perceived alcohol abuse to be a major problem in the area, he objected to union dues being spent in this manner. The division's superintendent attempted to remove the guidance faculty from the local bargaining unit, classifying Troyer as administration and thus avoiding the conflict with union membership. This effort was unsuccessful, and the local union president, Troyer claimed, decided that he would "see to it that that 'preacher' [Troyer] got fired." Both union and state representatives reminded him that he was part of the bargaining unit, but Troyer insisted that he was not, declaring that he had religious exemption and that forcing him to pay union dues was a violation of his religious rights. His claims, he said, were "met with laughter," so he went to the Mennonite Historical Library in nearby Goshen, Indiana, and obtained photocopies of papers that documented Guy Hershberger's efforts to achieve union exemption for Mennonites in the 1930s and 1940s, which he planned to use to support his decision. A local Catholic lawyer, Pat Kelly, agreed to argue his case pro bono. A counter offer was made to Troyer: to avoid a "legal battle with the Mennonite Church," the union was willing to allow him to pay the equivalent of dues to a mutually acceptable charity, minus unspecified "negotiating fees."

Troyer was reluctant to accept this compromise. He insisted that he would not participate in any work stoppages, strikes, or demonstrations. The union responded by demanding that the school board fire him. The precariousness of his economic position made this time a very difficult one for his family, as both he and his wife recalled tearfully. After lengthy meetings, the school board's lawyers recommended that he not be fired. Ultimately, the decision was made to establish the Manistique Foundation Fund to which Troyer would pay the equivalent of union dues which would then fund a summer camp scholarship for physically challenged children. Troyer was displeased that his contribution was "funneled through the union" so that it looked like a union donation rather than his own.[49]

The response of the Mennonite community to Troyer's circumstances was mixed. There was "no article in the [(Old) Mennonite church periodical] *Gospel Herald*" about his situation, Troyer noted, but he received "letters of support from everywhere." Job offers came from the Iowa Mennonite School, as well as Mennonite schools in Goshen and Fairview. Members of his church congregation were sympathetic at the time, but by the time of the interview, opinions in the congregation had shifted. The chair of his church council was a union member at the local paper mill, and did not see such membership as a religious compromise.[50]

Troyer remained employed at Manistique, but his battle with the union "created tension with faculty" who "intentionally paid [him] back" in ways he did not specify. The biggest issue with these co-workers, in his view, was not his refusal to pay union dues but his refusal to drink with them. Even the local ministerial association served alcohol at their meetings, Troyer commented, and he and a Lutheran were the only ones in attendance who would not drink. "They tried to get a glass in my hand so people wouldn't know" he was against alcohol, he commented.[51]

Troyer explained that he appreciated the role that unions had played historically in addressing injustice in the workplace, but he did not agree with their methods. Unions have "helped workers misused by industry," he commented. Slaves in the southern United States, he asserted, were in some ways better off than northern factory workers: slaves at least received food and medicine; the factory provided nothing. Such injustice, however, did not justify the use of force (union coercion) to make employers respond in the way desired. Mennonites should not use power, since doing so is inconsistent with their ethic of nonviolence, he explained. Unions have done more harm than good, but he "would not argue that the union has done the church's job" in addressing injustice. Nor was the church itself exempt from criticism: even in Mennonite church politics, "money talks." An ongoing problem, Troyer stressed, was Mennonites' tendency to address economic injustice only overseas rather than in their own communities. He noted that "MEDA [Mennonite Economic Development Associates] is no help in Michigan's Upper Peninsula" with respect to the struggling lumber industry, for example. Troyer hastened to add that he was not claiming that Christians should always side with the weak, but that the "economics of Jesus are to be generous and concerned regarding the needy, as everything is given by God. Start with those principles. We are past the time when we can have a monolithic answer [to labour issues]."[52]

Troyer's interview was both typical and atypical of these Mennonites' discussion of labour unions. He was the only one with whom I spoke who had tried to avoid the union membership his job required – and certainly the only one to defend his position through archival use of Hershberger's 1930s efforts! Where his story was similar to others was in his explanation of his convictions. Unions had value, as evidenced by both the historical and contemporary exploitation of labour. Their flaw was their embrace of coercion as a tactic, a mild form of violence but violence nonetheless. The church, too, was flawed in its inappropriate use of power in church relations and its limited engagement with economic issues close to home. Troyer's rejection of union membership was predicated on the union's methods, which he as a nonresistant Mennonite could not accept.

Other interview participants described the religious basis for their parents' objections to union membership, although in many cases their religious understanding was shaky at best. Business owner Vernon Erb explained that his parents, church, and community derived their anti-union position from "the scripture on two masters," an oblique reference to Matthew 6, verse 24: "No one can serve two masters; for a slave will either hate the one and love the other, or be devoted to the one and despise the other. You cannot serve God and wealth" (NRSV).[53] Presumably, the two masters in Erb's interpretation were God and the union. As a business owner himself, Erb's interpretation of this Bible passage is perhaps understandable. But similar religious rationales were not absent among working-class participants. Dave Klassen (a truck driver, farmer, and mechanic) was taught by his parents that unions were "bad" and originated "from nonbelievers." A union was a "group that didn't appreciate employers and demanded rights and higher wages" and thus was neither "right nor Godly." Making demands of others was not the action of a Christian, he stated.[54]

Others were more vague regarding the origins of their parents' stance on unions, whether for or against. Former auto worker Wilbur Roth simply stated that a "basic distrust of unions was indoctrinated."[55] Library worker Paul Friesen recalled that while there was no explicit discussion of unions in his home when he was a child, "someone must have said unions were bad or else it was subliminal."[56] Supply teacher Ellen Ibele was uncertain whether her family's pro-union views were a consequence of religious faith or "just dignity and respect" in general.[57] Teacher Barb Draper believed that her father's support of his union, even during a strike, may have been connected to universal "basics like fairness and justice." More important, though, was the idea that co-workers "have to stick together. You can't be a fair-weather friend."[58]

A few Mennonites connected their family's anti-union position and the church's early twentieth-century stance against Freemasonry.

While the biblical injunction to avoid being "unequally yoked" with unbelievers served to connect unions and Freemasonry in Mennonite theology, [59] interviewees did not offer this explanation. Asked about the religious reasons against Mennonite membership in unions, Alice Ramseyer's reply referenced only the Masons. She had "a strong feeling that we don't join, that it's not a Mennonite thing." She said she had not understood this position until she read Dan Brown's novels, at which point she realized that Mennonites disapproved of secret ceremonies.[60] Blaine Millar recalled that his grandmother disapproved of the Masons and equated unions with the army. All three organizations were off limits for Mennonites, in her view. It was "assumed that it was obvious" that Mennonites did not participate in strikes.[61] Barb Draper "wonder[ed] if in the past the Old Order Mennonite Church said organizations outside the church were not good." She knew that church resolutions had been passed that declared it inappropriate for Mennonites to join secret societies like the Masons. She was raised to believe that Mennonites did not participate in "Brownies, Scouts, organized sports ... [or] Lion Club" and speculated that "labour unions were the same."[62]

Some invoked a "Mennonite work ethic" as an explanation for their stance on organized labour. A pastor's son explained that he was raised with "a sense of pride in work." His recollections of his childhood were that people were happy to have a job and a salary and so were not demanding of their employers, since they knew that if they did not perform adequately on the job, they could easily be replaced. Conjuring up a nostalgic, rosy past, he noted that there was "different thinking" in those days, a "strong work ethic." People took "pride in their farms and homes. There was no litter. Everything was very clean and tidy. Everybody pitched in; everybody contributed."[63] Another interviewee, the child of a small-business owner, was raised with a similar perspective. It was important for "labour to fit in and respect the authority and investment the company owner puts in. Be thankful for your job and do it well."[64] Such a work ethic, religiously based or not, left no place for unions in the minds of these interview participants.

The interviews reveal that parents were important influences on Mennonites' attitudes toward unions. These findings are consistent with those of one of the few studies of predictors of union attitudes. A 1991 study of high school students and university undergraduates determined that parental attitudes were significant in shaping their children's perspectives on unions, while parental membership in unions was comparatively unimportant.[65] Randy Spallinger's recollections of his father's work experiences exemplify this distinction. His father was a member of the United Auto Workers for thirty-four years and was laid off by Ford in the 1980s; his unemployment benefits were calculated using accumulated credits based on seniority at the Ford plant. When his father returned to work in 1985, having saved many of these credits, the union claimed that he had used them all. Although he was greatly upset by this situation, he "never fought it. What are you going to do? It didn't seem right. A different person would fight," but his father disliked confrontation. His father's experiences shaped Spallinger's understanding of unions: one structured around, in his own words, "skepticism, stoicism, and wariness."[66]

Other adult children of union members noted that their Mennonite parents' frustration with their union shaped their perspective more than did their parents' decision to be union members. One academic recalled the economic insecurity that accompanied his father's strike activities as a member of the Canadian Auto Workers at General Motors. Strikes were "upsetting" for the family, particularly at Christmas, but her father believed picketing was necessary out of "loyalty to the people he worked with."[67] Both of Jonathan Janzen's parents were union members: his father belonged to the Manitoba Teachers Society, and his mother was a unionized nurse. From them, he had a "sense that unions were frustrating because promotions and raises were based on seniority, not skills." He had the "general sense" from his parents that unions were "both positive and negative." His parents were "not militant unionists, but not anti-union," a viewpoint similar to his own.[68]

Some children of farmers and immigrants were raised with suspicion of unions. Brian Hunsberger explained that his farming father saw himself as a small business owner, and thus distrusted unions.[69] David Giesbrecht's farming father associated striking unions with the Russian Communism he had struggled to escape as a 1920s immigrant to Canada. These memories were so "frightful and ingrained" that his father opposed "any protest of any kind by Christians." His father's "vision of the good life" was agricultural; the city and all that was associated with urban life (including labour unions) "represented evil."[70] Dave Klassen's farming parents taught him to be conscientious, to give an honest day's work for his pay, and to "go beyond the call." His parents were opposed to unions, believing they "flew in the face of the understanding that you can't tell your employer what to pay." If you were dissatisfied with working conditions, the solution should be to "work elsewhere" rather than "force demands by a strike ... If you don't like it, then work elsewhere." His parents taught him that unions were not part of a biblical view of labour.[71]

Tom Bontreger also was raised to believe that Mennonites "were to be nonunion." Unions were a "barrier in the relationship between employer and employee." The Bible passage that noted that a worker is due his wages[72] was a significant part of his upbringing, and the early teaching he received in home and church was "to go beyond what was agreed upon." For his father, the owner of a trucking company, this meant that he should "always buy the hamburgers" for his non-unionized workers and for his customers. Bontreger noted that union workers and their employers did not have this same friendly social arrangement. When he worked briefly as a driver for United Parcel Service, a unionized company, he attended union meetings out of interest. He believed the union "took away freedom" because of the necessity of following work rules. "You had to go by the book; you couldn't solve things your way." Unions had some value, however: he commented that he "didn't begrudge the extra benefits" of union contracts.[73]

Support for unions among these Mennonites as an extension of leftist political commitments was rare but not absent. Hans Houshower's grandparents had been members of the Industrial Workers of the World. In the 1920s and 1930s, his grandfather was Bluffton College's faculty representative for the socialist vote. In his family, the Presbyterian minister and Socialist Party presidential candidate Norman Thomas was "a hero." A favourable attitude to unions was part of his family's oral tradition, which combined the "Bible with higher education, creativity, justice, and progressive politics."[74] Wendy Chappell-Dick explained that because she had "grown up with peace marches," she was "comfortable in protests, and with interaction with union delegations" at such gatherings. She was raised in a family that idealized Pete Seeger and Woody Guthrie and so she "didn't question modern labour unions."[75] Stefan Epp, noting that he had "perhaps read too much Marx," declared that the Mennonite tradition of working cooperatively to benefit the whole in the formation of churches, schools, and insurance agencies was paralleled in the function of unions as an "opportunity for workers to work together, especially in a situation that can be adversarial." Unions helped the "marginalized and oppressed" to "participate more fully" in society and to "move beyond oppression and marginalization." His views, he said, were shaped in part by the social gospel of theologian Walter Rauschenbusch. If Christians "answer the Biblical call and read the Old Testament prophets and Gospels and letters" then there is a "clear obligation to feed and clothe and house which requires structural change."[76] Marianne Coleman was taught as a child that "anything that helped the plight of the common worker" was good. Her father was a strong supporter of Canada's New Democratic Party. Unions were viewed positively because they "helped the worker against capitalist evils."[77] Coleman held this perspective as well, until her own work experiences in union environments in later years altered her views.

Coleman explained that her experience as a health care worker left her "cynical about unions." She thought unions in her field had "fostered an attitude of 'what can you give to me.'" They focused on seniority, breaks, days off, and what was owed them. The result was that workers who were "old, tired, burnt out, and limping" were kept caring for vulnerable patients who "need better care than seems to be offered by those in it for money." She believed unionized health care workers were "not passionate for the work's sake."[78] Social worker James Yoder, a union member for seventeen years, had a more tolerant view of unionized workers with poor work ethics. He believed that unions were "terrific" and that "everybody should have one." He could not condemn union protection of colleagues who were "not the most competent" since "we all need meaningful work."[79]

Like Coleman, Randy Spallinger, an autoworker, was frustrated by what he perceived as the poor work ethic of his fellow union members. He had been employed by a non-unionized Japanese company and liked the "less combative" nature of labour relations at that workplace. He was profoundly affected by an encounter with a company vice-president who was cleaning sinks in a restroom; such a thing would never happen at Ford, he noted. While he appreciated union wages and the union foreman's efforts to ensure that the details of the collective agreement were fulfilled at Ford, he was dismayed by some union members' attitudes. Some refused to show up for work yet demanded their pay. Some were disruptive. Others abused alcohol and drugs, even while on the job, yet were protected by the union. His first factory job had been in a new factory with newly hired workers, and their attitudes were positive. When he moved to Ford, he was surrounded by older workers who "know how to handle the foreman, owned the place, and got away with murder." He claimed that these older, unionized workers took a forty-minute break every twenty minutes; "somehow, these old guys worked that." Others left the factory floor during their breaks, went to the local Elks Lodge for liquor shots, and "came back hammered." In the 1970s, there was much drug use on the factory floor, but this was no longer the case by the turn of the century. In those days, it was "not uncommon at 5 a.m. to see vodka on the floor. That was an eye opener." Spallinger blamed the union for protecting such workers. In his view, "smart folks don't want a union [representative] job, so loud mouths get them." The union representatives were usually "loud mouths with little or no education and no competitive skills."[80]

Such "loud mouths" were part of Brian Hunsberger's frustration with his experience as a union member. Hunsberger worked two-and-a-half years in the 1980s as a municipal planner, a job that required him to be a member of the Canadian Union of Public Employees (CUPE). As a university student, he had studied the historical background of the union movement and was sympathetic to its aims. As a CUPE member, he became aware that the union was divided between those who worked outdoors and those who worked indoors. Those who worked outside were more militant and less sympathetic to management, while those employed indoors worked directly with management and saw them as "less demonic." Those in union leadership tended to be outdoor workers. "Curiosity and self interest" led Hunsberger to attend union meetings regularly. Those experiences led him to conclude that there was room for improvement, since "the system didn't work well." The militant attitude of the union was part of the problem, in his view.[81]

An academic worker expressed similar frustration with the radicalism of his fellow union members. He recalled that Mennonite professors Roy Vogt and Henry Rempel had been keen supporters of university faculty associations. He himself had attended a few faculty association meetings but became irritated by the radical opinions expressed by some members, describing them as "off the wall" and declaring that he "couldn't handle that; it was too far left." Although he went on strike two or three times and participated in picketing, "life is too short" for serious union involvement and his faculty association "is not a priority" for him. Due to the "pettiness" of some of the faculty association's discussions and activities, he decided he would "rather not be involved" in the organization, although he retained membership.[82]

For others, the source of their frustration was neither the perceived incompetence of co-workers nor union militancy but a fundamental misunderstanding or dislike of the role of unions themselves. An elementary school teacher observed that she "struggles" each year with the question of union membership. Some aspects of the union are good, but there are also "voices that don't represent" her priorities or why she teaches or what is important to her. The union is most vocal about salary issues and is "teacher-oriented rather than student-oriented," which she finds problematic: "It seems like there is a level of self-protection at the expense of anything else." Most important to the union are union members' own rights and salaries and hours, she noted. This perspective is "a very different way of thinking about work," one with which she "can't identify."[83] Others echoed this critique. A doctor declared that he had no problem crossing picket lines because his "highest respect was to the patients."[84] An academic worker asserted that the problem with teachers' unions and faculty associations was that their "legal mandate is to promote the interests of faculty, not students."[85] A professional similarly claimed that unions were "not influenced by the attitudes and values of Christians" in that they placed their "own interest above the common good."[86] Such comments reveal that these Mennonites either did not understand or did not accept that the mandate of a union is to represent workers and not any other group.

Not surprisingly, some business owners observed that unions were irrelevant, particularly in a well-managed company. The owner of a non-union business said he has "stated at different times" that if his workers ever unionized then he would know it was "time to sell" because he "couldn't run" the company with a union.[87] Another business owner also declared his preference that his workers remain non-unionized. He believes that if employees are treated "properly," as "fellow team members," and as "family – though that requires discernment at times," one might be able to prevent unionization. While he acknowledged the historical importance of unions, he believed that working conditions at his business were such that unions were unnecessary. "The reasons for union membership are already covered: compensation is fair, and workers are well cared for and well paid." The nature of his business required the use of union labour at trade shows from time to time; there were places in the

United States where he deliberately avoided exhibiting his company's products because of the expense of the venues. "Often the most costly is a place with a strong union and services by union labour." Not that unions were the only reason to avoid these places, he hastened to add; the location and venues themselves did not "fit their needs."[88]

One individual cited such Mennonite-owned non-unionized businesses as models for labour peace. These workplaces offered job sharing and profit sharing to their workers, and used a portion of their profits for such charitable projects as building orphanages for AIDS orphans in Africa. Mennonites, he declared, had a "tremendous heart for business and labour relations." While it was true that some Mennonite-owned businesses were "not good," he asserted that Mennonite business owners were "not cruel like the Pharaohs" but rather "expect lots and fairly reward" their employees. "God bless Palliser" – the Winnipeg Mennonite-owned furniture manufacturer – since they were "good to labour." The Mennonite owner of Palliser, Art DeFehr, gave "solace and aid worldwide" through his charitable activities in Bangladesh and through Mennonite Economic Development Associates.[89]

While no workers cited Mennonite employers as "models," some shared the view that unions were unnecessary. Dave Klassen worked as a truck driver for thirty-five years, five of them in a union environment. He stated that unions "have done the good they set out to do" but that in the early twenty-first century they were too militant. He also disapproved of the political advocacy of unions, particularly of the allegiance between the union movement and the New Democratic Party in British Columbia. He dismissed union efforts to maintain or improve pension benefits, noting that most workers were neither organized nor had company pension plans, thus suggesting that unionized workers should be content with their lot. He relegated the value of unions to either the distant past or to "the third world where child labour and extremely poor conditions" existed and where employers and businesses situated in the industrialized countries took advantage of them and preyed on workers' needs.[90]

Another interviewee challenged the view that well-run businesses made union efforts unnecessary. Steven Webster recalled that he had been asked, as part of the human resources department at Bristol Meyers Squibb, to "lie to employees" during a union drive – an illegal act, he noted. He had worked with other businesses where organization efforts were unsuccessful, and one in Detroit where a union drive succeeded. He has "never felt strongly" about unions, he declared, but observed that it is a "challenge for Mennonites to be in a hard-core union environment." He has deliberately chosen not to work in union shops, in part because of his belief that union activities are "inconsistent" with Christian beliefs.[91]

Others' experiences with unions were less easily categorized, composed of a mix of positive and negative encounters. An academic worker described how he had fought actively and unsuccessfully against unionization at his place of employment. Following union certification, he participated in the writing of the union's constitution and served as a union steward. He explained these seemingly conflicting actions by saying that he "likes to tilt at windmills." He believed that once he no longer had a choice about union membership, it was his responsibility to "try to make it better or prevent it from being worse." Nonetheless, he drew the line at serving on the union executive.[92]

For at least one Mennonite, gender issues were significant in shaping her perspective on unions. Employed as a chemical technologist by the Canadian federal government, Valerie Paulley went to Ottawa in the 1970s as a young female bargaining representative for her predominantly male union. At the union convention, older male union members presented a demand for back pay for undervalued work as a topic "specifically for women." Paulley objected to this wording. She voted against a resolution on this subject, the language of which she said was "strictly female versus male." Ironically, the older male union leaders at the convention singled her out and demanded she explain her vote, an act she found intimidating. She explained to them: "Stop the separatist language. Talk about jobs, not gender, irrespective of who did the work." She felt it was "very risky to stand out" by voting against the resolution, but she believed it was a question of "social justice."[93]

Ironically, Paulley's gender was an issue for her fellow unionists, even as her union involvement was problematic for her fellow church members. She did not speak about her union involvement at church – "deliberately so because of the comments of others" in the church about unions, none of which were positive. By not discussing her union experiences, Paulley felt that what her co-religionists "didn't know didn't hurt them or me."[94]

Other workers, too, spoke of the careful line they had to walk to ensure that their union involvement, however limited, did not become a source of friction with fellow church members. A teacher explained that her union participation had been constrained by the fact that her husband was a Mennonite minister. While her husband worked as a pastor in Alberta, she refrained from joining her union (dues payment was compulsory but membership was not). She did so because she worried that if she went on strike, it would create conflict in her church congregation, the majority of whose members were anti-union. She herself did not approve of striking, however, describing it as a labour action that was neither "effective nor adult." When her family moved to Ontario and her husband changed professions, she joined the union. She noted that she could "really see the benefit of being part of a good union," citing the example of the ability of Manitoba nurses to secure wage increases within hours of threatening to strike.[95]

Attempts to limit conflict with fellow church members over differences of opinion on whether Mennonites should be unionists were common. One academic served as staff representative for his union, an experience he described as a "good learning opportunity." The efforts of the provincial government in the 1990s to eliminate teacher and health worker contract provisions significantly influenced his thinking on unions and labour relations. It was a "stress to see employers nullify provisions negotiated in good faith and lobbied for through strikes and sacrificed pay." He had "no problem seeing validity in workers mutually trying to bring positive change" and "no problem seeing Jesus opposed to the abuse of power and kinds of unfairness workers deal with in many situations." His support of unions, and the lack of support for them by the business people and professionals in his church, meant that his church "care group" had to "agree to disagree on labour issues."[96] Vernon Erb recalled an experience as a "snowbird" in Florida. A Mennonite trucker he had met there had spoken favourably of unions and had been "offended and surprised" to find that Erb was not similarly enthusiastic, since the trucker thought a very pro-union stance was "the only way to go." Since then, Erb has been careful not to criticize unions to fellow Mennonites.[97]

Former meat packer Henry Peters was impatient with the blanket condemnation unions received from most in his Mennonite community. He observed, "If you want a good union, then Christians should join and change what's wrong. But people would rather criticize without taking responsibility." He "never had any doubts" himself about whether, as a Mennonite, he should be a union member. Unions protect workers against the favouritism of foremen, he noted, and allowed workers to "talk back if spoken to without worry." He strongly rejected early twentieth-century Mennonite objections to unions on the grounds of their coercive violence, asking rhetorically, "How many church members don't live their Christianity the rest of the week? There are many hypocrites. I know some. How to relate to your neighbour is not important, they think." Those Mennonites who object to unions should get involved and seek to improve them: "Don't just criticize and do nothing about it." He himself, he declared, was a "living witness" in the union. The reason so many Mennonites were opposed to unions, he declared, was that they "don't hear about good ones; the bad ones are louder." He believed that negative attitudes to unions were rooted in Mennonites' hierarchical class system developed in the Ukraine and reconstituted in southern Manitoba: the land and business owners were the dominant group, followed by schoolteachers, with farm workers and hand workers at the lowest level.[98]

Such religious conflict was not always restricted to church members – in some cases the conflict was internalized. Paul Friesen was no longer an active Mennonite church member, but the legacy of his religious background interfered with his ability to take advantage of the union supports that were available to him. He could have grieved his dismissal from a job, but he did not do so because he "felt [he] was perhaps too much of a slacker. Not slacking, but taking too much time to get the job just right." Nor did he want to "use the sword" of the union to defend himself, using a phrase that echoes the religious language of the Schleitheim Confession of the Swiss Anabaptists.[99] Friesen felt some awkwardness attending union meetings because of the use of the terms "brothers and sisters." These words triggered memories of his religious heritage[100] and prompted the thought: "Oh great! Another cult." The Mennonite use of these terms he could understand "because we're all related. But this? Come on!" To him, the language of union fraternity "sounded weird" but he became "resigned to it."[101]

Tom Bontreger did not believe that those who objected to unions on grounds of religious belief were really so different in their labour relations from those who were unionized. Bontreger worked for a time as production manager in a non-union sawmill whose employees were almost all Amish. These workers had "their own way of establishing rules for themselves." He also had been manager of the trucking fleet at Jayco, a Mennonite-owned non-union business with a majority Amish workforce. Although the Amish were very "anti-union," he claimed they had "their own rules which made them a union unto themselves." Asked to clarify, he explained that the Amish bargained as a group and set their own work limits, similar to a union. They even "set their own holidays" through discussion with Amish workers employed at other businesses: "What do you think the Amish men are talking about standing together outside their church on Sundays?" In these ways, the Amish were "very union-like" but probably "would be offended" if anyone said so.[102]

A former pastor with an extensive career in Mennonite church-owned institutions, Lavon Welty observed that the Mennonite church itself was not immune from labour problems. There were days, he said, when he thought he should form a union of church workers so they could address the power imbalance in the church. Only recently were salaries improving in Mennonite churches, he noted. His decision to work in church-related organizations was motivated by values other than money, perhaps to the detriment of his retirement years, he observed. He had always been employed by church- or faith-based organizations and so was never a union member. He thought church ministers should form a union so they would be better paid, but joked that "strikes wouldn't work."[103]

A number of Mennonites had no doubts about the value – even the necessity – of active union participation. Barb Draper picketed during an Ontario teacher strike in 1996, explaining that Premier Mike "Harris was jerking us around."[104] Her church's attitude to unions was not as positive as her own, she noted.[105] Auto executive Greg Ring had positive experiences with unions both as a member of the Teamsters at United Parcel Service and as an account executive at Cooper Tire. Unions exist "for the common good" and to provide "a voice," he declared, and in this way, they are "no different than trade associations or accountability partners."[106] Former autoworker Wilbur Roth served as his union's treasurer. He declared that the union was "not the sacrament," but asked, "where else did workers have a voice? How else could they question their circumstances?" Unions were a necessary mechanism that provided fairness: "Good will is not enough." He recalled one summer without air conditioning on the factory floor. Workers asked for fans, which management denied, so half of them walked off the job. With the money saved on paying wages to these workers, fans were finally purchased. These workers were "not asking for the world," yet they had to "push to get action for simple things" since salaried managers working in their air conditioned offices were unaware of shop floor conditions.[107]

Not all workers relied on their unions to achieve workplace justice; some preferred to rely on their own individual efforts. Despite being unionized, Ellen Ibele took independent action to improve her working conditions. Ibele had been a union member at the John Forsyth Company sewing factory. She recalled that management at the company had offices with fans and transoms, but the factory floor had neither air conditioning nor fans. Ironing, particularly with the humidity of the summer, was hot work. Despite being unionized, Ibele did not rely on union leadership to address such issues. Her decision was based seemingly not on any objection to unions but on a preference to take action personally. She approached her supervisor directly and told him, "If you don't give us four fans on our station, I'm going home." She and her co-workers got the fans. She declared she did not think today she would dare risk losing her job over such an issue, but at the time, she was willing to threaten to quit – "over fans!" This incident was but one example she recited of the disrespectful treatment of unionized workers at the factory. Recalling her courage in standing up to management on behalf of her co-workers, she declared, "I had my moments!"[108]

Ibele's personal efforts to ensure decent working conditions extended to the workplaces of her children. Her second son worked at Tim Hortons as part-time supervisor in a building with ongoing problems with water leaks. Buckets were placed in strategic locations to catch the run-off, but despite these half-hearted efforts, "an old lady slipped and fell" and still the owner would not fix the problem. Her son wrote a letter to the health department, and she "bought him stamps to send the letter." He received no response, and Ibele "was so upset." Partial tarring of the roof failed to solve the problem. One day, Ibele recalls, she thought, "Why am I not doing something?" She spoke to the firemen at a local fire station who directed her to the health inspector. She did not inform her son of her actions. At one point he had told her that he was resigned to "just doing his job," so she "took action." Shortly after her communication with the health inspector, the business owner had the roof replaced, an outcome she viewed as a personal victory.[109]

Like Ibele, some Mennonites preferred to find alternate means of resolving labour issues. For a few Mennonites in British Columbia and (to a lesser extent) Ontario, the Christian Labour Association of Canada (CLAC) was just such an option.[110] Founded in 1952 by individuals in the Christian Reformed religious tradition (Dutch Calvinists), the CLAC portrays itself as a moral alternative in its objections to the "adversarial nature" of traditional labour unions and its opposition to the closed shop.[111] John Redekop, a Mennonite and former professor of political science, was influential in promoting this organization among Canadian Mennonites, both through his column in the national church periodical *Mennonite Brethren Herald* and through a series of seminars for Mennonites on labour relations sponsored by the Mennonite Central Committee Manitoba in 1976.[112] Redekop observed that the CLAC has been "close to [his] heart" and that he had spoken by invitation at three or four CLAC national conventions.[113]

Redekop provides an interesting contrast to the other interviewees discussed in this chapter, in that the views he expressed during the interview can be compared to the views he expressed earlier as a columnist for the *Mennonite Brethren Herald*. Such a comparison reveals that Redekop's memory of his attitude to unions (as expressed in his oral history interview) differs in some ways from his earlier written statements. The contrast between the two raises a number of questions worth exploring, particularly since his position as a columnist for the official publication of a national church body meant that he played a role in shaping historical Mennonite attitudes toward labour in a way that other interviewees did not.

In his interview, Redekop presented a careful account, both accepting and rejecting critiques of labour unions. He asserted that, having "listened in vain for sixty years for the subject to be addressed" by Mennonite churches, he himself tried to promote a balanced understanding of labour issues among Mennonites. He attributed the anti-union position of many Mennonites to two causes: their agricultural background and their association of unions with socialism and communism. He asserted that unions "fed the stereotype" by holding their main sessions at national conferences on Sunday mornings (thus preventing church attendance) and by sending delegates to the Socialist International and to Cuba to "stand alongside people who don't support democracy." He claimed that, for Mennonites, the "bone of contention" was their "desire to be exempt from using union dues to support the NDP [New Democratic Party]."[114] He noted that the church itself was divided: "A huge issue for church members and leaders has been the bifurcation where the rank and file take their ethical cues from secular leaders, and the clergy and the academy take their cue from US or traditional anti-labour views." While Redekop critiqued pastors for exacerbating this divide in their congregations, he emphasized that unions "fed these [negative] assumptions by their behaviour." He stated he had collected voluminous files of newspaper clippings about union violence, claiming that union pickets who participated in "serious physical assault" were not condemned by either police or news reporters. "Christians use power in a more restrained manner and are hopefully not totally self-serving," he noted. Unions, by contrast, "use the same power ethic but in more obvious, and sometimes more brutal, and maybe more negative ways."[115]

Following this blanket condemnation, Redekop qualified his views. He noted the historical necessity and achievement of unions. "Sometimes union power is used in enlightened ways," he observed, as when organized labour forced a reduction in the length of the workday. The "readiness to use violence in a very immediate sense has turned many off unions" despite a similar (ab)use of economic power by management and employers. The economic success of many North American Mennonites has led to conservatism and a desire to "protect their economic well being." "Theological and ethical guidance" in Mennonite churches on the question of labour is "largely absent. Does Anabaptism have anything to say to societal issues?" While nationalism, patriotism, and economics (in a general sense) have been addressed, "very little" has been said by Mennonites about labour. And there was the problem of bias. "When God helps management, He blesses; when God helps employees, they exploit society. But management does the same thing – and sometimes brutally."[116]

Redekop's writings for the *Mennonite Brethren Herald* present a rather different perspective. One of Redekop's earliest columns on labour unions was written in response to a 1965 account of a Mennonite's decision to leave his union. Jake H. Dueck joined a union in 1949 as a helper for an electrical construction and engineering firm: "Previously, I [Dueck] had heard references made in the morning church messages against unionism. It was even called communism, but this I could neither see nor believe. However, as the requests to join our developing union came repeatedly, I consented. I recall very vividly the evening I was accepted and took upon myself the responsibilities of membership. There was a dread and heaviness of heart that was hard to explain then. I was able to shrug it off with time, but never completely."[117] In 1956 Dueck read Guy F. Hershberger's "The Christian Attitude to Labour Unions" and in 1960 he refused to participate in a strike, for which he was fined. "I paid the fine but not without some severe inner struggles." Several months later, he had a religious experience. "One day as I was working alone on a job, the Lord spoke to me again and in agony I broke down and promised the Lord that at the first opportunity I would make a clear break with the union." He eventually found work with a non-union contractor.[118]

Redekop responded to Dueck's story in a subsequent issue, asking why the Mennonite church community did not address the question of union membership. "Brother Dueck has graphically portrayed one of the basic dilemmas facing us as a brotherhood as many of us rush headlong off the farms and to the cities. The problem of ethics in employment is one of those problems associated with urbanization which will likely be with us for a long time and we had better give it a little more attention."[119] In this article, Redekop did not specifically advocate any particular answer to the question of whether or not Mennonites should be members of labour unions. Nor, in later articles, does he explicitly state such a position. It is, however, difficult to infer anything other than an anti-union stance from his writing.[120] Redekop asks, for example, whether Mennonites "are afraid to spell out the harsh demands which may result when we apply to the area of economics those lofty principles which we claim to believe?" He suggests that upcoming conferences of church members address the topics "The Disciple and Wage Demands; The Role of Group Pressures; When Is a Strike Ethical?; What Union Claims Are Legitimate?; Should Christians Organize Unions?; and, What Is the Labor Law of the Land?" He concludes his response to Dueck's story with the question: "We have provided leadership on issues from lipstick to liquor, from tobacco to television, why hesitate on this?"[121]

Subsequent articles by Redekop on the subject of unions make his anti-union (if not anti-labour) bias clear. Writing about strikes in Canada in 1976 by teachers and by pulp and paper workers, he asks: "Is all-out economic warfare more acceptable than military warfare? Is class hatred more acceptable than race hatred?" He lauds Mennonite postal workers who refused to participate in the 1976 strike for being "ready to stand up for their convictions."[122] Two years later, he criticizes the head of the union at the Canadian nickel mining company INCO: "Are the union leaders so upset by the fact that the entrepreneurs, who have risked their capital, are making a [$90 million] profit that they are willing to have more jobs go overseas and lose millions in employee income just to whittle down that profit? Apparently. How sad. Let me remind you, the union leader did not say that employee wages were too low, his point of concern was the profit!"[123] Redekop then addresses whether employees should have a share in this profit or whether it should all accrue to shareholders through a discussion of the biblical parable of the talents. "For a person with money the earning of a profit is as proper and natural as is harvest time for a farmer. Let us not begrudge people their due." Further, that profit or harvest can be used to "serve our fellowman" since the "major test of our spiritual commitment" is whether or not we practise "good stewardship" – that is, spend the profit wisely. "What we do with what we earn is a basic moral question; whether we earn our income as wages or as reasonable profit is not."[124]

A 1979 article by Redekop is even more revealing of his anti-union sentiments. He presents a litany of abuses by lazy workers he encounters in the course of a day. He complains about a plumber who spent three minutes in his home diagnosing a problem and charged $17 for the call. He grumbles about secretaries who gossip and take long coffee and lunch breaks, and refers to them dismissively as "lovely ladies" and "dear things." He claims to have timed the actual number of minutes they spent typing, and concludes: "I calculated a total of 4 hours and 15 minutes of work in what was counted as a 7 hour work day." He then carps about the alleged demands of the Canadian Union of Postal Workers who, he asserts, want "paid wash-up, rest break, travel and lunch time" totaling anywhere from 2 hours 10 minutes to 3 hours 30 minutes of a six-hour day. The column concludes: "Of course I know that not all plumbers are rip-off artists, or that all secretaries goof off almost half the day, or that all union demands are so outlandish! Most working people are responsible. And yet, it seems to me that the work ethic is becoming ever more anemic. Many people, apparently, simply don't want to work anymore. Surely we Christians have a major responsibility to be the kind of diligent, reliable, and thorough workers which our society needs. In this area, too, we need to be salt and light."[125]

During a series of strikes and lockouts in British Columbia in 1982, Redekop again condemned unions. In his column for the *Herald*, he writes that when he read the news that postal workers refused to cross airport picket lines on Vancouver Island, "the temperature of my tax-drained blood rose several degrees; were it not for its Anabaptist component, it might have reached the boiling point. As it was, righteous indignation very nearly evolved into unrighteous anger."[126] He declares that those who refused to cross picket lines "should have been given one warning and then, if non-compliance continued, should have been fired. There are tens of thousands of unemployed men and women ready and willing to work responsibly and to fill the resulting vacancies." As for those Mennonites who found themselves members of unions engaged in such labour action, they should realize that union "membership does not make wrong behavior right ... And to our governments let us state clearly that abuse of confidence and continuing toleration of employee dereliction is an affront not only to the supporting citizenry but ultimately also to God."[127] Reading such articles, it is clear that if Redekop did countenance Mennonite involvement in labour unions in the 1970s and 1980s, it was only when those unions were not active.

While Redekop's columns do not declare unequivocally whether or not Mennonites should be union members, they are forceful in their advocacy of the CLAC. He writes in 1969 that the real problems in labour relations are greed and selfishness and antagonism, and concludes, "From a philosophical and theological point of view I find the clear-cut stance of the Christian Labour Association of Canada to be the best option." He observes that as "union problems" increase, Mennonites "are going to have to take some kind of a stand sooner or later. It is fine to talk about loving our enemy in wartime but our immediate problem is how to get along with our employer (or employee) in peacetime." He notes that the "Calvinistic emphases" of some CLAC representatives are at odds with Mennonite theology, but stresses that the CLAC is more in accordance with Mennonite values than "any other labour union with which I am familiar."[128]

A few Canadian Mennonites I interviewed agreed with Redekop in this assessment of the CLAC. An anonymous male academic worker in British Columbia said he appreciated the historical contribution of labour unions, but felt that "today in many cases they go too far." The problem, he noted, was that union executives have to "show progress." Not many elected union officials will tell the rank and file that they "have it good; be satisfied." This man had relatives who worked for the CLAC, and he expressed admiration for how the

CLAC "attempts to bring together employer and employee."[129] Another British Columbian, employed as a business manager, echoed the belief that unions had outlived their usefulness. He, too, had relatives who worked for the CLAC. The CLAC, he declared, was a "different type of union," one that took a "balanced approach. If all unions were like the CLAC, more people would be pro-union." He hastened to add that one should not "paint the whole organized labour spectrum with the same brush" since there were different levels of militancy and causes supported. The CLAC was to be credited with shifting perceptions on unions, however, allowing them to be viewed more favourably.[130] A business owner in Ontario invited the CLAC to organize his employees in the 1970s, but was informed that the impetus had to come from his workers. He reflected that he "would have been interested to work with" the CLAC because of their "Christian principles."[131]

Oral historians and postmodern theorists alike remind us that people's identities and understandings undergo constant change, both as the result of external circumstances and as a consequence of their efforts to interpret the effects of those circumstances. The act of participating in an interview creates new interpretations of a person's story, for both the narrator and the oral historian.[132] Interviewing John Redekop was a very different experience from reading his magazine column. Had his views on labour unions mellowed over the ensuing decades? Or did an interview with me, a business and labour historian who presented him with a consent form with the project title "Mennonites and Labour Activism," result in a recasting of his story to suit the perceived biases of his interviewer? Redekop's is only the most obvious example of this phenomenon. Other narrators, too, presented conflicting accounts, in part because they were trying to interpret their experiences for a new and strange audience. They were limited by the time frame of the interview and – in some cases – intimidated by the presence of the recording equipment. Their efforts to describe their experiences and understandings of labour issues in general and unions in particular were unavoidably influenced by individual and collective perceptions of contemporary events, such as the auto industry crisis.

These oral histories reveal that North American Mennonites did not have a unified religious approach to the question of unions. Mennonite churches themselves have not had such for fifty years. The Mennonite church's solution to the problems of late twentieth-century capitalism has been to advocate more (albeit modified) capitalism through the economic relief and development efforts of Mennonite Central Committee, Mennonite Economic Development Associates, and fair trade and micro-credit programs. These efforts have tended to depict capitalism as problematic primarily in its manifestation in the peripheral world, not the core. Thus Mennonites largely ignore labour issues in North America, except insofar as unions make what are perceived to be unreasonable demands. Indeed, unlike the Profiles of 1972 and 1989, the 2006 Mennonite Church Membership Profile does not even ask about attitudes toward and involvement in unions.[133]

The individualism of North American Mennonites increased as they became more urban and more involved in the industrial capitalist economy and its values. Using religious rhetoric and symbols to support their narrative of unionism, Mennonites made their personal decisions regarding union membership primarily on the basis not of class or religious identity but their individualized experiences of unions (which extended to their communicative memory of unions, i.e. their parents' experiences). Far more than religious convictions, what shaped North American Mennonites' attitudes toward unions in the late twentieth century was individual experience. Certain broader historical processes undoubtedly were significant. The movement of Mennonites from family farms to towns and cities meant the transfer of rural biases against labour unions to an urban context. Class position influenced some Mennonites' views, but not in any crudely determinative way. Nor was gender determinative, although it is clear that some Mennonite women – like their non-Mennonite counterparts – did not find the labour movement in the 1970s to be as liberating an experience as they might have hoped.[134] Place was significant only in that the majority of Mennonite support for the CLAC was situated in British Columbia – not surprising, given that province's history of alternative political movements.[135] A religious legacy was cited by some Mennonites as central to the construction of their view of unions, even though in many cases their ability to articulate that legacy was limited. Most important, however, were parental attitudes to unions and individuals' own workplace experiences, whether in a unionized environment or not. In the second half of the twentieth century, Mennonite church leaders like Hershberger and Mennonite academics like Redekop were no longer authoritative voices on the labour question for North American Mennonites.[136]

Mennonites instead found their own, individualized answers, and in so doing, developed attitudes toward unions that may not have differed much from those of the non-Mennonites around them.

Is there anything Mennonite, then, about this study? Social class, religious conviction, and family influence were all important factors. A common religious heritage was not sufficient to overcome class differences or to replace communicative histories of union participation shared within families. Mennonites were more likely than non-Mennonites to refrain from union membership, as many of their churches had taught (or required of) them until the mid-twentieth century. Mennonite attitudes toward unions, however, differed little from those of non-Mennonites, because these were shaped by class position and personal experience more than by theological conviction. Thus, there were significant differences between belief and practice for North American Mennonites on the question of organized labour. And, as will be seen, their response to specific labour challenges – such as those posed by the United Farm Workers in California or by the "conscience clause" in Manitoba – were further complicated by denominational and ethnic differences.

3

"What would *you* say, for the archives?"

California Mennonites and Migrant Workers

"What would *you* say, for the archives?"[1] I was asked this question during an interview I conducted near Fresno, California. It had been difficult to find Mennonites in California who were willing to talk about their work lives and religious beliefs. More than any other community to which I travelled, the Mennonites of the San Joaquin Valley were hesitant to participate. Many ignored my emails and phone calls. A few agreed to talk, but then changed their minds about participating immediately after the interview – or during the course of the interview itself. Many who did speak with me were reluctant conversationalists – a sharp contrast to the open and communicative Mennonites in the Midwestern United States I had interviewed earlier. Even the Canadian Mennonites with whom I had spoken, although reserved by comparison to the loquacious Americans of the Midwest, were more forthcoming. True, many of those I had interviewed in Abbotsford, British Columbia, mentioned an unwillingness to speak too openly of their religious views, citing as their rationale the conservative and close-knit nature of that particular Mennonite community. But the degree of reticence among Mennonites in the San Joaquin Valley was unique.

The first person I interviewed in California was Melvin Enns, the general manager of WesPak, a packer and distributor of tree fruit. His agreement to be interviewed was tinged with caution, as he noted that, although raised within the Mennonite Brethren church, his adult church affiliation was Presbyterian. He added that he did not make an effort to connect work and religion, which I had said was one of the main topics of the interview.

The interview was held in his office in the administrative building adjacent to the packing shed; both buildings were located on the

Enns family's original farm near Dinuba. I encouraged participants to choose the interview location, and most chose their home or their workplace for convenience and comfort. Meeting Melvin Enns at the company's head office gave me an opportunity to see the WesPak operation. The interview itself, however, was sufficiently awkward that I did not request permission to look inside the packing shed or wander about the grounds. Instead, I contented myself with a few hastily taken post-interview photographs of the exteriors of the office building and packing shed and of the surrounding tree fruit orchards and vineyards.

I had completed more than seventy interviews in other provinces and states before I interviewed Melvin Enns; however, his interview stands out in my memory of that year's research trip. It was the most uncomfortable.[2] I had the impression that he was not convinced of the value of my research – indeed, he hinted as much during the interview. He sometimes broke the fourth wall of the interview by speaking directly to the recorder, deliberately and dramatically addressing the unknown future researchers (and at one point, my employers) who might listen to the yet-to-be-archived recording. At times he made what I thought were jokes. Not wanting to offend him, I refrained from laughing in case I was mistaken and he was being serious. When he paused and stated that he had been joking, my relieved laughter was self-conscious. Listening to the recording, I am struck by the number of times my nervous laughter intrudes on the conversation. At many instances, he challenged me to answer my questions from my own experience instead of offering a reply. Asked about whether the Mennonite church ever offered advice or assistance with business questions, he turned the question back to me, asking if I, as a chemistry teacher, would accept advice on teaching the subject from someone I respected but who had no chemistry experience.[3] I said that yes, as an employee in a church-owned secondary school, I did receive such advice from non-chemists. He then suggested I turn the leave of absence I had taken for postdoctoral research into a permanent leave of absence, and, speaking directly to the digital recorder, stated, "For the archives, she's in a *terrible* situation that should not ever be in academia. Okay, so this cannot be edited now! It's in the archives. And I feel *extremely* sorry that a chemist has to have that put on her."[4] I laughed and thanked him, but despite the joking, we never quite established a rapport.

During the third stage of the interviews I asked participants how they had experienced spirituality or faith or God in their lives. The question was purposefully open-ended, to allow participants to discuss possibilities outside the realm of conventional religious practices like church attendance and devotional reading. In many cases, the responses involved recollections of specific personal experiences about which the interviewer could not have known to ask. Melvin Enns immediately dismissed this question. He declared that he did not believe the question was valid because the only reasonable response to how he had experienced God was either "always" or "never." His response was thus "always."

Interpreting this answer as a reluctance to discuss personal religious beliefs and experiences, I attempted to encourage a more detailed response by rephrasing and redirecting the question. I explained that some Manitoba Mennonite Brethren businesspeople that I had interviewed had emphasized the importance of their business as a Christian witness and asked whether that held true in any way for his own business. This question prompted a lengthier response, but one that was equally dismissive. He asked me: "For the archives, would you agree it's impossible, it's a misuse of the English language to say 'Christian business'?" I pressed that some who misuse the language in that way argue that their business structures or employee benefit plans reflect their religious values. He replied that the question was "redundant" and that certainly one's values as an individual were reflected in the decisions made in a business, but that the business itself was driven by the bottom line. Any business that fails to break even financially can last only so long, even in the face of reserve funds and loans. There must be a positive balance at the end of the year. So how much positive balance is valid? Everyone has different ideas about the amount and different definitions of the end of the year. Is capital investment included? Does one simply consult the bank statement? or the report to the IRS? What about purchases and prepaid expenses? How do these factor into the decision? To suggest that one gives benefits because one is a Christian – "Hello! How can you say that?"[5]

Finally, I asked him to respond to a suggestion made by economist Roy Vogt that Mennonites tended to prefer occupations that allowed them to critique class conflict without becoming involved in it themselves. He replied by reviewing the economic history of the region and critiquing the methodology of my research project. His father's generation employed farm workers who were Japanese, Armenian, Portuguese, and Italian. Mennonite farm workers worked neither more nor less hard than these others. Today, the new immigrants were from India and Laos, and they too were hard workers. Main street businesses, such as independent car dealers and drugstores, had been forced to close. The family farm was gone. These economic changes over the last half-century had occurred for people of all occupations and all religious beliefs. Third-generation Americans, the grandchildren of immigrants, were on the way to more knowledge-based jobs as medical doctors, lawyers, professors, and software engineers. The only way to tie these social changes to Mennonite or Mennonite Brethren identity would be to collect a large social science data set and mine the data for hypotheses and differences to determine whether changes in the third and fourth generations were tied to Protestant religious beliefs. If the results showed that Mennonites were more likely to be urban cognitive workers, he would be shocked, because he did not believe it.

Before turning off the digital recorder, I asked if there was anything he would like to add about which I had failed to ask. He replied, "I think some of the things we say, we're using them as crutches." Asked for clarification, he explained, "To some of the statements that you said, like 'we are a Christian business.' It's something we like to say, and it's a crutch for something. 'I do this because I am a Christian.' It's a crutch."

The next workday, I had an appointment with the archivist at the Center for Mennonite Brethren Studies in Fresno, who suggested a number of people I should contact for interviews. The list included Melvin Enns and his siblings. For a day-and-a-half, I debated the wisdom of contacting the Enns brothers, Eugene and Ken, after my awkward interview with Melvin. But finding willing participants was proving a challenge, so I decided to email them nonetheless. Two days later, I received a reply from Eugene Enns. He was aware that I had interviewed his brother Melvin, he said, and he was willing to be interviewed.

With some trepidation, I returned to the WesPak head office a few days later. I was worried about how to establish rapport, given the discomfort of the earlier interview there. I was concerned that I projected an image of a Mennonite keen to establish the superiority of Mennonite belief and experience – something I was not interested in doing. But I felt that was how Melvin Enns had perceived me. Caught up in my own worries, I had not anticipated that the Enns brothers also may have given consideration to my perception of them.

Before the interview formally began, Eugene Enns offered some comments on my earlier interview with his brother. He observed that

Melvin had been a university professor for most of his work life and so tended to ask questions and push for responses. He himself, he asserted, was not as educated and was just "a simple person." I noticed he had a clipboard of notes with him. During the interview, he referred to these notes when I asked questions about faith and work similar to those I had asked his brother.

Using these notes, Eugene Enns presented a very different view of the relationship between faith and work than did his brother. The Mennonite faith was their philosophical heritage whether they liked it or not, he stated, and the mindset of that heritage carried over to the business. This mindset was more prevalent with him than with Melvin since the family business and the Mennonite faith were all he had ever done or known. Melvin Enns had left the business for a period of twenty-five or thirty years and did not return until later in his life, so he had a different thought process. Eugene himself was grounded in this heritage mindset. He tried to lead with a Christian mindset – one that he admitted was hard to define. One could not always tell how it manifested, or know what to look at, but actions rather than talk were what was important. Examples of such action included giving of themselves and their equipment for use by church and school and the Mennonite Central Committee, not only in North America but in South America and Asia. Other examples included the company's refusal to use written contracts, preferring to rely on trust. Granted, such trust made the business vulnerable, he observed, but trust was received in return. In addition, a Christian spirit was needed to maintain an atmosphere of harmony in the workplace. The lack of such harmony, particularly among family members, was the reason there were more first-generation businesses in North America than second-, third-, and fourth-generation businesses combined. One could draw parallels between family businesses and the church. Why do churches split? Always because of the disappearance of harmony, and the debate over who has the last word.[6]

It seems clear that with such comments, Eugene Enns attempted to establish the Mennonite nature of their business and to smooth over the awkwardness of the earlier interview with his brother. There are perhaps other reasons, however, for the awkwardness of that interview than just Melvin Enns's conclusions about the nature of my research project and his rejection of the supposed unique character of Mennonite-owned businesses. Part of the problem may have been that I was a General Conference Mennonite in a predominantly Mennonite Brethren community, an academic interviewing businessmen, a Canadian among Americans, a woman interviewing older men. I was "the other" but saw myself as a part of the group. And there was the collective memory of Fresno area Mennonite Brethren growers and packers: other interviewers had asked questions along similar lines some decades before and, it was believed, unfairly passed judgment on California Mennonite Brethren without really understanding them. What made it worse, those earlier interviewers were co-religionists. In other geographic spaces, the fact that I was a fellow Mennonite had served to establish a comfortable rapport with interview participants. Although we did not necessarily share beliefs and experiences, there was at least some common ground between us that aided in creating an atmosphere of trust. As a Canadian Mennonite academic – an outsider who was also (masquerading as?) an insider – asking questions about faith and work, I may have reminded these California Mennonites (consciously or otherwise) of the betrayal of trust they felt when Mennonite delegations from the US Midwest visited in the 1970s. These delegations had come to investigate the migrant labour situation in California in response to Cesar Chavez's United Farm Workers movement.

The first Mennonites in California were late nineteenth-century transplants from other American states. The two major Mennonite denominational groups to settle in California – the General Conference (GC) Mennonites and the Mennonite Brethren (MB) – came from Ohio, Kansas, Minnesota, and Nebraska. At first settling in other parts of the state, Mennonites migrated to the San Joaquin Valley as early as 1903, settling in and near Reedley and Dinuba, both small towns located just south of Fresno. Although the GC Mennonites arrived before the Mennonite Brethren, by 1950 the latter group was the more numerous. The majority were farmers. At first, they cultivated grain and cotton, but soon changed crops to grapes and raisins, and later to tree fruit such as peaches, plums, and nectarines.[7]

Over the past fifty years, various ethnic groups have done the job of harvesting fruit. The Enns family migrated from Russia in 1907–08 and began farming around Reedley in 1910. At that time, they employed their children and their Mennonite neighbours to do the work of harvesting. The family's first packing line, begun in 1948, comprised Mennonite women exclusively. As Mennonites' financial position improved and succeeding generations aspired to post-secondary education, they abandoned jobs as pickers and packers. Newer immigrants took these jobs. By the 1960s, harvesting was done by migrant workers, primarily Hispanic Catholics, who worked seasonally.[8] The shift to Hispanic labour began in 1942 with the creation of the Mexican Farm Labor Program, and culminated in the Bracero Program, which operated from 1942 to 1964.[9]

Work in the fields has remained relatively unchanged for the last fifty years. Peaches, plums, nectarines, and apricots need to be hand-picked. Mechanization is impossible, since the fruit has to be harvested – very gently – with multiple picks that remove only a part of the crop at a time as it matures. Citrus is a hardier product in comparison, and so the citrus harvest has become mechanized in a way that tree fruit has not.[10]

What has changed since the 1950s is the labour process in the packing plant. Here, the work had become more mechanized by the end of the twentieth century. Tree fruits were sized electronically. Colour machines were used in some fresh fruit packing operations to sort product, although this equipment tended not to be used for stone fruit. Automated box fillers sorted and packed fruit according to size. In most cases, however, women who were paid piecework rates but received a guaranteed minimum wage did the work of filling the boxes. The work was difficult and required considerable speed.[11]

By the early twenty-first century, the workplace had become highly regulated, in part to address the problems of employing undocumented migrant workers. Labour problems were an ongoing concern, including worries about immigration reform and border tightening. Despite unemployment levels in Fresno that had been in the double digits for decades, Eugene Enns noted that growers always feared labour shortages. In 2009, at the time of my interviews in California, the unemployment rate in Fresno was the highest it had been in twenty years.[12] To avoid the complications of dealing with migrant workers, some of whom might be undocumented, some California Mennonite growers, such as Gordon Wiebe, decided to change from stone fruit production to olives. Olive production is less dependent on labour, since much of the harvest and subsequent processing is mechanized. Although WesPak had not made such a shift, the company had made "major philosophical changes."[13] They broadened their product offerings to include pomegranates and grapes. They employed an individual whose job it was to ensure that the company was in compliance with the myriad of regulations that govern the industry. They also were active in grower organizations that lobbied government for specific legislative changes. Their farm management tasks expanded to include governance of diesel engine emissions, water purification, waste disposal, and farm sustainability with respect to fertilizer and insect control spraying.

A major transformation of the fruit industry in California occurred in 1962, with Cesar Chavez's formation of the National Farm Workers Association (later known as the United Farm Workers or UFW). The Delano grape strike of 1966, several public fasts by Chavez, and an international boycott of table grapes – together with the work of union organizers – resulted in UFW contracts for farm workers with some of the largest California grape growers. Motivated by his Catholic faith and his reading of Gandhi, Chavez saw "La Causa" as not only a workers' movement but also a religious quest for justice.[14]

Fresno area Mennonites were aware of the problems that the UFW sought to address, and had their own solutions. At first, they were interested only in meeting the perceived spiritual needs of migrant workers. Mennonite Central Committee (MCC), the Mennonite peace and service agency headquartered in Akron, Pennsylvania, created a voluntary service unit (VS) in 1950 to address these supposed needs.[15] MCC VS workers visited children in migrant work camps and taught Bible stories using religious films and flannel board pictures.[16] Some VS workers perceived Catholicism as one of the oppressive conditions from which they tried to liberate these children. One worker reported that the decision of Catholic nuns to offer catechism classes in one camp made the VS unit wonder if the migrant children would "all accept the teachings of Catholicism, or will there be those few who will take a stand for Christ?"[17] While religious conversion was their main objective, VS workers "also wanted to share with them our better education and other privileges and to help them to live as much as possible normal lives. In camps where the different races were represented, one of our goals was to teach tolerance of racial differences and ideas."[18] Tolerance of religious diversity, however, was not a goal.

The Mennonite Brethren churches' efforts to evangelize Hispanics in California began in 1956.[19] The work was successful – a number of Hispanics were converted to the Mennonite faith. They were not integrated into existing Mennonite Brethren churches, however;

instead, the MB Conference created separate churches for Hispanics, with Hispanic pastors to serve them. Such separation, together with the financial dependence of these Hispanic churches on non-Hispanic Mennonites, "fueled paternalism within the church."[20] Researcher Jordan Penner argues that, while their recognition of racism and ethnocentrism in broader society occurred earlier, Mennonites of European background did not attend to these problems within the church itself until the 1980s.[21]

While MB church planting continued apace, by the late 1960s, MCC had shifted from the offer of religious assistance to exploration of the possibility of social assistance to migrant workers. In 1969, the MCC West Coast Relief Committee investigated how they might be of service to non-Mennonites in the city of Fresno. The problems experienced by many in the city were rooted in both class and race. An MCC report from that year noted that "West Fresno is a typical 'across the tracks' community, looked down on by the self-righteous as a bunch of no goods who, if they would work, could get out. The paradox of this is, no matter how hard they work they are still black or brown and not really welcome in any other part of town."[22] Some Mennonites in Fresno had requested that MCC take advantage of the opportunity presented by the many Mennonite young men who needed to do alternative service in lieu of participation in the Vietnam War: MCC should help these men find volunteer work with social agencies in the Fresno region.[23] Internal correspondence on the subject reveals that MCC was aware that the social problems that needed to be addressed were institutionalized, and that many Mennonites preferred not to get involved. Allen Linscheid, chair of MCC's West Coast Relief Committee, noted: "We have been tuned mainly towards overseas relief contributions and have not been intent upon the social concerns around us in our own communities. Perhaps our churches here are unique in that I sense considerable reluctance to engage in service programs supported or directed by governmental agencies. To be honest, I don't think we have provided sufficient leadership for stimulating serious explorations in other fields."[24] The problem stemmed in part from the economic prosperity many Mennonites enjoyed by the 1960s. Edgar Stoesz, MCC Akron's VS director, observed, "As I get into the churches I am impressed with the number of people who have achieved normal middle-class expectations but who have not found meaning in life."[25]

Migrant farm workers' issues as a *labour* problem (and not solely a religious or social problem) came to the attention of Mennonites in 1966. That year, news of the Delano grape strike was carried in *The Mennonite,* a national periodical produced by the US branch of the General Conference Mennonite Church. An article on the strike quoted Don Ohlson, a Presbyterian minister: "To be neutral on this grape strike issue is to take sides ... The growers are big and strong. The field workers have no strength. If the church stays out of the controversy it supports the growers."[26] While the news item made no mention of Mennonite attitudes toward or involvement in the strike, it sparked a flurry of letters to the editor.

The first such letter came from a Mennonite grower in Reedley. The writer defended large farms, asking rhetorically, "How many grapes do you eat, Mr. Editor?" and condemned the Delano strikers' march to Sacramento as "just as much communist inspired as the Berkeley college mess." He claimed that the strikers were not grape harvesters themselves. While he conceded that unions "have their good points," he hastened to add that it was "a sad but true fact that many are headed by hoodlums and racketeers." He chastised the editor for publishing the news item, declaring, "I feel ashamed that my church paper would even print a confusing thing such as this without understanding the real facts."[27] A brief but critical response came a few issues later via a letter from a Mennonite from Pennsylvania: "The grapes in the epistle by the fruit grower were souring. He really ought not to have used the word communist so loosely."[28]

A second Mennonite from Reedley came to the defence of the original letter writer, whom he described as a friend of his. This author concluded that the entire question of the treatment of farm workers could be dismissed since "this whole thing started among migrant people."[29] The strikers were condemned as communists (as evidenced by their clothing), as Catholics, and as lewd individuals who, "with their behavior, with dancing, and the kind of girls that went with the bunch, sure did not show any religion or respect." The letter writer concluded, "I can't see how a paper like *The Mennonite* can call itself a religious paper and then get mixed up with an affair like this."[30] Both this letter writer and a third one from Reedley forwarded an issue of the *California Farmer* for the edification of *The Mennonite*'s editorial staff.[31]

The editor of *The Mennonite* responded to the criticism, carefully avoiding contradicting the letter writers. Instead, he commented on the forwarded issue of the *California Farmer,* noting that it gave "eighteen pages ... to present the growers' point of view." The editor highlighted two quotations from the issue, which subtly undermined the letter writers' arguments. The first was a quotation from the editor of the *California Farmer:* "Honestly we don't know what is going on in Delano." The second was taken from an article titled "Can We Avoid Another Delano?" in which the author observed that the most important issue "is that growers know their labor supply and know the problems of their employees."[32]

Mennonite engagement with this labour issue reached a crisis point in 1973. That year, the draft for the Vietnam War ended, two UFW members were killed while picketing, grape boycotts were resumed, and the UFW held their first national convention – in Fresno.[33] Media reports of the boycotts and deaths of picketers, as well as the proximity of the UFW convention to Mennonites living in the San Joaquin Valley, must have caught the attention of Mennonites in California. Farm labour issues were a topic at the 1973 national assembly of the (Old) Mennonite Church in Harrisonburg, Virginia. MCC's Peace Section had been preoccupied with assisting Mennonite young men in applying for conscientious objector status during the Vietnam War, but with the end of the draft, they could turn their attention to other social issues. MCC Peace Section had been encouraged over the years by various Mennonites to investigate the farm labour issue, particularly by Mexican-American Mennonites who wanted MCC to mediate the conflicts between growers of European Mennonite descent and Latino/a migrant workers.[34] In addition, MCC's executive secretary, William Snyder, had been told by a Mennonite from Fresno that some California Mennonites "were beginning to carry guns and clubs in connection with this matter." Snyder pushed MCC Peace Section to investigate.[35]

MCC Peace Section took action that winter. They decided in November 1973 to "work with other interested Mennonite agencies" on the migrant farm worker issue. The following month, Lupe De Leon, a Hispanic Mennonite who was associate executive secretary of the (Old) Mennonite Church's Minority Ministries Council, invited Ted Koontz from MCC Peace Section to attend a National Farm Worker Ministry Board meeting in Cleveland, Ohio. MCC considered establishing a VS unit relating to farm workers.[36] Peace Section also decided to discuss the migrant worker situation with unnamed "persons in California," together with representatives from the General Conference Mennonite Church and the Mennonite Brethren Church. This decision resulted in the sending of a delegation of Midwest and East Coast Mennonites to California to investigate the farm labour issue.[37]

California Mennonites were not pleased to hear about this forthcoming MCC visit. Phil Hofer, who was employed at Fresno's Pacific College (a Mennonite Brethren institution), arranged for himself and three other Fresno area Mennonites to meet with MCC Peace Section in Washington in January 1974. MCC's Ted Koontz and Luann Habegger met with them and the result was summarized as a "helpful exchange of views and an indication on their part that a visit from Peace Section staff on this issue would be welcome."[38] A more detailed memo by Koontz reveals that Phil Hofer was the most welcoming, and that the "helpful exchange of views" included the sharing of some surprising opinions by the other three Californians.[39] These men believed that the nonviolence of the UFW was merely a front, and claimed that UFW workers threw rocks at non-union workers who continued to work in the fields. They asserted that "their workers told them that they were better off not being a member of the union. They also indicated that little can be done to improve the lot of the farm workers since even when nice new housing is provided, within a year it is in the same condition as the shacks which farm workers had previously lived in. This was particularly the view of Richard Hofer who repeatedly indicated that 'that kind of people do not want nice houses. They're not like us.'"[40] Part of the problem, the men said, was that the UFW was more than a labour union. "It is a movement for the self identity and dignity of the Mexican American people in California. Because of this there are some tensions with other racial and ethnic groups." When questioned by the MCC representatives, these men acknowledged that some Mennonite growers – whose religious beliefs included a commitment to pacifism – had been carrying guns, and some had been brandishing sticks against organizers while standing between them and their workers in the fields. Phil Hofer, however, noted that a significant (and often ignored) issue was the class difference between farm workers and growers. This difference, he insisted, should "tend to make us sympathize with the plight of the farm workers and work to improve their lot whether that be through the United Farm Workers or through some other means." Justice must be considered, he asserted – not just growers' "economic viability" or violence perpetrated by either side.[41]

Alvin Peters, a Mennonite Brethren farmer from Reedley, launched a campaign of his own against the impending MCC visit. He called MCC in Akron in February 1974. He had been invited to speak about the farm worker issue at Goshen College, Indiana, and Bluffton College, Ohio – two Mennonite post-secondary schools – to "present the farmers' point of view." He asked that an MCC representative attend, and expressed "concern about rumors that MCC either was or was planning to support the [grape] boycott."[42] Lynn Roth, MCC Akron, wrote a letter in reply. Roth noted that Hispanic Mennonites, "together with other minorities in the Church, are asking questions about the Mennonite employers' approach to the labor situation on the West Coast." [43] MCC intended to send two people to California to investigate – probably MCC Peace Section secretary John Lapp and Eastern Mennonite College professor George R. Brunk II.[44] Roth added, "In the meantime it is my understanding that you have invited some people you met at Goshen College and Bluffton College to visit your area. These do not have any relationship to MCC, however. You must feel free to do that kind of thing as you feel led." Meanwhile, MCC would send its own delegation, which would not hold large public gatherings but would instead meet quietly with "the Mennonites who are better informed and who are directly involved in hiring people. It is not our intention to make a crisis situation nor would the Mennonite Church wish to do so I am sure."[45] MCC invited Peters to their headquarters in Akron, Pennsylvania, shortly after his college presentations. The result of the meeting was that Peters agreed "to have Mennonites from the colleges, conference groups, and MCC visit in the Fresno area to see the situation for themselves."[46]

Other California Mennonites also contacted MCC to express concern. Phil Hofer (Pacific College, Fresno) warned that "there was a near unanimous feeling that it may not be wise for you to come at this time. This because of the already ambivalent feelings among local MBs toward MCC."[47] Another Pacific College faculty member, Paul Toews, cautioned that "anyone who comes on any sort of investigative mission is regarded as suspect because of the emotionalization of the [farm worker] issue."[48] Leo Miller, pastor of Reedley's First Mennonite Church, wrote in response to a phone call and letter from Harold Regier, who inquired about what the local reception of the MCC delegation (of which he would be a member) might be. Miller noted that some Californians thought the MCC delegation would be talking only to unions, whereas others believed MCC would take sides. "Others interpreted your visit as 'experts' coming to California to help Californians solve their problem since they seem incapable of solving it on their own."[49] Miller himself viewed MCC's trip as a learning experience "so that you might take these facts back East where truth as reported by the unions seems to be horribly distorted." He suggested that MCC meet with growers before meeting with union representatives to "be better prepared to ask questions of the union." He noted that there were no UFW supporters in his congregation because "the activities of the union have negated any credibility, and there are only negative feelings toward the union."[50]

MCC itself was divided on the wisdom of sending a delegation to California. The chair of MCC's West Coast Relief Committee, Allen Linscheid, wrote to the organization's executive secretary, William Snyder, in March 1974: "The [West Coast MCC] Development Committee was of unanimous opinion that such a visit should not be conducted at this time ... We believe that it would be virtually impossible to avoid a very negative reaction among our people if MCC is known to be having discussion with farm union officials. Such repercussions would likely be widespread and long lasting."[51] Lynn Roth, MCC Akron, also worried that the trip would have negative repercussions for the reputation of MCC on the West Coast. Instead, MCC should leave the issue to local area Mennonite pastors.[52] Plans nonetheless were made to conduct such a visit from 12 to 16 March 1974. The month prior to the delegation's departure, MCC received a number of phone calls from the West Coast that expressed "both concern ... and encouragement."[53] In light of the expressed concerns, MCC developed a cautious approach to the upcoming trip. Ted Koontz, MCC Peace Section, insisted that the delegation follow the guidance of the MCC West Coast Relief Committee and not hold public meetings but only "individual discussions." The purpose of the visit was to be "primarily one of getting more information rather than one of taking direct action or assuming a position."[54]

The March 1974 MCC-led delegation to California consisted of five men: Harold Regier (representing the General Conference Mennonite Church), Ted Koontz (MCC Peace Section), Guy Hershberger (a leader in the (Old) Mennonite Church), Lynn Roth (a Mennonite Brethren who worked with MCC in Akron and Fresno),[55] and Phil Hofer (a Mennonite Brethren employed at Fresno's Pacific College).[56] On their brief tour of the Fresno-Reedley area, they spoke with both Mennonites and non-Mennonites, growers and farm workers, as well as representatives from the UFW, the Teamsters Union, the Nisei Farmers League, and the Central California Farmers Association. An MCC press release noted that the delegation "concluded that the issue is more complex than many people, particularly Easterners, realize."[57] The previous summer, Mennonite growers had been picketed by the UFW (the only union active in the Reedley region, although the Teamsters were challenging the UFW elsewhere in California). The Mennonite growers with whom the delegation spoke asserted that California had the highest agricultural wages in country, and they viewed the UFW very negatively. They blamed the UFW for vandalism, and some believed it was "part of a communist conspiracy or an attempt to reclaim the Southwest for Mexico." The UFW blamed violence largely on the growers, with some isolated exceptions. Farm workers interviewed by the delegation were divided on their views of the UFW and of their own working conditions, but few believed the conspiracy theories about the UFW. Guy Hershberger, quoted in the press release, observed that what was needed was "some talk – and a little humor. Open communication is the key to solving such disputes."[58] Some of the Mennonites the delegation interviewed agreed with Hershberger's view and believed the Mennonite church could play a role by encouraging dialogue. Most, however, believed "strongly that the church should not take sides, some arguing that the church should stick to preaching the gospel."[59] As a result of the California visit, MCC Peace Section ultimately decided that their organization should not take a stance on the farm labour question, but instead work with churches "to try to understand who is being hurt and to increase communication between polarized groups."[60] They also determined that MCC would take no further action without consultation with California Mennonites.

MCC's visit was reported on at length in *The Mennonite* in May that year.[61] Lois Barrett Janzen reported that MCC learned that class and ethnicity stratified the California Mennonite community: Russo-German Mennonites tended to be growers; Hispanic Mennonites tended to be farm workers (both unionized and nonunionized). There was little communication between the two groups. The article detailed the conspiracy theories of growers regarding UFW's communism and the potential annexation of California by Mexico. "In all the disagreements and confusion, the visitors found one point on which nearly everyone agreed: some kind of legislation is needed." Finding agreement on what that legislation should entail, however, would be a challenge. Nor was it possible to reach consensus on what role, if any, the church should take in the matter. "Some Mennonite growers felt their side had not been heard in the church." The article concluded with a summary of the commitments by various national church bodies: neither MCC, the General Conference Mennonite Church, nor the Mennonite Brethren Church would publicly take sides on the farm labour question. The only Mennonite organization to do so was (Old) Mennonite Church's Minority Ministries Council; as a member of the National Farm Workers Ministries, the council worked with other religious denominations to support the UFW.[62] Ironically, the (Old) Mennonites were the least prominent Mennonite group in California.

In the same issue of *The Mennonite*, MCC delegation member Harold Regier contributed an editorial. Regier noted that the experience touring the San Joaquin Valley drew attention to the broader question of "Christian ethics in management/labor practices."[63] Mennonites needed to investigate how wages and benefits for workers and management in various occupations were determined, and why the wage differential between management and labour was so great. Questions to be asked included: "How do we decide what people ought to make? For Christians should this be determined by position and responsibility, or by need? Is there a Christian basis for a wide disparity between the net annual income for those in management positions and those in worker roles?" He added that the question of compensation was not the only problem: "The issue is also one of power and self-determination." As for the UFW, Regier was undecided about both its purity and its future. He did laud it, however, for its attempt "to provide a voice to the voiceless and a measure of power to the powerless." Whether the UFW's efforts were the best means of doing so, and whether Christians should align themselves with it accordingly, were uncertain.[64]

The Barrett Janzen and Regier articles prompted a Washington, DC reader to write a lengthy letter to the editor in response. The author condemned the Christian church as a whole for being "callously insensitive to the injustice of such a continuing situation." He recalled his own childhood experience with Puerto Rican migrant workers in Lancaster County, Pennsylvania. These workers picked tomatoes for a Mennonite farmer under poor working conditions and for low pay, yet no Mennonites protested the injustice. "Maybe it was because as Christians 10 percent was given to the church, and that was the accepted definition of 'good stewardship.'" Mennonites had conformed to the economic system as they found it. The UFW, by contrast, was challenging that system and attempting to create one that was more just. Further, the UFW, in its effort to "seek recognition for [farm workers'] identity as persons of equal worth to the growers," was living out the "good news of Jesus." As such, they provided a lesson to the church itself, whose decision-making process too often was dominated "by only the professionals, by only the middle and upper class folks ... Participation, as opposed to representation. Do our churches seek this?"[65]

The MCC delegation of March 1974 was not the only investigation by Midwestern Mennonites of the farm labour situation in California. Undergraduate students, under the auspices of their Mennonite college professors, made similar visits to the San Joaquin Valley, acting on the invitation issued by California farmer Alvin Peters after his visit to Goshen College and Bluffton College in February 1974.[66] Beth Sutter, a student at Indiana's Goshen College, kept a diary of her participation in such a trip in May 1974.[67] She was appalled by the seeming unorthodoxy of Californian Mennonites, as when the mention of Anabaptist heritage by a speaker in chapel at Fresno was met with laughter from the Mennonite audience. Writing of the incident, she asked, "Is Anabaptism here a joke, a novelty, a hobby?" Sutter was challenged by some of the Mennonites with whom she met. One Mennonite grower told her "there are worse problems in Appalachia, Ohio, Georgia, and other countries" and "question[ed her] sincerity." Detailing encounters with various area Mennonites, she noted their prejudice against Roman Catholics, casual racism against Mexicans and Japanese, and emphasis on religious conversion as the solution to economic problems. She summarized a discussion with a Mennonite Brethren pastor, who stated that "if the [Mexican American] people 'had a Mennonite background' they'd be successful and know how to save ... After these people 'get the gospel' they'll move up economically." [68] Sutter's diary reveals that, as a result of these experiences, she saw the Californian Mennonites as "the other" and was troubled by that realization. "The conflict comes when I do not want to be identified with the MB growers here. 'We're a different *kind* of Mennonite,' I (or we) quickly add now when we say we're Mennonites. It just doesn't seem like it's the same gospel. The things Mennonites here say about 'the gospel' really frustrate me, and hearing people that I should have an identity with as Christians saying these things tears me up. We are supposedly believing in the same God, the same Jesus, and here I am, not wanting to be classified with 'them.'"

Goshen College professor John R. Burkholder took an active role in promoting such student interest in the plight of migrant farm workers. At an August 1974 meeting of the (Old) Mennonite Church's Board of Congregational Ministries (MBCM), he recommended that Goshen College design courses on the migrant worker issue (with the "California experience-based course as a model for others"), hold a public forum, support boycotts, and invite Chavez as a speaker (or failing that, "a public official who knows the issues").[69] At least one of Burkholder's Christian Ethics students, Daniel Hertzler, wrote an essay on the UFW for Burkholder as an undergraduate at Goshen.[70]

Hertzler's paper called for greater understanding between Mennonites and the UFW: Mennonites needed to acknowledge the UFW's commitment to justice "and they should speak out and say so."[71] The UFW, in turn, should treat California Mennonite growers "in the manner of Philemon, rather than as unbelievers hostile to social justice." The biblical reference was a suggestion that the UFW use the same forgiving approach to correction of Mennonite growers that the apostle Paul had used with the slave owner Philemon.[72] There was much among Mennonites that required correction: "prejudice, anti-Catholicism, nationalism, paternalism, rabid fear of Communism or even of social change, and love of money, power, and social respectability." Hertzler cautioned that if the UFW were to become "established and part of the power structure like most unions today (not too corrupt but not too helpful or dedicated either)," then Mennonites might have to adopt the strategy promoted by Guy Hershberger in the 1930s and 1940s. Hershberger had assisted eastern Mennonites at that time to secure arrangements with labour unions that allowed them to remain employed in union shops but redirected their dues to charitable organizations. Hertzler noted, however, that Hershberger's method was "not quite up to Jesus's example; the Christian should state where each side is wrong and right in each given circumstance." Nor should Mennonites reject striking or picketing out of hand: "As Jesus broke restrictive Sabbath laws, so it may at times be [necessary for] Christians to break restrictive laws and court orders."

While MCC was much concerned about migrant labour in California, they did not completely neglect similar issues in other parts of the country. The organization made a much less publicized and much smaller scale investigation of farm worker conditions in Ohio.[73] William Longenecker, MCC VS, took two days in March 1974 to meet with a variety of organizations in that state that addressed migrant worker issues. He met with the chair of Ohio's Fulton County Migrant Association, which taught the Bible to migrant workers, an approach to migrant assistance that Longenecker described as "quite conservative." He spoke with the department director for the Spanish-speaking Roman Catholic diocese of Toledo, noting that they were "a bit unsure of their direction ... They seem to have their fingers dabbling in everything and possibly not accomplishing anything." He also met with representatives from FLOC.

FLOC, the Farm Labor Organizing Committee, was founded in Ohio in 1967 when twenty-year-old Bluffton College student Baldemar Velasquez organized a small group of migrant farm workers – including his father.[74] When Longenecker met with FLOC representatives, the organization had changed from targeting small farmers to corporations. Longenecker saw this shift as "a much more viable position. It begins to hit at the trunk rather than the branches."[75] He hesitated to recommend that MCC establish voluntary service opportunities with FLOC, however, "because of identifying ourselves with a labor movement. I feel it would hamper us in the types of things we are trying to accomplish with both the growers and the migrants." Instead, he suggested that MCC partner with La Raza Unida de Ohio, a social service agency that provided day care and recreation activities for migrant workers' children. He concluded his report with an expression of sympathy for Ohio farmers, "who often find themselves on the receiving end of a kick, [and] are in somewhat of an awkward position." The migrant labour problem in Ohio was an "extremely hot issue" and there were "sparks that could ignite very easily," so MCC needed to keep close watch over the situation. If serious conflict arose, Longenecker thought farmers would either mechanize or simply stop growing labour-intensive tomatoes.

Joyce Schumacher's father raised tomatoes in Ohio, a crop that required migrant labour to handpick the produce. Migrant workers were provided with housing made by converting chicken coops. These one-room facilities were scrubbed clean, and the workers "lived across the lawn" from the Schumacher family. Schumacher remembered how Velasquez and FLOC made area farmers feel like they were "under attack" because of their treatment of migrant labour with respect to housing and wages. Her father was "deeply hurt" that Velasquez was a Bluffton College student and that his local pastor took FLOC's side. As a consequence, he withdrew his financial support from Bluffton College, the school his children had attended. Schumacher acknowledged that FLOC had been successful in establishing wage rates and overtime pay for holidays, ensuring that there were restrooms and clean drinking water in the fields, and preventing children from working during school hours. She insisted that these were all demands that her family was either "doing already or were willing to do."[76]

Ohioan Jeff Boehr observed that it was the local farmers' perspective on farm labour issues that was the dominant view. Migrant workers in Ohio tended to come from Texas or Mexico, and although Midwestern farmers "cared" about these workers, the housing they provided was "minimal" and they complained about their workers' greed. Boehr asserted that many migrant workers were indeed well cared for, and many eventually settled permanently in Ohio, but tension or "fear" remained. The two groups – farmers and farm workers – were "somewhat insulated, moved in different circles." Farmers saw their workers as "friends" but they did not socialize with them: to do so was not socially acceptable.[77]

According to Bluffton University business professor George Lehman, many Mennonite farmers in Ohio in the 1960s and 1970s thought they were treating their workers well, and some still resent FLOC and Velasquez today.[78] Local frustrations with FLOC extended to frustration with Bluffton College for a time, as had been the case with the Schumachers. There were other reasons for this frustration than simply Velasquez's association with the college. When Sally Weaver Sommer was a student at Bluffton College in the spring of 1972, the student senate voted to boycott lettuce in the college dining hall. A classmate started a petition to hold a referendum to bring back lettuce. It was an "exciting time," and the only referendum ever held against the senate. A public debate on the question in the college's Founders Hall included a Montreal priest who worked in California and spoke in favour of the boycott and California MB farmer Abe Peters[79] who spoke against it. Both students and local farmers attended the debate. Although Weaver Sommer believed the priest won the debate, the students voted to bring back lettuce. She remembers the early 1970s as a difficult time: with students protesting Vietnam and Velasquez promoting FLOC, many people hated Bluffton College.[80]

Mennonites in Indiana, Ohio's neighbour to the west, experienced similar challenges with migrant farm workers. In the late 1960s and early 1970s, Pine Manor Incorporated, a hatchery and feed business owned by a Mennonite family in Goshen, began to use Hispanic migrant workers in its processing plant. To house these workers, chicken coops were converted and sited beside a wastewater pool. According to historian Theron Schlabach, the workers themselves "asked if they could live in an unused storage building near the processing plant."[81] When a Pine Manor worker's shooting death was ruled a suicide in 1969, his family protested that it was an accident, while others insisted the death was related to working conditions at the plant.[82] The incident attracted the broader community's attention, and in 1971 various social action groups and non-Mennonite churches boycotted Pine Manor turkeys. The CBS documentary "Harvest of Shame" was shown in the community, drawing further attention to the migrant worker situation. Pine Manor's owners protested that they had made improvements to housing, had been denied zoning permission to bring in mobile homes for the workers, and had no access to city sewer lines. Lupe De Leon announced in 1971 that the church would build a housing complex to replace Pine Manor's housing. The housing was not replaced, nor was the complex ever built. In the end, despite the lack of results, the boycott of Pine Manor turkeys was called off.[83]

Denominational, ethnic, and class differences divided Mennonites over the question of the UFW in the 1960s. Mennonite institutions failed to take a leadership role on the issue, fearing the potential negative consequences for financial donations to their organizations. This story is an example of the broad extent of capitalist commodification: Mennonites with a religious commitment to social justice stifled the public expression of those values in favour of institutional persistence.

Despite the existence of farm labour problems in other parts of the country, it was the situation in California that created a legacy that persists to this day. Mennonites in the 1960s and 1970s found it a challenge to address the ethical concerns regarding wages and, especially, working conditions raised by the UFW. The religious, ethnic, and class differences among Mennonites at the time – together with the political and financial concerns of Mennonite institutions – prevented them from achieving a united response to the farm labour issue. And their failure to do so, as I discovered through other interviews with California Mennonites, continued to shape their memories of these events many decades later.

4

"What is said publicly must be carefully framed"

Mennonite Memory of California Conflict

Oral history interviews are not the only sources that record the story of this conflict in California. Numerous documentary sources, such as letters and reports, exist as well. While these differ from interviews as memory sources, they are nonetheless part of the analysis of memory.[1] Documentary sources are often part of an "official" record and for this reason can be limited in what they reveal about intentions and conflicts. They reflect their authors' understandings of the events at the time those events occurred. By contrast, oral sources are a record of the interview participants' later efforts to make sense of the past, to place past events within a larger narrative that gives those events meaning. As such, oral sources provide insights that supplement those provided by written sources. Both oral and written sources are subjective, of course, but historian Alessandro Portelli has made historians aware that their subjectivity is their strength rather than their weakness.

There is no way to determine whether MCC's March 1974 visit to California affected donations to that organization, but there is evidence of MCC's concern about its potential financial impact. Together with a donation receipt, MCC executive director William Snyder sent a personal reply to a criticism from a Californian donor. He explained that MCC was *not* sending money to the UFW. "All that we did in relationship to the grower-union problem was to ask Ted Koontz of our staff to get background on the grower-union problem that has been receiving a great deal of attention in the East." While students at two Mennonite colleges had joined the lettuce and grape boycotts, "it is my understanding that at least one of those colleges rescinded its action after a visit by some representatives of the growers." MCC itself preferred "not to make a statement one way or another [with respect to the boycotts] because the Mennonite Central Committee is far removed from the scene." It was the responsibility of local Mennonites to resolve the situation. Snyder concluded with a reminder that the letter writer's stance against Chavez was not the only position held – even by California Mennonites. "It is true that there are Mennonites who believe as you do that Chavez does not have a case, but there are also Mennonites, largely those who are not on the West Coast, and largely those who are of Mexican or Spanish-speaking extraction, who believe that he does." Thus MCC, with the support of Mennonites on the West Coast, would not "make pronouncements one way or another on this particular issue."[2]

MCC leadership, Mennonite church leaders, and Mennonite academics alike worried about how to balance the moral need to speak against injustice and the financial need not to antagonize donors to their organizations.[3] J. Winfield Fretz, an American Mennonite professor at Conrad Grebel College, a Mennonite school in Waterloo, Ontario, wrote to a fellow Mennonite academic at Goshen College in September 1975. "I am wavering between the sense of urgent need to do something by way of the agencies we represent on the one hand, and not doing anything because of the feeling that, at least by the growers, it would be interpreted as 'outside interference' on the other hand." He suggested that two seminars be held – one for growers, one for workers – organized by the Christians in Business Association, the Mennonite Community Association, and "possibly" MCC Peace Section. The seminar for workers should not be limited to union representatives. Fretz forwarded copies of his letter to two of the members of the 1974 MCC delegation to California: Guy Hershberger and Ted Koontz.[4] Ken Neufeld, MCC West Coast director, responded to the letter. California was about to pass some new labour legislation and elections were coming; to schedule seminars now might further polarize the situation. "It seems to me that even very open minded people are resistant to the idea of a group of people coming from the East to solve the problems in California." MCC was still "getting waves" from their March 1974 visits. Besides, the California Mennonites were taking action themselves. Mennonite academic Calvin Redekop had been invited by Pacific College in Fresno to give a seminar on employer-employee relations; MCC was exploring peace education; Reedley's MB Church had shown "increased sensitivity" by asking for a larger budget for salaries of church leaders in four Spanish-speaking churches to which they contributed financially. "My hope is that we would not undo the progress, however small, which has been made locally."[5]

Ted Koontz, as an MCC representative and delegate on the 1974 trip, initially pushed for a strong public stance on the part of MCC. In a December 1973 letter to a fellow MCC worker, he expressed his uncertainty about what exactly that stance should entail. "I am developing a deeper conviction, however, that we should seek to relate to this situation in some way. I feel we have some things to contribute in terms of aiding people in need and that we have a lot to do in terms of educating our people on this matter. We also may have a lot to learn about using non-violence for social justice."[6] Following the 1974 tour, Koontz prepared an internal report for MCC.[7] This report was more detailed than that published later in *The Mennonite* and included reflections by Koontz on the broader implications of the delegation's findings.

The farmers interviewed by the delegation were adamant that the problems experienced by migrant farm workers were either non-existent or of their own making. They asserted that California growers paid the highest farm wages in the US at $2.30 an hour. Migrant workers' poverty, therefore, was the consequence of their unwillingness to work or their financial mismanagement. The use of child labour was at the behest of the farm workers themselves. Such familial assistance was part of their Mexican culture, not an attempt by growers to exploit labour. As for claims that field work was hazardous due to pesticide use, the statistics were misleading. What was needed, the farmers said, was not unionization of farm workers but legislation to prevent secondary boycotts and strikes during the harvest. If a union was unavoidable, farmers preferred the Teamsters to the UFW.[8]

Farm workers' views were harder to categorize, Koontz reported. There was no agreement on their perceptions of the UFW. Nor was there agreement between the experiences of workers on non-Mennonite farms and those on Mennonite farms. Koontz concluded that what was needed was "a process whereby workers could freely choose whether or not they wish to be represented by a union and, if so, which one." He sympathized with California farmers' assertions that they felt singled out for criticism. "There is a great deal of truth to this. There is a need to discuss the issue of fair wages and fair treatment of employees in general by Christian employers in the

East who manage factories and who employ other laborers, as well as in California." The situation had arisen as a consequence of the shift to agribusiness, and the effects on (comparatively) smaller Mennonite farmers in the region were not yet known. Koontz wondered if MCC should research national farm labour legislation and encourage its constituency to "support appropriate legislation."[9]

Guy Hershberger, also a trip participant, wrote a supplement to Koontz's private report.[10] Believing that Koontz left the door open to MCC support of the UFW, Hershberger slammed that door shut. Mennonites could not support boycotts, since economic coercion was simply a disguised form of violence and thus off limits to Mennonites as religious pacifists. Further, to abandon pacifism in order to support the UFW "would be promoting a lost cause" and would have "a divisive effect within the Mennonite brotherhood, with much to lose and little to gain."[11]

An expurgated version of Koontz's report was submitted for publication to *The Mennonite*. Even this edited version was too explosive for publication, however. Instead, it was rewritten by one of the periodical's editors, Lois Barrett Janzen, as the article discussed above. Harold Regier, who had been on the 1974 MCC trip, observed that although "there may be dangers in this from our perspective, I think it is simply an editorial privilege to report news as seems appropriate to the editors."[12] Regier speculated, "Though I have not seen the final rewrite [of the article for *The Mennonite*], I feel that it will be a bit less guarded than the Ted Koontz article."[13] In the end, the published version was far *more* guarded.

Regier, too, was challenged by the need to censor his views when it came to his own editorial on the delegation's visit for *The Mennonite*. He told Guy Hershberger that he was "uncomfortable" with the publication of a factual account of the trip without any accompanying reflections. Nonetheless, he censored himself in the writing of his editorial, trying not to be "strongly opinionated. However, I recognize the risks involved in publishing even a statement such as this."[14] Regier's confidential reports to MCC, like those of Koontz, were more forthcoming.[15] He questioned why migrant farm workers' wages were condemned for being too low, but eastern manufacturers escaped critique for paying even less to factory workers. He noted the ethnic and class division among Mennonites in the area: the original Mennonite Brethren Church in Reedley had growers as members; the four other MB churches in the area were filled with Mexican farm workers. The division was also denominational: Mennonite Brethren were growers, General Conference Mennonites were not. Thus Reedley's GC Mennonite Church on one occasion used a church bulletin cover "with a picture of Chavez and a quotation by him," a situation that would never have occurred in the Reedley MB Church.[16] *The Mennonite* published articles on Chavez, and a children's game in *The Builder* (an (Old) Mennonite Church periodical published in Pennsylvania) included a playing card with the words: "You got a bellyache from eating too much non-union lettuce. Lose one turn until your stomach compassion improves."[17] Such incidents only further divided the Mennonite community.

Regier noted that there was much misunderstanding – and more than a little racism – in Mennonite growers' attitudes to the UFW. He learned from Selma's UFW Service Center director, Tanis Yberra, that the criticism of the UFW as "not business-like" was the consequence of its being a new organization and one with different methods. Farm workers accompanied union representatives to negotiations with growers, and thus "may not have looked very business-like to the growers."[18] Regier observed that comments from Mennonites during the California visit revealed a need for education against racial prejudice. "A comment heard by one of the team members from a Mennonite, 'I hate Mexicans,' and the comment of the person saying that it would not hurt her conscience to shoot troublemakers may be evidence that some work on this could be done." That a Mennonite woman should make such a remark must have been particularly startling. Open conversation between growers and workers was unlikely to transform the situation, however. Chris Hartmire of the National Council of Churches' National Farm Workers Ministry cautioned Regier that such dialogue was "hardly fair play. This is the powerful talking with the powerless."[19] Ultimately, Regier wondered whether the loss of family farms to the corporate model of agribusiness was not, in the long run, a more important concern than the UFW.[20] Noting that reconciliation was possible only as justice prevailed, he concluded that the California farm labour problem was just one aspect of the broader question of equitable labour relations that Mennonites needed to address.[21]

Ted Koontz and John R. Burkholder corresponded privately about the challenge of tailoring their opinions to the needs of their Mennonite employers. Koontz noted that he had deliberately avoided value judgments in his report to MCC, as "an attempt to keep dialogue going among people on the West Coast without simply making further communication between us and them impossible."[22] In his letter, he compared the migrant workers' struggle to the African American struggle for civil rights, observing that "the expressed desires of an oppressed people do not necessarily reflect their real desires and also that in some cases people do not support movements for changes which would to us appear to be in their long range interest."[23] Despite inconsistent support for the UFW by migrant workers and some questionable UFW tactics, Koontz felt the union was "pushing in the directions which I would like to see things go ... especially when you look at the alternative – the Teamsters."[24] But he also felt a connection to Mennonite farmers in California, whom he believed were "caught in a struggle which is far larger than themselves, a struggle between the large corporate growers and the unions in which they are really powerless."[25] Someone needed to convince the Mennonite farmers to stop identifying with the larger growers – but it could not be MCC. "As you probably know, feelings on this issue run terribly high. It is extremely difficult to engage in any kind of rational discussion with farmers about this issue. Sitting as I do at a desk of an inter-Mennonite agency, you can understand that what is said publicly must be carefully framed so that farmers do not simply put us in the 'enemy' camp."[26] Thus, Koontz explained, he wrote a neutral report for MCC (which was nonetheless highly edited when it appeared in *The Mennonite*). That decision left him with "some uneasy feelings" but was nonetheless "the proper course for us, given our circumstances."[27]

Burkholder replied that he, too, had to walk a difficult line as an employee of a Mennonite organization. Working as a professor at Goshen College, he was "in the difficult situation, as a self-styled supporter of the oppressed (armchair style, I must confess), of trying to help the kids who see Chavez, etc., as unparalleled and impeccable heroes, to see the complexity and ambiguity of the issues." He had created a new course, titled "The Church and Farm Labor in California," which would involve a study tour to California, but feared enrolment would be too low to offer it. Like Regier, he felt trapped between opposing camps. "I'm pleased to know that there are Mennos in the Fresno area who are not as ___ (you may fill in the blank) as [California Mennonite Brethren grower Alvin] Peters. Through FOR [the Fellowship of Reconciliation, a Christian peace organization formed during the First World War], etc., I have contacts who are extremely pro-Chavez, and I find myself in the usual situation of trying to steer between."[28]

It was these pro-Chavez supporters that worried Guy Hershberger in particular. He wrote a letter of complaint to *Gospel Herald* editor Daniel Hertzler in April 1974. He noted that positive comments on Chavez in the Mennonite press were straining relationships within the national church. Sunday school literature and articles in *The Mennonite* were placing Chavez and the UFW "on a rather high pedestal." Worse, they appeared to support the UFW boycott, a situation about which Hershberger had long made his views known. Mennonite tongues were wagging not only in California but in Indiana and elsewhere, and "some people do not feel very happy about it. Indeed, we have a real problem to remain on good terms – that is the eastern section of the church on good terms with the San Joaquin Valley section."[29] What Hershberger's letter did not mention, however, was an additional problem facing the Mennonite churches – not only a geographic divide but an ethnic one.

Behind the scenes, Stanley Bohn, as Peace and Social Concerns secretary for the General Conference Mennonite Church in the Midwest, was engaging in the kind of activity to which Hershberger objected. Writing to pastors in states with significant migrant labour populations, he asked that they support legislation to include migrant workers in the National Labour Relations Act. Bohn's letter testified to the tensions within the Mennonite community that Hershberger described:

> Some of you can tell me much better than I can tell you that writing to Congressmen to get bargaining powers for migrants will cause trouble. In the first place, farmer members of your congregations will be drastically affected and members generally will have to pay higher prices for food. If you have members of the American Farm Bureau, you will perhaps find that they have received materials recommending they write their Congressmen urging the opposite of what this letter recommends. Not only do we get irritated when people hit us in the pocketbook but we know that labor unions were never a favorite concern of churches. In the big labor battles several decades ago the Protestant church was not particularly helpful to labor unions. (We have paid the price for that with a middle class church). Many members do not see unions any more sympathetically now than they did then.[30]

Bohn asked that, at a minimum, the pastors address the issue in Sunday school classes, which would "help church members look at migrants in a little more understanding way and help them read newspaper accounts of migrant strikes with a little more sympathy." The need to do so was pressing, both because of the necessity of bringing an end to violence between migrants, growers, and state troopers, and "to get migrants the power to bargain for better housing, sanitation, wages, and fair labor practices."[31]

The views of Hispanic Mennonites on the California farm labour question are more difficult to trace. In addition to the second-hand descriptions of their views as recorded by the 1974 MCC delegation, the perspectives of those in church leadership – albeit within racialized committees – are part of the record. In the late 1960s and early 1970s, Hispanic Mennonites formed the Concilio Nacional de Iglesias Menonitas Hispanas (Council of Spanish Mennonite Churches), and later joined African American Mennonites to establish the Minority Ministries Council.[32] Hispanic Mennonites in these organizations were far less hesitant and equivocal in their assessment of the migrant farm worker problem. Members of the *concilio* reported in July 1974 on conversations they had had with a number of California growers, including Alvin Peters, the Reedley MB grower with whom both the 1974 MCC delegation and John R. Burkholder had met.[33] The *concilio* noted that California Mennonites' interest in farm workers was largely limited to the provision of churches for them. They noted as well the growers' ignorance of the diversity of the Hispanic population.

> We all made a mental note that most of the growers, and especially Mr Peters, referred to the people of Mexican ancestry who work on their farms as our workers, our Mexicans, not taking into consideration that while some are Mexicans, others are Mexican-Americans and some Chicanos. We don't accuse them of making these generalizations in a malicious manner, but we would like to point out that these are allusions that are very offensive to a great majority of us who are of Mexican ancestry, and furthermore, they need to be eliminated from a Christian's vocabulary. It has connotations of slavery and racism.[34]

While the Mennonite growers claimed they were "poor, average businessmen," the *concilio* found this claim difficult to accept in light of their own observations. They supported Koontz's description of the farm labour situation in his private report for MCC, but strongly rejected Hershberger's addendum. "His suggestions [to not be involved] smell of '*gringismo*' (or is there such a word?). Those of us who support the farm workers do so not because we want to promote a lost cause, we promote it because it is hurting us and we want our brothers and sisters in the church to know where we hurt so that they can take their foot off of our sore spots."[35] The *concilio* equated the silence of Mennonites in the face of such injustice with the culpable silence of others during the Japanese internment and the Holocaust.[36]

Lupe De Leon, associate executive secretary of the Minority Ministries Council, was particularly vocal about Mennonite neglect or distortion of the farm labour problem. He wrote a letter to the editor of *Guidelines for Today*[37] in February 1974 regarding an article titled "Cesar Chavez – Church Leader?" De Leon corrected the article's author: Chavez did not claim to be a church leader. In an impassioned passage, he wrote, "The fact that you and your 'authority' attempt to denounce Cesar's organizing efforts from a Christian perspective proves very little ... Cesar Chavez is a man of the people and the people will triumph because God hates injustices and He will send his men like Cesar just as He sent Moses to liberate the Israelites. The migratory workers in this country are enslaved and their liberation is in unionization and unionization by the FARM-WORKERS OF AMERICA." De Leon suggested that if the author had worked in the fields for at least one summer, the article would have taken a completely different stance. The final words of his letter were the rallying cry of the UFW: "*Si se puede!*" (Yes, it is possible). The letter was stamped in green and purple ink with the words "BOYCOTT LETTUCE" and "BOYCOTT GRAPES."[38] De Leon's position was completely opposed to Hershberger's.

In June 1974, De Leon wrote an article for the *Gospel Herald,* a weekly periodical that was the official publication of the (Old) Mennonite Church. The article detailed the deplorable working and living conditions of migrant farm workers in many parts of the United States – not just California. Poor pay, together with inadequate food and housing, meant that migrant farm workers were "the most exploited human beings in the American labor market." The economic necessity of moving from state to state, following the harvest, meant that farm workers had no stable social or economic base that would allow them to bargain effectively with growers. Reflecting on his own family's experience as migrant workers, De Leon "wonder[ed] where the church was." It was the responsibility of the church to care for farm workers. Therefore, his family was boycotting non-union lettuce and grapes. Without actually mentioning Hershberger, De Leon addressed Hershberger's concern about such boycotts: "We do not want to be members of an oppressive force. Some of you may not wish to follow this route. Whatever you decide to do, please, please don't be a party to the forces that continue to oppress *mis hermanos y hermanas* [my brothers and sisters]."[39] While Hershberger worried about the violence implicit in the strike and the boycott, De Leon was more concerned about economic violence by those in positions of power.

Ted Koontz wrote a letter of encouragement to De Leon shortly after the MCC delegation returned from their visit to California. He noted that the MCC delegation's meeting with Chris Hartmire (National Farm Workers Ministry) had taken place without either informing California Mennonite farmers or including it in the official report. Nonetheless, without naming Hartmire (to avoid offending Californians), some of what Koontz had learned from him was incorporated into the report. He reassured De Leon that although the MCC delegation respected the sincerity of the Mennonite growers, they did not agree with some of their "political, religious, social, and economic views" nor were they "at all convinced by their views about what the UFW is and what it is seeking to do."[40] Koontz warned De Leon that he "may well be disappointed with some of our findings and views" and that the report attempted to take a neutral tone to avoid ending dialogue prematurely. Doing so was a strategic but necessary move on the part of MCC, yet it did not mean that the organization was "any less committed to justice for farm workers than others who take a different stand."[41]

De Leon met with a group of Mennonites at Fresno's Pacific College in September 1974, a meeting later discussed by Ken Neufeld with his MCC co-workers (including Lynn Roth and Ted Koontz). Neufeld noted that the problem was that Mennonites of European descent "like to hear about the salvation of 'Mexicans' but not their physical needs. Often they are not even referred to as Mennonites." Accordingly, he suggested that rather than the seminar on farm worker issues that De Leon had requested, the discussion be broadened to address other problems faced by minority Mennonites as well as the general issue of integration of faith and economics.[42] De Leon agreed with the suggestion. He noted that the Minority Ministries Council was not the group to make the arrangements for the seminar. Instead, "to be realistic and in order to respect channels that have been established long before we were around," MCC should take the lead.[43]

Hispanic Mennonites took action not only within church organizational structures and in the pages of the Mennonite press but on Mennonite college campuses and at youth gatherings. At their meeting in August 1972, participants in the first Cross-Cultural Youth Convention voted in support of Cesar Chavez and pledged to boycott lettuce as well as calling on the (Old) Mennonite Church to join them.[44] In August 1975, an unidentified author presented the Mexican American Student Association (MASA) at Fresno's Pacific College with a statement demanding that MASA take a bold stand.[45] It was the responsibility of Christians to bring "justice and equality into the lives of farm workers." MASA needed to be aware of the tensions that existed at Pacific College, to which both workers and farmers had connections. The author recommended "that MASA sensitively recognize the implications of the choices it has and then concretely pursue involvement having chosen which direction it will go." Three options were presented for consideration: outright support for the UFW; support for farm workers apart from the UFW; or support for social service outreach to farm workers. The author suggested that the latter two options were best because they encouraged the possibility of further dialogue. Whatever the decision, MASA was called to "be aware of the implications of its choice and intelligently, peacefully and in responsible Christian love deal with the consequences of those choices."[46] It is not known how MASA addressed the author's suggestions, if at all.

I had no success in interviewing Hispanic Mennonites in California. I placed advertisements in local newspapers, church bulletins, and MCC offices, and I contacted Hispanic Mennonite professors, the Fresno Historical Society, and family members of a Mennonite lawyer who used to work for the United Farm Workers. The son of the Mennonite UFW lawyer had attempted an oral history project involving California migrant workers, but despite his excellent personal and familial contacts with the UFW, he was unsuccessful.[47] Of course, being interviewed poses more risks for those who were migrant workers in the 1960s than it does for those in more privileged occupations.

Other interview challenges include the fact that many migrant Latino Mennonite workers on Mennonite farms in the 1960s cannot be identified through farm records and may no longer be living in the United States. The few Hispanic Mennonite contacts I obtained using the snowball method did not reply to my emailed requests for an interview. The scarcity of oral histories of Hispanic farm workers is not restricted to the Mennonite community, unfortunately.[48] Oral historians Lu Ann Jones and Nancy Osterud note that Hispanic migrant workers, although forming "the majority of the California farm labor force throughout the twentieth century," are nonetheless "seriously underrepresented in the region's oral history collections."[49]

Those Californians I was able to interview were Mennonites and Mennonite Brethren of European background – and their interviews reflected some of the same reticence and inconsistency exhibited in the Enns brothers' interviews discussed in the previous chapter. Steve Penner, minister of Reedley Mennonite Church, recalled that although his father was a grower in California, he never spoke about farm labour issues. At harvest time, he would put a sign on the corner of the road saying grape pickers were needed, and hope people would show up. If there were insufficient workers, the crop would rot in the field. The work was hard, dirty, dusty, and hot, and workers were plagued by wasps. Workers would pick the grapes and place them on trays 3 feet by 1.5 feet. They were paid by tray: Penner's job as a child was to walk the rows and count the trays to double check the workers' counts. He recalled an instance when one worker suddenly vanished one day, only to return much later. The man had been deported, but returned to the Penner farm in the company of a "coyote" (the name for individuals who help people emigrate illegally into the US from Mexico). The coyote demanded hundreds of dollars for the return of the worker. Penner's father was faced with a dilemma: if he refused to pay the coyote, he put the worker in jeopardy; if he paid the coyote, he supported human trafficking. Ultimately he decided to pay the fee demanded.

The Penner family lived in a conservative community, but Penner guessed that his father was probably more sympathetic than most to Chavez. He speculated that the lack of interest in the farm labour issue may have been because the church in which he grew up, full of "warm-hearted salt of the earth" people, had no way to talk about such issues. Even in 2010, at the time the interview was conducted, the Reedley Mennonite Church was "one church but [composed of] two distinct groups" of farmers and farm workers. Stories existed in the congregation of farmers whose fields had been picketed by the UFW, of farmers during the Japanese internment of the Second World War who had cared for their Japanese neighbours, and of local reactions to the 1974 MCC delegation. Of this latter, the "general feeling" was "who are these uppity Mennonite Easterners to say how to behave" – a kind of "throwing dirt clods feeling."[50]

Gordon Wiebe, owner of Wiebe Farms in Reedley, asserted that although his father (a tree fruit grower) was opposed to Chavez, he was "not opposed to what Chavez was saying or trying to do." The UFW, Wiebe noted, had improved working conditions. One heard less about labour issues because growers "can't cheat like they used to." In the past, some had "taken advantage" of workers. It was necessary to try to pay fairly, give them what they deserve, and treat them humanely. Every election year, the same debates about labour and immigration issues arise, as with the "Arizona immigration mess" of 2010. If government seriously wanted to solve the problem of undocumented migrant workers, Wiebe asserted, the solution was simple. All that was needed was for government to make it possible for employers to check their workers' names against an online database of legal migrant workers. Such a solution, however, would "destroy the economy" because the necessity of migrant labour – undocumented or not – meant that the US was "past a simple answer." Wiebe was attempting to find his own solution to the labour problem. Tree fruit was labour intensive. What could he grow that would require less labour? The solution, to which he felt God had led him, was to raise olives for oil.[51]

Duane Ruth-Heffelbower, director of Fresno Pacific University's Center for Peacemaking and Conflict Studies, recalled that Chavez was "a big deal" in the Reedley General Conference Mennonite Church in 1974.[52] The grape boycott left Mennonite farmers "confused" since they believed they took better care of farm workers than most growers did. What was interpreted as a "civil rights" movement on the part of Hispanics was thus unpopular among Reedley Mennonites, not because they were opposed to such rights but because they "felt beat on for something that was not their fault." Further, they objected to breaking the law (through picketing and strikes) as a means of pushing for equality. The UFW was even more unpopular in the Reedley Mennonite Brethren Church, but their congregation was composed of bigger farmers than the GC congregation. The pastor of the Reedley MB Church, however, had little to say regarding Chavez or the MCC delegation, asserting that Mennonites had few encounters with the UFW.[53] The 1974 MCC delegation, Ruth-Heffelbower claimed, was perceived as a group of "busybody idiots, just causing trouble, self-righteous know-nothings." Part of the problem was the history of misunderstanding between Mennonites from East and West: "Eastern Mennonites think the far west is Pittsburgh. Pastoral searches see [California] as foreign mission: they come and serve and go."[54]

Lynn Jost, president of Fresno's Mennonite Brethren Biblical Seminary, had been pastor of a rural Mennonite Brethren church in California in 1974. He had "a sense they were more understanding" of the UFW. The congregation was not anti-labour, he said, because many had farm workers as their friends. It was true that others were more suspicious of Chavez, but the Mennonites he knew at the time were sympathetic to their workers. The farm worker issue was raised in student discussions at Pacific College, but Jost did not know if it was formally discussed in public venues as it had been at Goshen College and Bluffton College. Some wealthy Mennonite farmers at the time were uneasy about labour rights and had the sense that the campus was misrepresenting biblical justice with respect to the issue. The *Christian Leader,* a biweekly periodical that was the official publication of the Mennonite Brethren Conference, "forced conversation" on the issue, as did various MB Conference resolutions and conference floor discussions (none of which, however, resulted in resolutions that passed). Academics, Jost noted, pushed agriculturalists to think about how Jesus would treat the workers.[55]

As for the Enns brothers, when asked about his family's responses at the time to the MCC delegation, Melvin Enns observed that he was not living in the Fresno-Reedley area then, and so could not reply. He then redirected the conversation, interrupting my next question to ask one of his own: "What's a fair wage?" I laughed and replied that it was a good question, but he persisted: "What would *you* say – for the archives?" I gave a general answer, and he responded by agreeing and expanding somewhat on my reply. We did not return to the subject of the UFW. His brother, Eugene, gave a very different response to questions about farm worker unions in general and Chavez in particular. He noted that there had not been any real union activity in the area (much less at WesPak) since Chavez's day. No one had the same "entrepreneurial dogmatism to lay their life on the line like [Chavez] did." Chavez's work "definitely strengthened the laws of California and the nation" with respect to pay, and placed tough restrictions on contractors regarding housing, food, transportation, and paperwork. Peach picking, he commented, was a dirty job, but there were many such tough jobs – mining, for example. If workers were treated respectfully, were able to make a living, were paid better than minimum wage, then "what is there to rise up against?" Nonetheless, such "uprising can happen anywhere." He used a sports metaphor to explain the sentiments of California Mennonites during the UFW movement: suddenly you see "your best friends with flags," screaming, caught up in cheers, "propelling their team to success" and "caught up in the frenzy of excitement of winning."[56]

What is of interest in these interviews is how Mennonite collective memory of Chavez provides insight into relations within the Mennonite community itself. Natalie Zemon Davis and Randolph Starn declare that "whenever memory is invoked we should be asking ourselves: by whom, where, in which context, against what?"[57] Mennonites' collective memory of Cesar Chavez is divided by ethnicity, by geography, by religious denomination, and by class.[58] East Coast and Midwest Mennonites were divided against West Coast Mennonites, General Conference and (Old) Mennonites against Mennonite Brethren, Hispanic American Mennonites against Euro-American Mennonites, Mennonite academics and professionals against Mennonite agribusiness owners.

It is not possible to assess whether Mennonite growers in the 1960s and 1970s treated their farm workers (Mennonite and non-Mennonite alike) better or worse than did other growers.[59] Records do not exist, and oral testimony (as we have seen) is difficult to obtain, particularly from Hispanic Mennonite farm workers. Nor is it the historian's job to determine whether Mennonites' support or failure to support the UFW was the "right" choice. In the same way, Anna Sheftel and Stacey Zembrzycki, discussing the perceived racism of a Holocaust survivor they interviewed, have argued that their responsibility as historians was not to make "moral judgments" but to understand "people's lives, and how their experiences have formed their identities."[60] This chapter, then, has attempted to uncover US Mennonites' collective memory of Chavez. At stake with the "forgetting" of Chavez is the ongoing ability of Mennonite institutional and community leaders to define Mennonitism – to construct an identity that elides the class and ethnic divisions that persist in the community. The ability to do so is assisted by what memory scholars and oral historians have termed "reticence" and "covert silence."

Covert silence is "not about the complete absence of talk, ritual or practice" but "the absence of content."[61] The reluctance to speak of a subject, or the insistence on speaking in a veiled manner, are ways to address memories that involve "issues of accountability and guilt" when outright silence or refusal to speak is impossible. In other words, when overt silence would result in conflict between social groups (or would draw attention to existing conflicts), individuals and communities resort to covert silence.[62] "The power of veiled silences as a mechanism for coping with a difficult past lies precisely in their ability to minimize the potential for social conflicts."[63]

Reticence is one means of creating covert silences. Reticence is not the failure to remember but "the exercise of the narrators' agency through conversational shifts intended to limit dialogue on specific matters."[64] There are numerous possible reasons for the reticence of an interview participant, and scholars warn against automatically leaping to the conclusion that an interviewee desires to produce a sanitized history.[65] The many demonstrations of reticence and covert silence by numerous interview participants in this case suggest that these were not simply individuals making independent decisions about how to present their story. Rather, interview participants structured their story to fit into an existing discourse on the subject of Chavez and the 1974 MCC delegation. In so doing, they reveal the way power relations in the Mennonite community have shaped collective memory of this subject, in much the same way as Romans' collective memory of a Nazi massacre was shaped by "popular belief and political distortions of memory, perpetrated by the popular press, the media, the Church, and conservative political forces."[66]

Interview participants were aware that what they said, what they chose to recall, would become part of a permanent archival record that could be consulted (subject to restrictions to access they could choose to impose) by subsequent researchers for generations to come. Caution in the sharing of experiences that occurred in difficult circumstances in the past was therefore only to be expected. What is more difficult to determine is how the researcher should respond to reticence and covert silence.

Oral historians disagree about how (or whether) to interpret uncomfortable interviews.[67] Tracy K'Meyer and Glenn Crothers discuss their interview of an African American woman who passed as white, and the ethical dilemma of persisting in asking her questions about race when she expressed clear disinterest in the subject.[68] Their article not only discusses the content of her interviews but also describes and interprets comments and stories she shared when not being recorded. Unlike the woman interviewed by K'Meyer and Crothers, however, my interview participants were not disempowered by society, nor does my interpretation of Mennonite collective memory rely on off-the-record remarks by these interviewees.[69] Sheftel and Zembrzycki considered asking their discomfiting participant directly to reflect on their interpretation of his remarks, but decided not to do so because they "did not have the courage to ask such difficult questions" and they "dreaded the idea of going back" to the interviewee.[70] While I did not "dread" a return visit to the Enns brothers, nor were their views objectionable in the way that Sheftel and Zembrzycki's interviewee's observations were, I too opted not to ask interview participants to comment on my interpretation of Mennonite collective memory of Chavez. Whatever methodological choices scholars make, it is clear that uncomfortable interviews need to be seriously considered, in part because of the academic responsibility to "shed light on controversial topics"[71] but also because such interviews are "a prism through which we can understand how [interview participants] continually grapple with their experiences."[72]

Histories and collective memories "help create and maintain our identities" and "help maintain institutions and traditions."[73] They do so in part through "the selective forgetting of the past," a "forgetting" that includes "acts of 'representation' and 'repression.'"[74] Mennonites' collective memory of Chavez allows Mennonite institutional and community leaders – still primarily of European background – to regulate discussion of issues of class, ethnic difference, and power in the Mennonite community, issues that are not only historical but also contemporary. Daniel James, speaking of a problematic interview he conducted with an Argentinean supporter of President Juan Perón, notes that the result was "a dialogue between himself and his listeners/his public and, at a remove, with myself, the outsider." The story he told "could be manipulated truth. Not at will, according to individual whim with arbitrary intent, but rather according to tacit, largely unspoken consensus between both audience and narrator about present needs, priorities, and imperatives.

These were in turn arrived at through negotiation and concession with other alternative narratives within this community."[75] In their interviews with me, California Mennonites presented a similarly carefully crafted narrative. Melvin Enns's question, "What would *you* say, for the archives?" is thus a very interesting question indeed – one that reveals the ongoing struggle for authority in definition and interpretation of a community and its history.

This case study, then, contributes to an analysis of Mennonite attitudes toward unions in that it is an example of the broad extent of capitalist commodification. Mennonite religious commitment to social justice could lead to union support, as was the case for some Mennonite supporters of the United Farm Workers. Racial divisions within the North American Mennonite community, however, undermined widespread Mennonite support for the UFW. Most significantly, when the ongoing financial support of Mennonite institutions was threatened, Mennonite leaders preferred to withdraw from the debate and present their inaction as neutrality. These Mennonites viewed their position not as anti-union but as supportive of ethnoreligious unity. In essence, they chose to commodify their religious values, trading a commitment to the work of the UFW and to social justice at home for ongoing access to the funds needed to alleviate social injustice overseas through the work of MCC.

5

"They work with troubled conscience"

Conscientious Objections to Unions in Manitoba

There is no Canadian counterpart to the American Mennonite experience of the Farm Workers movement; no single labour issue attracted similar nation-wide attention. A more localized experience, however, serves as an interesting comparison: conscientious objection to unions in Manitoba. While California Mennonites' recollection of the UFW may have been a "manipulated truth,"[1] very few Manitoba Mennonites have any memory of the events discussed in this chapter. The Farm Workers movement involved thousands of people and drew the attention of not only California but also much of North America for several years. By contrast, Section 68(3)'s conscientious objection to unions in Manitoba existed for only four years, and directly involved only some two dozen Mennonite workers as well as Mennonite community leaders. Nonetheless, the events described here provide some insight into how Mennonite arguments against unions shifted in the 1970s, from religious (nonviolence) to secular (human rights) grounds.

The 1970s were a watershed era with respect to Mennonite relations with labour unions in Manitoba. The province elected its first New Democratic Party (NDP) government in 1969, led by Premier Edward (Ed) Schreyer. Manitoba's labour legislation had not been revised in many years, a fact that had prompted the previous Progressive Conservative government (led by Premier Dufferin (Duff) Roblin) to create a Manitoba Labour-Management Review Committee in 1964.[2] By the early 1970s, the committee had made some recommendations, and a proposed bill to amend the Labour Relations Act was produced in the fall of 1972. The revisions introduced Section 68(3), an amendment that would cause, in turn, jubilation, frustration, and disappointment for the province's Mennonites.

Section 68(3) – known as the "conscience clause" – provided for individuals with religious objections to unions to apply to the Labour Board for exemption from union membership. The clause stated, in part: "Where an employee has satisfied the [provincial labour] board that because of his religious beliefs he is by conscience opposed to joining a union and to paying union dues, the employer will be required to remit the amount deducted from the employee's wages as union dues to a charity agreed to by the employee and the bargaining agent, or, if they cannot agree on a charity, to a charity designated by the board. In such a case, where a closed shop agreement is in effect, the employer is not in breach of the collective agreement."[3] Successful applicants under Section 68(3) had fourteen days in which to reach agreement with the union on a charity to which to remit the equivalent of union dues. Failing that, the Manitoba Labour Board would appoint a charity. The clause was patterned after changes to Ontario's Labour Relations Act that had been made in 1965, and was created in response to requests from Manitoba's small Plymouth Brethren religious community.[4] It was consistent with the newly consolidated Canada Labour Code of 1966–67 that incorporated the provisions of the famous 1945 Rand Formula (which required payment of union dues by all workers but allowed for religious exemptions).[5]

The Plymouth Brethren, a non-hierarchical Protestant group with origins in early nineteenth-century Ireland, numbered only some two hundred in Manitoba. Several Plymouth Brethren appeared before the Standing Committee on Industrial Relations regarding proposed amendments to the Manitoba Labour Relations Act, requesting a conscience clause. At that hearing, Harry J. Enns, a Mennonite and a Progressive Conservative member of the legislative assembly (MLA), expressed his support for them. NDP MLA Cy Gonick asked Plymouth Brethren member Norman W. Plater whether he and other workers had not benefited from unions; Plater agreed but said he was "not compelled to contribute to other groups whose activities result in benefits to him." NDP MLA Jim Walding then asked Plater if the Bible mentioned unions; Plater countered that scripture forbade Christians from association with unbelievers – referencing 2 Corinthians 6:14: "Be not unequally yoked with unbelievers." Another Plymouth Brethren member, Anthony MacLachlan, quoted the prophet Amos at the hearing in support of his anti-union stance: "How can two walk together unless they be agreed?"[6] A third Plymouth Brethren, George Henry, asserted his belief that compulsory union dues check-off was a violation of the Human Rights Act. A few other Plymouth Brethren members claimed that compulsory union membership undermined the master-servant relationship that defined industrial relations.[7] Whether the government found these arguments convincing, or why they decided to pattern their amendments after those in Ontario, is not clear. Whatever the case, the Plymouth Brethren got their conscience clause.

The amendments to the Labour Relations Act – including the new Section 68(3) – took effect on 1 November 1972, despite reservations on the part of some government members. Labour Minister A. Russell (Russ) Paulley noted that "the requirement of labor board approval for conscientious objectors" to union membership would discourage "'frivolous' applications." However, government member Sidney Green "warned that by making a special case, the government might be making a bad law" in that non-religious people also could have conscientious objections to union membership but were excluded from applying for exemption. Government members T.W. Johannson and Jim Walding opposed the amendment, but were willing to support the caucus majority who favoured it.[8]

The Ontario legislation on which Manitoba's conscience clause was modelled had resulted in its first exemption from union dues on religious grounds in 1971. Klaas Stel was a sixty-one-year-old Parks Department worker in North York, Ontario; he had been a member of Local 94 of the Canadian Union of Public Employees (CUPE) for sixteen years. As a member of the Christian Reformed Church – whose objections to unions resulted in their creation in the 1950s of the Christian Labour Association of Canada (CLAC), a union alternative that opposed strikes – Stel had sought exemption from union membership. By 1971, some twenty-five other such applications were scheduled to be heard by the Ontario Labour Relations Board.[9]

Applications for union exemption on religious grounds in Manitoba were similar in number to those in Ontario. While the Archives of Manitoba notes that they have case files of the Manitoba Labour Board's "applications, hearings, and rulings regarding Section 68(3) of the Labour Relations Act," the board themselves noted in response to a Freedom of Information request that these records "do not exist."[10] The records of the Deputy Minister of Labour, however, state that within four years, twenty-three applications to the Manitoba Labour Board were made under Section 68(3).[11]

One of the first to file for exemption under Section 68(3) was not Plymouth Brethren, but a member of the Christian Reformed Church. Chris Vander Nagel applied for exemption from membership in the United Steelworkers; the Labour Board rejected his request in August 1973.[12] Vander Nagel had argued that the Steelworkers union "does not subscribe to the Christian view of life and does not acknowledge the Scripture (the Holy Bible) as normative for their actions. They are committed to a materialistic view of life and labour relations. And pursue policies inspired by a class struggle mentality. This is against the Lord Jesus's Greatest Commandment to love thy neighbour as thyself."[13] The board refused to give reasons for their rejection of Vander Nagel's application, explaining that they did "not have the personnel or resources necessary to give reasons in all cases." The Committee for Justice and Liberty (CJL), founded by members of the Christian Reformed Church, decided to involve themselves further in the case.[14]

CJL founder Gerald Vandezande and CJL lawyer David G. Newman made plans to challenge the Manitoba Labour Board's rulings against applicants under Section 68(3). Newman complained that the Labour Board was misinterpreting the conscience clause, in that "it is necessary in Manitoba to show both an opposition to joining a union *and* to paying union dues."[15] Vandezande asked Newman if it was possible to use the courts to force the board to give written reasons for their decisions. Since the Vander Nagel ruling was a "first, precedent-setting decision," Vandezande wondered if it could be reviewed. Part of his concern was that workers' ability to join the CLAC might be hampered by the board's interpretation of Section 68(3). "As you can appreciate, we are much concerned about the Board's negative decision, for it virtually renders section 68(3) meaningless if it is only considered to apply to workers who are opposed to 'any union.' If this narrow interpretation is allowed to stand then all CLAC-affiliated workers would not be in a position to apply for exemption from secular union membership and dues payments."[16]

Lawyer Newman noted that there was no way to force the board to provide their reasoning or to review their decision. He suggested that churches be encouraged to write to the minister of labour and send copies to the press, since "the power of public opinion is more likely to be effective than legal procedures the way the Act is presently worded and interpreted."[17] Vandezande wondered whether a less public approach could bear fruit: he suggested that board members or the registrar be "approached *informally*" (emphasis in original) for advice on how to file future applications to obtain more successful results. He observed that this method had "been possible and 'practice' in Ontario." As to who should make the informal approach, Vandezande suggested, "Sometimes, ministers of the Gospel are less likely to be refused information than 'ordinary' churchgoers."[18]

After a further exchange of letters, Vandezande decided to focus instead on the upcoming applications of two nurses that *Mennonite Brethren Herald* editor Harold Jantz had drawn to his attention.[19] Jantz was particularly active in the cause of Mennonite conscientious objection to labour unions. Before the 1970s, Mennonites in Manitoba had made individual decisions regarding union membership – although joining was "a problem," Ted Regehr notes, "particularly for the (Old) Mennonites and in churches with many urban employers."[20] The increased labour militancy in North America in the 1970s, together with the passage of the conscience clause in Manitoba, presented an opportunity for Jantz and Vandezande to promote a cause that was dear to them. That decade saw the greatest number of strikers in decades, coupled with the first postwar decline in real wages, in both Canada and the United States.[21]

Jantz believed that the Labour Board was misinterpreting Section 68(3) by ignoring individual conscience and focusing instead on church doctrine. "It appears that the government never had any intention of truly recognizing conscientious objectors to union membership (aside from those in the Plymouth Brethren churches). The Labour Board is interpreting the act as the government would have it interpreted (though the wording itself would give rise to other hopes)."[22]

The two nurses in question, Trudie Barkman and Hilda Friesen, sought exemption from the Selkirk General Hospital Nurses' Association. The Labour Board asked them rhetorically, "Does the Bible not teach us that there are times and places where it is better to work together against conditions which are not in your own best interests? If people hold such strong opinions against unions, why would you accept the raises?"[23] The board rejected their applications, ruling that the Mennonite churches to which Barkman and Friesen belonged did not have explicit statements against union membership. Progressive Conservative MLA Robert (Bob) Banman wrote to the labour minister, asking that he investigate the board's ruling and "help to restore the personal rights and freedom" of the two women.[24] Banman also raised the issue in the legislature, and received a reply in the house from Sid Green, who declared that the nurses probably had not made their case.[25] Banman explained that the women were opposed to unions because they were opposed to violence. Green observed that it "would be ridiculous for the labor board to accept such a reason because it would suggest that unions were in favor of violence." Green then challenged his own governing party by declaring his opposition to Section 68(3) "because it undermines the entire system of collective bargaining."[26]

A week later, legislative debate on a proposed Human Rights Act was derailed by further discussion by MLAs of Mennonites and labour unions.[27] Progressive Conservative MLA Werner Jorgenson declared that non-violent Mennonites teach "that they can't deny help to people, particularly sick people in hospitals" – thus Mennonite nurses could not, in good conscience, go on strike or be union members. In reply, Sid Green drew an interesting distinction between church doctrine and individual belief, declaring that "wasn't what the Mennonite religion actually teaches, but what the Mennonites see in their religion." Strikes, he said, are actually "the complete absence of force" and those who use violence during a strike are punished under the law. "If a strike is called, it doesn't mean people can't work. They may be hooted at and called scabs, but if they hold a belief, they must make that sacrifice."[28]

Mennonite community leaders reached out to each other and to other interested Christians in both Manitoba and Ontario to explore ways in which to assist applicants under Section 68(3). A network of support developed between Ontario's CJL, MCC Manitoba, and John H. Redekop (whose views on unions as a columnist for the *Mennonite Brethren Herald* were discussed in chapter 2).[29] Harold Jantz wrote a letter on behalf of MCC to four nurses in Virden to "let them know of MCC's willingness to give assistance" with their applications for union exemption. MCC Manitoba's Peace and Social Concerns Committee also issued a press release to broadcast their "willingness to help individuals in applying for exemption from union membership."[30] Jantz sent articles from the *Mennonite Brethren Herald* on Mennonites and union exemption to the province's MLAs and to Premier Schreyer.[31] Gerald Vandezande indicated his willingness to travel from Toronto to assist applicants at his own expense. John Redekop answered requests for advice from Manitoba Mennonites concerned about unions, and expressed his support for the work of MCC Manitoba in that area: "May God continue to bless you and your committee in your innovative and aggressive ministries."[32]

Further evidence of trans-provincial and trans-denominational networks in this area was the decision by MCC Manitoba to invite Redekop and CJL's Vandezande to present three seminars on labour relations for the Manitoba Mennonite community.[33] These seminars were offered in Winnipeg, Winkler, and Steinbach in January 1976. Redekop was asked to present "the Biblical basis for an Anabaptist Christian position regarding labor management relationships." Vandezande was invited to present "his model [the Christian Labour Association of Canada] which might help us to get into the practical aspects of the problem."[34] Advertisements for the seminars situated the discussion in contemporary events: "With the present unhappy spirit in relations of labor and management toward one another, many Christians are increasingly asking themselves what their response ought to be. These seminars will attempt to give some answers, from a biblical understanding, of the kind of relationships which acknowledge the Lordship of Christ and bring about reconciliation."[35]

Larry Kehler arranged a meeting with Labour Minister Russ Paulley for Jantz and leaders of MCC Manitoba. Kehler was the former editor of *The Mennonite* (the official publication of the General Conference Mennonites) and was either a member of MCC Manitoba's Peace and Social Concerns Committee or the MCC Manitoba board at the time. Jantz, MCC Manitoba chair Peter H. Peters, and MCC Manitoba Peace and Social Concerns Committee representative Diedrich J. Gerbrandt met with Paulley on 17 December 1974.[36] According to Jantz, Paulley said at the meeting that he was talking to Premier Schreyer about a more liberal interpretation of Section 68(3), and that those individuals rejected by the Labour Board could appeal. Jantz reflected, "It seemed to us that we were helping to educate the government on issues of which they had not been aware when they originally drafted" Section 68(3). "We will have to give the government some time to see whether the growing understanding about our concerns actually bears some fruit."[37]

Jantz's hopes were dashed when Peters received a follow-up letter from Russ Paulley. In it, Paulley explained that there were very few applicants under Section 68(3) and that the Labour Board functioned independently of the government: "I indicated to you I could not instruct the Board as to the direction of their decisions." Paulley noted that he had told board members informally of the Mennonite delegation's concerns, but that "the general opinion is that the Board's decision was based on an impartial approach to the situation."[38]

The catalyst that had prompted this group of Mennonite leaders to confront the Labour Minister was the Labour Board's rejection of the application of a Mennonite baker. Henry Funk, a Mennonite Brethren Church member, had worked for twelve years as a teacher before taking a job at McGavin Toastmaster in June 1974, where he refused to join the Bakery and Confectionery Workers International Union. He was fired after one month on the job because his co-workers "threatened to go on strike unless he joined" the union.[39] Accompanied to the Labour Board hearing by his pastor, Jacob Bergen, and by Mennonite professor of religion William Klassen, Funk declared his religious objections to the union membership oath and "violent tactics" of unions. Two of his brothers worked at McGavin Toastmaster and were union members, he admitted, but he insisted that both would have preferred not to have joined the union. While Funk was not the first Mennonite applicant rejected by the Manitoba Labour Board, his was the first case in which the board, under the chairmanship of Murdoch MacKay, gave written reasons for its decision. The rejection of Funk's application was criticized by Harold Jantz in the *Mennonite Mirror*: "The fact that Funk has spent four years in Bible school, knows the Scriptures well, believes himself to be taught that the violent tactics employed by unions are wrong, has discussed union membership with a minister of his church (and was discouraged from joining), could testify that no union could have his 'first allegiance' and that his church teaches beliefs which can be interpreted as being in opposition to union practices – all of this did not seem to distract the Board."[40] Funk would go on to challenge the Labour Board's ruling in the courts, with the support and assistance of Jantz and Vandezande.

It was not only Mennonites who were interested in the Funk case; as the first decision for which the Labour Board offered written reasons, the case attracted broad public attention. Dudley Magnus, labour reporter for the *Winnipeg Free Press*, observed that the case was one "to watch; it may alter the thinking of labor boards across Canada."[41] After Funk's appeal to the Labour Board was rejected, he appealed the ruling at the Manitoba Court of Queen's Bench. Magnus believed that the Labour Board would be as interested in a resolution of the case as Funk himself, since "there have been several different views as to what exactly was the intent of the legislation."

Magnus asked rhetorically "what would happen to unions" if all churches decided to prohibit their members from joining them, rather than leaving the matter to individual conscience as did the Mennonite Brethren.[42]

Funk's appeal to the Manitoba Court of Queen's Bench was rejected by Justice Louis Deniset, but was upheld by Chief Justice Samuel Freedman at the Manitoba Court of Appeal in October 1975. Freedman ruled that "the labor board had stepped out of its jurisdiction when it dismissed Mr. Funk's application." The Labour Board had rejected Funk's application because the Mennonite Brethren Church did not have an official position against union membership. Freedman declared that the absence of a church rule against unions was irrelevant; the board should have asked about Funk's – not the church's – beliefs, and whether those beliefs were "sincerely and genuinely held."[43] Freedman also commented on inconsistencies in the act: while the application for exemption had a space for the signature of an official of the church of which the applicant was a member, the act itself mentioned personal – not church – beliefs.[44]

The appeal court's ruling provoked a response by the government. Labour Minister Russ Paulley warned that "a corrective amendment" to the Labour Relations Act might have to be made as a result.[45] Murdoch MacKay, the chair of the province's Labour Board, commented that the board would consider taking the case to the Supreme Court. Funk's lawyer, Kenneth Regier, replied that they were prepared for such an eventuality.[46] Gerald Vandezande asked that Regier or Harold Jantz inform him if Russ Paulley took the Funk case to the Supreme Court: "Frankly, I hope he does. I am rather confident that Funk could win, provided a solid, well-researched legal argument were made," preferably by CJL's lawyer, Newman.[47] The *Free Press* remarked on the subsequent "stir in the provincial labor department. Labor Minister Russ Paulley's reaction indicates that he, at least, is not much concerned with the rights of individuals." The *Free Press* speculated that if the case did not go to the Supreme Court, then the Labour Relations Act doubtless would be amended to remove the conscience clause.[48]

Harold Jantz wrote to the editor of the *Winnipeg Free Press* to express his frustration with the responses to the Funk decision by both the provincial government and the Manitoba Federation of Labour (MFL). Both groups, he declared, "seem to be saying that a law respecting the convictions of genuine conscientious objectors is perfectly all right until it is used."[49] The government had stated it would review the act and the MFL president had insisted it be changed. "For the government to make such statements amounts to virtual fraud," Jantz charged. "The problem is that neither the labor board nor the government of this province has understood the nature of religion and of conscience. You cannot go to a person's church to determine what his beliefs are, no matter how sincerely he believes and how close he feels himself to be to his church. The issue must be what the person himself believes."[50] Churches, Jantz explained, do not make rules for themselves as do governments; individuals must determine their position on unions, since "you can read the Bible from beginning to end without finding a single reference to labor unions. Nothing there." He asked that government avoid turning conscientious objectors to unions into economic martyrs: "I would like to believe that we would value people who are so faithful to their conscience that they will even give up economic security before they will compromise it."[51]

Jantz, together with Larry Kehler and CJL founder Gerald Vandezande, considered his next move. Vandezande recommended that lawyer Kenneth Regier "should probably *not* continue to act for people concerned with Section 68(3)" (emphasis in original). He asked whether particular applicants should appeal their rulings, and wondered, "What does [MCC] Peace and Social Concerns [Committee] think of it all? What does it conceive its role to be in relation to labour issues such as this one?"[52] CJL's lawyer, David Newman, suggested that "a reasonably good case could be made before a Court to quash these decisions."[53] He recommended challenging "just one of the decisions" as a test case.

Jantz also continued to follow Mennonites' cases before the Labour Board. He contacted Hazel Barkman, a nurse, after her request for exemption was denied, asking for a copy of the Labour Board decision and whether Barkman was interested in challenging the decision in the courts. Barkman's father, a minister, replied that they had lost their copy of the decision, but would not send it even if found: "Some of the questions were of quite a personal nature, and I as a minister was also involved." Nor were they interested in court action, since "our principles of non-resistance would not permit us to use coercion."[54] Jantz explained that he and other Mennonites were working to "help [the government] understand our concerns about union membership. They are for the most part not believing men and don't understand what it means to try to live with a good conscience before God."[55] Jantz and others had "sought to use a variety of means" including meeting with the labour minister, presenting at legislative committees, and writing letters to the newspapers – "always we trust without malice and disrespect." The goal was to demonstrate that "there are Christians in our province who do not want to be a part of the violence and intimidation with which the unions have become associated." In doing so, "a positive testimony for Christ" could be made while simultaneously alerting both government and Labour Board that "we too know what the law is about and what the limits to their powers are."[56]

In the aftermath of the Funk decision, two other Mennonites' applications to the Labour Board were successful – those of Gertrude Friesen and Gordon Dyck.[57] Friesen, who refused to join the Swan River Nurses' Association, had filed her request in the spring of 1976.[58] As a member of the Evangelical Mennonite Church, she objected to the union's use of coercion as a negotiating tactic. Friesen was the first in the province to be exempted by the Labour Board under the conscience clause;[59] lawyer David Newman, whom Harold Jantz had recommended to her, had presented her case.[60] That same spring, Gordon Dyck, an employee of International Harvester, also had his application (for exemption from membership in the United Steelworkers of America Local 8283) approved.[61] Four nurses' aides in Virden's Westman Nursing Home, however, had their request for exemption from membership in CUPE rejected.[62]

Friesen wrote detailed accounts of her experience with the Labour Board for Jantz. Her lawyer, David Newman, had asked her before her hearing whether she would quit her job if the Labour Board denied her request for exemption. She decided "there really was no other option if for conscience's sake I was opposed to paying union dues."[63] She prepared for three hours with her lawyer and her minister before the hearing. The hearing itself lasted almost two hours, during which time she had the "great privilege to give my testimony before 3 austere men plus 12 or 15 others who had come to listen in for what ever reasons I don't know."[64] After the board ruled in her favour, Newman told her, "Your prayers were answered." She later reflected, "We did not pray to win; we prayed to be a testimony and God answered as He so often does over and above what we have asked."[65] There were few consequences for her on the job, she observed. "I had 1 person congratulate me but at school the son of one of the pro-unionists said to my son, 'It would serve her right if she got fired!!' No doubt those were his mother's sentiments."[66]

Friesen's and Dyck's success, and the overturning of the ruling in Funk's case, necessitated either changes in the way the Labour Board interpreted Section 68(3) or revisions to the Labour Relations Act. Was the purpose of the conscience clause in the act to provide a religious exemption for members of churches with tenets against union membership? Or was it to allow exemption for anyone with any conscientious scruples against unions? The alliance of Mennonite leaders and the CJL determined that their focus should be "on retaining the section. We should *not* flood the Board with applications until we know what the Government has decided to do."[67] Since there was some talk that the government might amend the act, Vandezande recommended that MCC Manitoba "send a clear, positive communication" to the premier, the labour minister, all members of the legislature, the province's Standing Committee on Industrial Relations, and the media "again outlining your position re religious objectors." Doing so "would hopefully make the Government think twice about introducing a last-minute amendment and, thus, catch us and the 'opposition' parties by surprise."[68]

Amendment of the act was clearly on the NDP government's agenda by the spring of 1976. The province's Labour-Management Review Committee recommended that Section 68(3) "be reviewed in light of the recent decision of the Court of Appeal with a view either to repealing or amending it."[69] The chair of Manitoba's Labour Board recommended that Section 68(3) be amended to "correspond with the B.C. legislation."[70] The consequence of such amendments would mean that conscientious objectors would not have to become union members, but *would* have to pay union dues.[71] The *Winnipeg Tribune* explained that such a change would satisfy Plymouth Brethren but not Mennonites, since the former had church tenets against union membership (unlike the latter). Section 68(3) had been written with the intent of granting exemptions to those with church teachings against unions, but recent court rulings meant that individual beliefs rather than church tenets were to be the test.[72]

Mennonite leaders in the province took an aggressive approach to persuading both fellow church members and fellow citizens of the need to challenge the government's efforts to erode the conscience clause. A news release from the Mennonite Brethren church conference asked rhetorically, "Why should a person, who does not want to join a union because of his conscience, still be forced to financially support the very organization from which the law has granted him exemption?"[73] The proposed amendment "flies in the face of precedents set by the Labour Board" in the cases of Gertrude Friesen and Gordon Dyck. "The public should be aware of the threat to civil liberties and freedom of religion" represented by the government's amendment of the Labour Relations Act, the Mennonite Brethren warned. "A democratic, freedom-loving government will allow a responsible minority to express their religious beliefs openly – even at their place of employment. But that doesn't seem to be true in the case of people who believe that following the teachings of Jesus does not allow them to associate with a union that operates on the adversary principle and is willing to use force (strikes, coercion) to get what it wants." The Mennonite Brethren news release listed as contacts not only *Mennonite Brethren Herald* editor Harold Jantz and Mennonite Brethren Bible College dean Abe Dueck, but also MCC Manitoba executive director Art Driedger, MCC Canada personnel director Reg Toews, former *Mennonite* editor Larry Kehler, and Evangelical Mennonite Church pastor Ben Friesen.[74]

Several Mennonite church conferences spent thousands of dollars to place a half-page advertisement promoting their perspective on the conscience clause in the *Winnipeg Free Press* and the *Winnipeg Tribune*.[75] The ad was endorsed by MCC Manitoba, the Mennonite Brethren Conference of Manitoba, the Conference of Mennonites in Manitoba, the Evangelical Mennonite Conference, and the Evangelical Mennonite Mission Conference of Manitoba, as well as the Christian Reformed Churches of Manitoba.[76] The ad noted that "increasing militancy and disregard for Christian standards of justice among many Canadian unions" resulted in the desire of "increasing numbers of persons to ask for the right to stay out of unions and withhold their dues from such unions." That right, guaranteed by Section 68(3) of the Manitoba Labour Relations Act, would be eroded by the government's proposal to end the withholding of dues: "This is a serious loss of human and civil rights." The ad explained that "many Mennonite Christians" as well as "a large portion of the broader Christian community" opposed the adversary nature of unions and did not want to support, through membership or dues, "a union which will use force and intimidation against someone else. They do not wish to take part in movements which place their own interests above the interests of the sick, the aged, or the

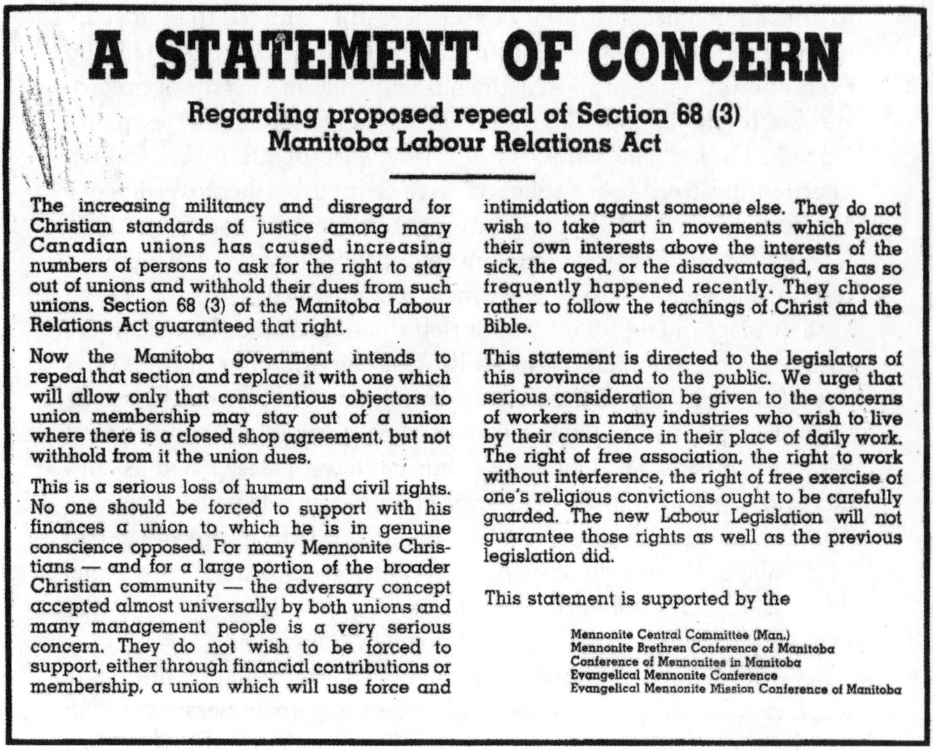

A STATEMENT OF CONCERN

Regarding proposed repeal of Section 68 (3)
Manitoba Labour Relations Act

The increasing militancy and disregard for Christian standards of justice among many Canadian unions has caused increasing numbers of persons to ask for the right to stay out of unions and withhold their dues from such unions. Section 68 (3) of the Manitoba Labour Relations Act guaranteed that right.

Now the Manitoba government intends to repeal that section and replace it with one which will allow only that conscientious objectors to union membership may stay out of a union where there is a closed shop agreement, but not withhold from it the union dues.

This is a serious loss of human and civil rights. No one should be forced to support with his finances a union to which he is in genuine conscience opposed. For many Mennonite Christians — and for a large portion of the broader Christian community — the adversary concept accepted almost universally by both unions and many management people is a very serious concern. They do not wish to be forced to support, either through financial contributions or membership, a union which will use force and intimidation against someone else. They do not wish to take part in movements which place their own interests above the interests of the sick, the aged, or the disadvantaged, as has so frequently happened recently. They choose rather to follow the teachings of Christ and the Bible.

This statement is directed to the legislators of this province and to the public. We urge that serious consideration be given to the concerns of workers in many industries who wish to live by their conscience in their place of daily work. The right of free association, the right to work without interference, the right of free exercise of one's religious convictions ought to be carefully guarded. The new Labour Legislation will not guarantee those rights as well as the previous legislation did.

This statement is supported by the

Mennonite Central Committee (Man.)
Mennonite Brethren Conference of Manitoba
Conference of Mennonites in Manitoba
Evangelical Mennonite Conference
Evangelical Mennonite Mission Conference of Manitoba

5.1 A Statement of Concern regarding proposed repeal of Section 68 (3) Manitoba Labour Relations Act: advertisement in the *Winnipeg Free Press* (8 June 1976): 8.

disadvantaged, as has so frequently happened recently. They choose rather to follow the teachings of Christ and the Bible."[77]

The government invited interested groups to make their views on proposed amendments to the Labour Relations Act known to the Standing Committee on Industrial Relations. Hundreds of letters were written and scores of presentations were made in response.[78] Sixty telegrams and an eighty-signature petition were received, asking to preserve Section 68(3).[79] The Winnipeg Civil Liberties Association voiced their support of the conscience clause.[80] Plymouth Brethren church member John Henry, employed at the Swift meat packing plant for forty-six years, said he would have to quit his job if the act was amended; he could not in good conscience pay dues to a union.[81] Both the CJL and the Winnipeg Newspaper Guild recommended the interpretation of conscientious objection be expanded to include people who "hold religious beliefs without belonging to a recognized church" and to non-religious people.[82] Union leaders voiced their dissent. Retail Clerks Union Local 832 president Bernard Christophe advocated for universal dues check-off: "People objecting to war were still obliged to pay taxes, although a considerable amount went to support the armed services," he argued.[83] Art Coulter, MFL executive secretary, declared the conscience clause should be eliminated "because too many workers were prepared to use it to avoid paying dues to the unions representing them."[84]

MCC Manitoba Peace and Social Concerns Committee drafted a lengthy brief to the standing committee, one that was both more critical and more theological than the brief they ultimately chose to present. In their draft, they explained that Mennonite values of non-resistance ("you do not use force to gain rights or benefits for yourself") and loyalty ("under God, we cannot take positions in opposition to those for whom we work") made support of unions through membership or dues payment "very difficult."[85] The Labour Board's decisions in the cases of Selkirk nurses Trudie Barkman and Hilda Friesen and baker Henry Funk were a "clear injustice" since the "entire thrust of the Bill of Rights and our own laws ought to be to protect the rights of conscientious objectors."[86] Citing (Old) Mennonite theologian Guy Hershberger and various Bible passages, they asserted that union coercion, including strikes "used for clearly selfish ends," was incompatible with Christianity. Defiance of back-to-work legislation, closed-shop agreements, membership oaths, rising militancy, and the adversarial nature of unions were "intolerable and unacceptable" at worst and problematic at best for Christians.[87] The fact that some Christians were nonetheless union members, they noted, "should not obscure" their argument – many did not want to be "economic martyrs" while others hoped to influence the union by their Christian witness. They ended by clarifying the question of individual conscience versus church dogma that had confounded the Labour Board in the Funk case: "in order for a belief to be religious, it need not be bound to some specific ecclesiastical body."[88] The voluntarist nature of the church meant that "individual members may in cases interpret ethical practice quite differently. Yet the genuinely religious conviction which may be involved should never be in doubt."[89]

Harold Jantz presented the final version of the brief on behalf of MCC to the standing committee. He noted that the Funk, Friesen, and Dyck decisions were "encouraging and gratifying" and called for the preservation of Section 68(3).[90] The brief he presented retained the draft's discussion of adversarialism, militancy, intimidation, selfishness, and disrespect for contracts, and introduced critique of the class struggle, but refrained from citing either theologians or scripture. A new discussion of comparative wealth was included: North Americans "already enjoy one of the highest standards of living in the world" and so union demands not only "do not correspond to the real increase in our productivity" but are made "at the expense of others who are worse off than we." Unions "no longer ask about the needs or concerns of others. 'To hell with society,' would sum it up for many." To compel people to pay dues to such organizations "is in direct contradiction of the human rights code of both this province and our nation."[91] "Paying dues to a union with which one cannot identify in principle means that one has to give tangible, material support to the tactics, leaders, political affiliations and goals of the unions in question. We are concerned because of the growing disrespect for both a signed contract and for the law of the land which has been demonstrated by many unions."[92] Also problematic was that the amendment to Section 68(3) that the government proposed would shift the emphasis from individual conscience to church tenets, seemingly "a conscious attempt to set aside the results of the Funk decision." Mennonite churches, like most others, did not have specific teachings on unions, MCC noted. "They never will. They do not function that way." Churches teach biblical principles and individuals must apply them to their own situations. The government's proposed amendment was "counter ... to a proper definition of what is religious. When conscience is emphasized, religion is clearly whatever is of ultimate significance to the person involved. A definition for religious or religion which appeals only to church rules or clearly stated church positions, however, will ultimately have little meaning, since there is no reason to assume that this will shed a definitive light on the real state of the individual's convictions." Requiring payment of union dues, Jantz declared once again, would turn some Mennonites into "economic martyrs" as they would have to quit their jobs to honour the claims on their conscience.[93]

After presenting the MCC brief, Jantz was questioned by standing committee member Sid Green. Green asked whether Jantz "knew of any Mennonites who refuse to sit on the board of directors of a corporation, or refuse to be an employer because those positions may involve being engaged in conflict with employees."[94] Jantz said he did not, but that many employer organizations had been "formed to help its members act like Christians in their business practices." Green responded that "employees work in unions on the same basis" and asked if Mennonites could "work, in conscience, in a union." Jantz replied, "They work with troubled conscience." Green commented that as a lawyer he paid dues and could not redirect them to charity, and that the same held true for other professionals. Union leader Bernard Christophe joined the conversation, agreeing that "employees should not be forced to join a union" but adding that he had "never seen these same employees refuse to accept the benefits attained by the union."[95]

Debate continued in the legislature and in the newspapers. A *Free Press* editorial reprinted in the *Steinbach Carillon* asserted that the removal of the conscience clause would "give to the labor movement an authority and legitimacy now enjoyed only by the state."[96] Doing so was perhaps "natural" for the NDP, as "the political arm of the trade unions," but it was nonetheless "an attack on the freedom of the individual."[97] Two Mennonite MLAs (both Progressive Conservatives) voiced their objections: Bob Banman protested that there was no need to change the existing clause, since "there had been no 'mass exodus' from unions on religious grounds in the last four years." Harry Enns observed that "a government is often measured by its tolerance to minorities."[98]

Meanwhile, Labour Board hearings on applications under Section 68(3) continued. On 24 June 1976, the board ruled against eight Mennonite nurses who were seeking exemption from membership in the Bethel Hospital Nurses Association. The ruling was decried by a Winkler Mennonite Brethren pastor in a letter to the *Free Press* as "a total and flagrant disrespect for the rights of individuals and human conscience."[99] The pastor cited the usual arguments against union membership: strikes, selfishness, membership oaths, withholding of essential services. By contrast, "God's word teaches us: 'Be content with your wages,' and 'Godliness with contentment is great gain.'" He warned Christians of "the serious and systematic erosion of our dearest freedom – the freedom to hold religious beliefs, and the right to live according to these beliefs." "The issue is not whether it is right or wrong to belong to an association and pay dues, nor whether a church teaches this or not; the issue is clearly whether or not a person in our society still has a right to exercise his religious beliefs and remain true to his conscience, without coercion or discrimination from any group."[100]

As in the MCC presentation made to the standing committee by Harold Jantz, the emphasis of the Mennonite argument against unions had shifted here. Less important was whether or not unions violated religious conscience – clearly there were a variety of perspectives on this issue within the Mennonite community, where some were union members while others sought exemption. Rather, the emphasis was on the *right of the individual* to determine God's will for his or her self. Lawyer Kenneth Regier, who had represented some Mennonites at their Labour Board hearings, shared this viewpoint. "The present provincial government … always voiced strong views on the rights of individuals."[101] Their proposed amendment to the Labour Relations Act, however, revealed that they were "quite prepared to say one thing and do another." Government "should be ashamed of itself" and "out of a sense of basic honesty" should state clearly that they do not support individual rights and "are prepared to subvert those rights when they deem it in their own interest."[102]

The Schreyer government was clearly annoyed by these public pronouncements of Mennonites against unions. The premier's executive assistant, Herb Schulz, took the unusual step of writing a lengthy and candid letter to the *Mennonite Mirror* (a magazine independent of the churches) to chastise them for published commentary on the forthcoming legislation. Schulz declared that the *Mirror's* article "Conscientious Objections Irk Manitoba Government, so It Changes the Labour Law and Thereby Subverts a Right" was a misrepresentation.[103] Outlining the history of both the 1972 amendment to the Labour Relations Act and the origins of the Rand Formula,[104] Schulz asked, "how does a society distinguish between the conscientious objector and the person who is willing to eat off organized labour's table but refuses to contribute?" The government had avoided the challenge of determining individual conscience by instead applying the amendment only to those whose churches taught that "unions were evil and an abomination in the eyes of God." Mennonites did not have a church proviso against union membership, so the Funk case "forced the Labour Board, an agency of the government of Manitoba, into the invidious position of having to decide if a stranger appearing before it was indeed a conscientious objector just because he said he was." The new amendment to Section 68(3) instead would allow individual conscience to be decided by the union. Schulz added sarcastically, "The members of the Mennonite society for whom you claim to speak now presumably having everything you claim they want: firstly, their conscientious objections will now be considered on an individual basis; secondly, the authenticity of their conscientious objections will be judged by their peers – the people they work with and who presumably know them best." Noting that Harold Jantz and others claimed that part of their objection to unions was that they cause confrontation, Schulz ended his letter with a cynical request:

> Would you please send us a list of Mennonite businessmen who resigned from boards of directors of firms that caused confrontations by locking out their employees? Would you please send us a list of Mennonite doctors who stopped paying their union dues to the Manitoba Medical Association last January when the MMA caused a confrontation by threatening to strike against their patients? Would you please send us a list of Mennonite doctors who resigned from the Saskatchewan Medical Association during the doctors' strike in 1962? Finally, would you please send us a list of Mennonite lawyers who have applied to the courts to be exempted from paying union dues to the Manitoba Law Society whose members generally thrive on "confrontations"?[105]

Although *Mirror* editor Roy Vogt was sympathetic to unions, he was not sympathetic to Schulz's letter, which he said "reflects rather badly on the type of leadership found in our government."[106] Forcing conscientious objectors to apply to their union rather than the Labour Board was unjust: "Has our notion of justice really sunk to the level where we can pretend that it is just to force an aggrieved party to appeal to the very body against which he is grieving?" He further noted that Schulz still insisted on separating personal conscience and religious belief: a "dangerous distinction" which had been "knocked down" by the Court of Appeals in the Funk case and from which the government clearly had "learned nothing." Vogt concluded, "The mischievous nature of Mr. Schulz's closing paragraph does not deserve comment. If the current government continues to depend on spokesmen such as this, then it deserves to be replaced."[107]

Vogt had written earlier, in the aftermath of the Funk decision, to argue for a more nuanced approach to labour issues by Mennonite leaders. Funk, he noted, was opposed "to the 'violent tactics' of unions and to the pledge of primary allegiance which the union seemed to demand."[108] Funk's objections to unions were "based on solid Mennonite beliefs and have clear and obvious roots in the teachings of Jesus."[109] Vogt, however, took his fellow Mennonites to task for their "almost exclusive focus on employee abuses." "Many of our Mennonite people are in management positions and they are as prone to abuse power as are employee organizations. This is not meant to excuse unions in any way but to point out that the Christian faith speaks about the universality of evil. It is to be found in all human beings and in all forms of power."[110] Vogt emphasized that the universality of evil was not an excuse to reject such organizations but a call to transform them. Mennonites, he declared, should not necessarily refrain from membership in groups that were at times guilty of such failings: "We should be humble enough to admit that even church membership might be hard to justify on such terms."[111] Vogt also pointed out the irony of Funk objecting to union coercion while embracing the coercion of the courts, describing it as "another example of how impossible it is to get around our use of some form of resistance in order to accomplish certain objectives ... Let us, therefore, quit pretending that we don't engage in resistance of others, or that unions somehow engage in it in a unique way when they use their power to withhold services. The image of a manager firing his worker in private doesn't jar us as much as workers resisting their managers on the picket line, but the difference is merely a sentimental one and has nothing to do with Christian ethics."[112]

Ultimately, the conscience clause was repealed. The government's amendments to the Labour Relations Act came into effect in December 1976; Section 68(3) was replaced with a revised Section 68(1): redirecting union dues to charity would continue to be allowed, but unions – rather than the Labour Board – would determine conscientious objector status.[113] Labour Minister Russ Paulley insisted that the spirit of Section 68(3) therefore was preserved, in that exemption from union membership was still possible.[114] The conscience clause was rewritten to read: "where a union is satisfied that an employee is a member of a religious group which has as one of its articles of faith the belief that members are precluded from belonging to or financially supporting any union or professional association, the union may, on such terms as the union and employee may agree upon, exempt the employee from paying union dues. In such a case, the union ceases to be obligated to represent or act on behalf of that employee." The new Section 68(1) also annulled all decisions made by the Labour Board under the former Section 68(3).[115] No longer would Mennonites and others in Manitoba be able to use religious beliefs as an exemption from the Rand Formula, unless their church expressly forbade membership.[116]

I conducted oral history interviews with three of the Mennonite men who played significant leadership roles in this story of conscientious objection to unions in Manitoba: former *Mennonite Brethren Herald* editor Harold Jantz, former MCC Manitoba chair Peter H. Peters, and former *Mennonite* editor Larry Kehler. They offered radically different accounts of these events: Jantz maintained that his position in the 1970s had been pro-union, Peters expressed a change in his perspective since his actions in the 1970s, and Kehler asserted that he had followed the lead of more assertive personalities such as Jantz.

Reflecting on his experiences almost forty years later, Harold Jantz commented that some fellow Mennonites had criticized him for the active role he took regarding Section 68(3): "I know I also had some of our [Mennonite] business people who thought we were too involved with issues like this and who thought I was a Communist [laughs]. *A Communist even though you were supporting people not being union members?* Yeah. Well, you know, I wasn't arguing against unions. I was really arguing against unions that imposed certain conditions on people, rules on people. I was very supportive to Christians coming to, you might call them, associations, but something that would allow employees to speak together to their employers."[117] The association that received Jantz's endorsement, both in the 1970s and decades later, was the CLAC. In 1976, his support extended to encouraging Mennonite workers at a Winnipeg construction company, whom he said were "harassed by the Carpenters and Labourers Unions," to join the CLAC.[118] He assisted them in writing a letter of petition to the Labour Board: "If it goes through," he told a CLAC leader at the time, "it will be a good test of what the Labour Board might be willing to accept."[119] In his interview with me, Jantz declared that his position on unions had not changed since then: "Workers have an investment in the workplace, and employers obviously feel they have an investment there. But both of them are accountable to God."[120]

Jantz noted that Mennonite interest in the ethical dimensions of union membership had declined since the 1970s, but not because labour relations were not still problematic. "I do think that the momentum in our time ... has really gone against working people. We've moved toward very powerful entities in the labour market, and I'm talking now about business enterprises – many business enterprises are *very* strong. And if one follows what's happened to unions in general, they've disappeared in many places, and become weaker."[121] Although the CLAC had expanded since the 1970s, "the issue has sort of disappeared for many people," this despite the fact that the income gap between workers and managers has "widened hugely." "And many people would be quite, quite unsupportive to a labour movement. Part of that of course has to do with the way labour itself has behaved. Many unions, at least for the Christian community, have lost support because of their tactics."[122] For Jantz, the CLAC was the moral alternative to unions.

Peter H. Peters, by contrast, recalled that he had found the conscience clause "a bit confusing."[123] He was familiar with Gerald Vandezande's stance on unions, having known Christian Reformed students in his previous career as a high school principal at Winnipeg's Mennonite Brethren Collegiate Institute. And he was aware that many Mennonites were anti-union, associating unions with Stalinist socialism. He himself, though, "didn't quite understand that." Harold Jantz, however, had pushed MCC to take action on the issue, he claimed. Peters recalled himself in the 1970s as being "naive about those things" and filled with "feelings of ambiguity" regarding the question of Mennonites and unions. When the issue was raised at MCC Manitoba meetings, in part because of "the Schreyer ferment that was percolating" in the Mennonite community, Peters found he "had to do something about it and I didn't know what." Harold Jantz was "very fond of" the CLAC and "he pushed MCC Peace and Social Concerns to make a study of it here in Manitoba. That was the agenda. I was chair. That's how it came up. Innocently enough. I certainly didn't drive it." John Redekop, the speaker at the MCC workshops, "always appeared as though he knew everything" and "he spouted freely and frequently." He says he admired both Jantz and Redekop at the time "because they were articulate; I wasn't. They had the gift of writing and speaking and so on, which I don't. So I followed them. Today, it's not where I am. Really not."[124]

Larry Kehler also asserted that he had followed the lead of others in the 1970s.[125] He says he only "very vaguely" remembers the events in question, but does recall the "loud and very thought-through positions" of people like Harold Jantz and Peter Peters. He states that he did not have anything to say at the meeting he attended with Russ Paulley, since the others present served as spokespeople. He recalled that he was in fact "pro-union" in the sense that he was "for the common person getting more help and protection in such things as salary and so forth ... The issue of getting money [union dues] diverted elsewhere somehow just slipped totally from my mind. I'm sorry about that." He thinks his feelings about unions "remain the same as then: unions are efforts at giving the common person more rights and more protection." Harold Jantz, he said, took the lead on the issue in the 1970s: "Articulate people such as Harold Jantz – in spite of the fact that we were both editors – I felt very inferior to people like that. For one thing, the certainty of position on everything was so strong and I was much more of a searcher ... I know I was always – sort of odd – How come they're asking me [to lead]? I'm just a poor farm boy from Altona ... I have to admit also I had very little nerve to speak up, even later on when I became in a leadership position, I was always very reluctant to speak up on a controversial issue. Just so you see inside me." Part of the context for the effort to preserve the conscience clause, Kehler recalls, was conflict between Mennonite Brethren and General Conference Mennonites in those days that led the GCs to allow the MBs to take the lead on the issue.

> In many ways, we wanted to be recognized as as spiritual as the Mennonite Brethren, but on the other hand, not this far. I'm overstating it here, but the tensions were very strong, You know, if you have a strong group, and you're a secondary group that's struggling for existence and for identity, then you somehow block those [issues] out rather than take a careful look at some of the details of that. And that was happening ... "If this is an issue they want to get all knotted up about, that's for them to say." And that points a negative finger at our [GC] side of the scale as much as at them [MBs] because we felt so inferior that we felt we had to say no. This is going to look bad if we record any of this. *I'm sorry?* This is going to look bad. *[laughs] Well, we can talk about that on the consent form after, sure.* Some of those things needed to have been said then and were not and they sometimes sort of linger below the surface for a long time, just the basic testimony. *Well, that's one of my interests in*

> *writing this book, is that I think many Mennonites and many non-Mennonites alike think they know what Mennonites believe about unions or have practised about unions and* – Because somebody spoke up so loudly.

The "somebody" in question was Harold Jantz. "Harold had this strong provocative approach that I think really turned many of us off rather than – There were some who really grabbed at it and said, 'Yeah, that's right,' but for others of us, and especially if we wanted to take a more neutral two-sided approach, that sort of shut that out. I'm not saying that about Harold but that's sort of how I recall the – And it wasn't as though I didn't feel that sometimes we have to listen to the Harold Jantzes when they point a finger and say we are really falling short in this area."

What do we make of these three disparate oral histories? Oral historian Sandy Polishuk notes, "It is our responsibility as the experts on our narrators to make sense of the contradictions between our interviews and other sources, or between conflicting accounts related on different occasions by the narrators themselves. We must try to figure out why the contradictions exist as well as what the truth is."[126] I have less confidence than Polishuk that I am the "expert" on these three narrators. It is difficult to sift the words of soft-spoken men in their senior years with whom I have shared time and food.[127] Jantz was happy to discuss these events with me in detail, and to loan me his rich documentary collection on the subject. It is clear that he continues to believe that his actions in the 1970s were right. Peters and Kehler, however, expressed some reluctance to discuss these events, and deflected some responsibility for their earlier decisions to Jantz's forceful personality. The documentary record, however, suggests that Mennonite leaders in the province – whether General Conference, Mennonite Brethren, or Evangelical Mennonite – were willing to take a public stand in support of the conscience clause, as evidenced by their signatures on the half-page ad in the *Winnipeg Free Press.* Kehler, the "poor farm boy from Altona," was appointed general secretary of the Conference of Mennonites in Canada in 1981.[128] It seems unlikely that men who held such positions of authority in the Mennonite community – provincially and nationally – were intimidated sufficiently by one individual, though editor of a national publication, to take up his cause. Nor does it seem likely that feelings of spiritual inferiority could persuade the leadership of so many organizations to support him unless they agreed, at least to some extent, with his position.

The post–Second World War rural-to-urban shift of Canadian Mennonites, together with increased labour militancy across the nation in the 1970s and the election of the first NDP government in Manitoba, led to a confrontation between Manitoba Mennonites and the labour movement. The government's provision of a conscience clause in the revised Labour Relations Act of 1972 provided Mennonites with a means to express their religious objections to organized labour. Yet those objections were rooted in late-twentieth-century individualism as much as Mennonite theology, a fact that Mennonites and non-Mennonites alike acknowledged at the time. Mennonite MLA Bob Banman had spoken in the legislature of the "personal rights and freedom" of conscientious objectors to unions. Government member Sid Green had noted the difference between "what the Mennonite religion actually teaches" (a collective understanding of faith) and "what the Mennonites see in their religion" (individual interpretations of that collective faith). Chief Justice Samuel Freedman had ruled that the conscience clause referred not to congregational but to individual religious beliefs. *Herald* editor Harold Jantz had criticized Labour Minister Russ Paulley for his lack of concern for "the rights of individuals," and had argued that it was not the church but the individual that determined belief. The leadership of a number of Mennonite denominations, in their half-page newspaper ad, had asserted that the issue of the conscience clause was one of "human and civil rights." MCC Manitoba had argued that the Bill of Rights and other laws must "protect the rights" of conscientious objectors. They also had claimed that religious beliefs need not be tied to a church, and that churches expected and encouraged individuals to reach their own (often disparate) religious understandings: "Religion is clearly whatever is of ultimate significance to the person involved."

The Mennonite Brethren and the non-Mennonite CLAC shared an evangelical perspective and a rejection of traditional labour unions. Mennonites recognized the waning authority of the church in their private economic lives: as early as the 1940s, Hershberger had found the ban on union membership essentially unenforceable. Instead, Mennonites in 1970s Manitoba invoked the authority of the state and of secular moral and legal principles as they appealed to government using the rhetoric of human rights to mobilize support for their anti-union cause.

For a brief four-year period, then, the conscience clause offered Manitoba Mennonites a means of asserting opposition to organized labour. Few took advantage of the opportunity, despite the efforts of community leaders like Jantz.[129] Mennonite leaders in Manitoba had led the drive to retain the conscience clause but had undermined their own religious authority with their arguments for individual belief over against church rule. After the repeal of Section 68(3), Mennonites could no longer count on religious or governmental authorities to resolve the tensions between religious beliefs and labour relations. Instead, some Mennonites adopted a more individualized solution by seeking employment with co-religionists, believing that a shared religious commitment would mitigate any workplace conflicts. As will be seen, this solution was, at times, no solution at all.

6

"It's easy to write a paper; it's not so easy to live"

The Faith-Based Workplace

In the late twentieth century, Mennonites no longer relied on government provisions for union exemption or on church authorities like Guy Hershberger to negotiate alternative contracts that exempted them from union membership. Nor did they devote time at conferences or column inches in church publications to debates about the morality of union involvement. Instead, some Mennonites acquiesced to the demands of their employment and joined unions, some may have become "economic martyrs" as Jantz and others had warned, while others made individual employment decisions designed to prevent potential labour issues before they arose. By working for fellow Mennonites, the latter hoped to avoid the labour discord discussed in previous chapters.[1] Some of these Mennonites found, however, that a shared religious commitment did not necessarily preclude workplace conflict.

A number of the individuals interviewed for this study were employed in workplaces that were affiliated with Mennonite churches. Some of these workers spoke of specific, work-related challenges that were caused by the religious ethos and practice at their workplaces. Some discussed the difficulties of espousing religious doctrine with which they privately disagreed or of maintaining a relationship of integrity with the church institution that was also their employer. Some described instances in which their employers' avowed religious commitments to justice and equality were contradicted by the way they, the employees and their co-workers, were treated. And some spoke of the problems of reconciling their religious beliefs in forbearance and forgiveness with their need to defend themselves and others against workplace injustices.

These workers often found it difficult to share their stories, since doing so could threaten their continued employment. The sharing of these stories also necessitated a questioning of religious identity, both their own and that of the larger religious group with which they identified. Commenting on the gap between religious belief and practice, one participant noted, "It's easy to write a paper; it's not so easy to live." Sharing these stories, while protecting interview participants' identities, allows the creation of an "alternative history" – one that presents a counterpoint to the "official" stories in the archives of corporate entities and religious institutions.

Four individuals' stories in particular address these issues in detail. In each case, the person's identity has been protected by the use of a pseudonym, although not all of these individuals requested to remain anonymous. All four were employed in professional organizations that were affiliated in some way with the Mennonite Brethren Church, in either Canada or the United States. Two of the four were fired from these jobs. Their stories address scholarly questions in a variety of fields – including the history and sociology of business, labour, and religion – and suggest potential avenues for further research.

Anna left a career in labour history to work for a Mennonite Brethren institution. Her story as told to me centred on her personal frustrations with the seeming loss of ability to integrate her religious commitment with her new job at the church-affiliated institution that now employed her. Barbara also expressed personal frustration, but her focus was on the changes in her religious beliefs and their seeming contradiction to those of her employer. Dan was released from his job, an experience that ultimately transformed his religious beliefs. Clara's story is somewhat more complicated. Clara at first spoke of the connections between her religious beliefs and her work life in fairly traditional terminology. As the interview proceeded, however, she dropped the religious rhetoric and voiced specific disappointment with her employer's termination of her employment.

Anna was raised by parents of conservative Mennonite background, a fact that affected her attitudes to labour in her early life. Her mother was more vocal than her father about work experiences. When Anna was young, her mother would speak of enjoying work outside the home, often telling Anna that she hated farming, gardening, and housework, but loved working in a grocery store and keeping accounts. While working outside the home was partly a financial necessity, it was also a joy of which she often spoke.[2]

Although her parents' conservative religious background meant that they did not support labour unions, Anna herself saw "strong connections" between union support and religious commitment. In the late 1980s, she attended a labour history seminar on relations between churches and unions. Unions had strong beliefs at their core, she noted, and although they were "not quite a church," there were commonalities with respect to their care for people. This commonality was not something either her church or her siblings acknowledged.[3]

Anna's stance on unionization was not reflected in her own history: she never became a union member, largely because her choice of occupations precluded that possibility. A union organized the lower-level staff at her former non-Mennonite workplace, but her supervisory position meant that she was not able to join. She sees a real rift between her current employment in a Mennonite Brethren church-affiliated organization and her earlier studies and employment in labour history, and is not sure why this is the case. Rejecting the early twentieth-century (Old) Mennonite Church condemnation of unions as inherently coercive, Anna said she believed that violence by management against employees, while not always overt, is far greater and far more powerful than union violence. The "real violence" rests "with those who have power." "In the end," she observed, "Jesus says he sides with those who don't have power and who are hurting the most and who have no recourse." She expressed hope in people who care about such issues both in and out of the church, but no hope in the church itself as an institution. The "true" church has less to do with doctrine than with how to live, she asserted.[4]

Anna said she was "hesitant" to discuss how she connected her religious beliefs to labour issues in any detail, describing herself as "a functional atheist at this point." She continued to "see the good in church." The Christian church had done, and continues to do, "horrendous things," but it "tries." The liberation of women was not an initiative of the church – "women have done it for themselves." Nor is the church a leader for the equity issues of "immigrants and gays and others." These failures on the part of the church do not explain her religious doubts, but they do not help, either, she noted. Anna concluded her interview with the observation that there is a "real issue" in her Mennonite Brethren workplace with respect to racism. She commented that it is "easy to say what you believe, but not so easy to stand up. It's easy to write a paper; it's not so easy to live."

She said she "can't be too critical of the church" because she was "not doing it either" – that is, not working actively for justice.[5]

Anna's deep concern about the issues of labour and religion became evident to me when, several days later, she requested a second interview. She said she had thought further about the issues of labour and religion, and wanted to share some more specific reflections. The first was about workplace training regarding sexual harassment. She had been angry, she said, in her first meeting for this training at her Mennonite Brethren-affiliated workplace when she learned that her co-workers were upset that they had to participate. "Every year, people fuss" about having to take part in this training. In frustration with these naysayers, she finally wrote an editorial for her workplace newsletter that explained why such training was necessary and that described "what happens to women in the workplace." Her earlier research on women garment workers "seems far and unrelated" but, she asserted, it *was* related, because such women "fought to get laws because anything could happen" to them in the workplace otherwise. For example, women could be fired for resisting sexual advances. Thus workplace training about sexual harassment was "really important" and there was good reason for it.[6]

Anna, for one, takes the well-being of her employees seriously even in her supervisory role. She clearly tells her employees what she needs from them; "open communication" is important to her. These issues came to her attention shortly after our first interview, when one of her female employees told her she had to quit her job because of sexual harassment. Anna said she was "devastated" by this information. "All of that comes together: my belief in why we are here, my belief and understanding of what labour means and what it has fought to get," including a workplace where one can work "in comfort and safety." She credits unions for these achievements, and notes that even her workplace – "where you can't hardly mention the word 'union,' because [unionization] would not happen, and [her employers] really don't like it" – nonetheless "reap[s] all the benefits" of union successes. For Anna, such activity is so keenly connected to her understanding of religious commitment that the two are almost equated.

> And I know I kind of equivocate in terms of my faith and what that really is, but if there is anything that it is, it's a very basic understanding of the dignity of human beings and that we need

> to be treating people with basic respect and providing them with safe workplaces among many other things. So ... I've been thinking about that a lot since [the first interview], and I realize that it is a part of who I am and what I'm doing here. And maybe it is for other people, too, who haven't had that kind of exposure to labour. I don't necessarily always see it. But for me that is why it's important.[7]

Anna further demonstrated her sympathy to labour issues by sharing that she had just learned about the death of labour historian Cletus Daniel, whom she knew. She expressed shock and dismay at his passing, and admiration for his legacy, providing me with a copy of his obituary. She noted Daniel's tolerance, generosity, and compassion, and quoted his observation (on being named the 1992 University Paramount Professor for Teaching Excellence at Cornell University's School of Industrial and Labor Relations) that being able to "love without limit is success." She reflected, "Those were the people and the kinds of things that really drew me to being [in her previous workplace]: the labour lawyers and labour historians – they really, really believed in the dignity of human beings."[8]

Anna's frustrations at negotiating between her ideals and her reality were expressed at the very end of the interview. Her work in labour history in a previous non-religious workplace had been "inspiring" because religion and labour "seemed so closely connected," in that the work she was doing was "exactly what the church says we should be doing." This connection is missing in her current Mennonite Brethren church-affiliated workplace, she noted. She observed that Mennonites often speak of immigration issues and the treatment of migrant labour, but seem to make no connection between faith and work in their own workplaces. Her frustration with this situation extends to her own inability to solve it. Why are Mennonites not the "first people out there," leading the way in workplace justice, she asked rhetorically. She herself tries to do what she can in that respect, occasionally writing articles to draw attention to various labour issues, but she observed with regret, "Mostly, I kind of just get tired."[9]

Anna's story exemplifies the importance of "vocation" or "calling" for many workers who have religious and/or spiritual commitments.[10] An extensive literature exists on vocation and calling, both scholarly and popular.[11] Keith Graber Miller, professor of religion and philosophy at Goshen College in Indiana, defines "calling" as an "inner sense of commitment to a people or a cause or to God, an unfolding sense of our gifts and skills (experienced both within and then also confirmed by others), and a gradual recognition of what we perceive as particular callings or passions."[12] Anna experienced this sense of calling in her previous employment in labour history, but was disappointed to find that her current workplace, while overtly religious, made living with a sense of calling more difficult. Graber Miller observes of himself:

> In my Mennonite gut I know that I want to attribute some *meaning* to the work that I and others do ... We are not just called to be Christians "in general," but to be Christians in concrete locations – as friends, as spouses, as parents, as citizens, and as laborers and professionals ... It is not possible for everyone, but my hope would be that followers of Christ would be able to commit their lives and energies to relationships and work that *matter* in the world, engagements that make a difference in others' lives and contribute to the spread of God's reign.[13]

Ironically, this "meaning" in work is what is missing in Anna's experience in her religious workplace.

The positive manner in which Anna's mother spoke of her employment outside the home doubtless encouraged Anna to view paid work as a calling. An early education experience resulted in her drawing a correlation, if not an outright equation, between the Christian church and unions. Her understanding of church as more about orthopraxis than orthodoxy is shaped by these experiences. Her commitment to workplace justice reinforced – and, at the same time, challenged – her understanding of a calling, as she was aware that her family and religious community did not share her positive view of unions and the labour movement. The gap between her understandings and those of her religious community has widened to the point that she hesitates to identify with the church.

The failures of her religious-affiliated employer with respect to questions of equity and justice reinforce these beliefs and assist in undermining her religious identity. Anna initially was very critical of herself, suggesting that in her current employment she was largely unable to connect her spiritual commitments with her job demands. On further reflection, she reconsidered this position in the second interview, one that she had requested. She was able to cite specific instances in which she had been able to take a strong stance in support of the workplace justice issues that mattered so much to her. She rearticulated her religious beliefs as a commitment to social justice, particularly in the workplace, citing Cletus Daniel as a model. Nonetheless, she concluded by re-expressing the doubts and frustrations she had voiced in her first interview – doubts and frustrations not only with her employer and her religious community but with herself.

Barbara's experiences differed significantly from Anna's. She grew up in an environment that was religious but not evangelical. Neither parent was a Sunday school teacher, and her father's only involvement in church activities was to serve as an usher. Although her parents "lived out their beliefs in an upstanding, moral way" and the family had devotions, in which they all gathered on an irregular basis to read *Our Daily Bread*,[14] Barbara was critical of them when she was younger because they would not use the evangelical language of religious conversion. She noted that she came to respect their beliefs only as she grew older.[15]

As a child, Barbara struggled with religious guilt. She was tormented psychologically, wanting "desperately to please God but [she] had no assurance of salvation." Her journals as a teenager reveal this angst, she said. She had a "sensitive conscience," and was a "pleaser" who tried to meet the expectations of her church and family but "always failed." She realizes now that she probably had adolescent depression as a consequence of her religious doubts.[16]

Barbara's spiritual identity shifted dramatically, she said, as a consequence of an inner-city experience with a non-Mennonite evangelical Christian organization. It required her to do social work with a large group of young people of diverse socio-economic and ethnic backgrounds. The organization was very hierarchical, with a "clear leader-follower distinction" and a "strong male dominant model." She noted that there "were extremes" in the organization's refusal to include women in leadership roles and in its abusive exercises of power. She felt much "dis-ease" with the organization, but would have remained employed there had it not been for "organizational chaos." In addition, she suffered "emotional burnout" and "trauma" from the intense social work, for which there was not much emotional support from the organization. She was "young and idealistic," she said, and felt stressed by living in an inner-city environment of violence and crime, and she "kept on giving."[17]

In her later view, the organization took the religious beliefs with which she was raised to an extreme, particularly with respect to "self-denial and self-negation and self-sacrifice." Barbara could not sleep because she was depressed, yet, as she recalled, she was unable to see her own depression. Finally, she told the organization that she was quitting. In doing so, she felt that she was "betraying the core of [her] self." She had joined in youthful idealism in her mid 20s, and left it as she was turning 40. The experience was "disillusioning" in that she was "not able to live out [her] own identity." She felt disappointed by the organization, characterizing the experience as "like divorce" since her departure cut her off from her employer-provided housing, her neighbourhood, and her spiritual community. The physical and spiritual are linked, Barbara asserted, so she "knew [her health] was vulnerable" when she left. She "felt God's silent presence," but also was "disappointed" with God. Three years later, she "crashed" emotionally and physically. She decided to attend seminary, which was "healing in many ways" because her studies allowed her to understand what had happened. She read Stephen Arterburn and Jack Felton's *Toxic Faith,* which counsels readers how to recover from unhealthy involvements with religious groups or religious practices, and prepared a research proposal on self-denial and self-affirmation. Mennonites did both, she noted, although she had "only picked up on the first."[18] Barbara observed that her studies led her to conclude that the Holy Spirit "indwells all, not just the hierarchy." To "choose both streams" of denial and affirmation was "life affirming," particularly since self-denial had "just about killed" her.[19]

After seminary, Barbara found an uneasy term of employment with a Mennonite Brethren church-affiliated organization. This new employer had clear expectations of Christian employees: they were to be "dedicated" and "missional" (that is, actively engaging with the secular world in order to assist in its reconciliation with God through its social transformation). Barbara, however, wanted a "sabbatical from being a missionary." She asked herself, "Do I have to live that [emotionally] lean for the rest of my life? I don't know beauty anymore, because I've stripped down to just what is useful." She wanted to "just enjoy" and not "witness." Joy had been "stripped away" from her life; she was "depleted of a sense of self." It was when she had recovered physically from her earlier work experience that her spiritual crisis hit, she declared. Yet she had returned to work for a Christian organization. "Don't you wonder why?" she asked me.[20]

Barbara said she needed a break from "Christian things" not with respect to the lifestyle, just with respect to her employment. She resigned from her Mennonite Brethren-affiliated workplace and took odd jobs. She "needed to learn how to say yes and no" since she "didn't know how to protect [her] self." She then returned to the Mennonite Brethren workplace part time, explaining that she wanted connections outside of Christian circles as well, and wanted to "reserve the right to say no" – a right that she felt part-time employment allowed. She "didn't want to be sucked into the vortex [of full-time commitment] again." She had learned to "pay attention to what happened to the body as an indicator of the soul."[21]

Barbara noted the problems many people have with religious discourse. Even in the midst of her "weakness and doubt," clients seek her out, because they want to speak with "someone who doesn't use traditional religious language." She relishes such opportunities and the "sacredness of being in a space where God speaks." Her challenge, she said, has been to "work out [her] faith in a genuine and authentic way," despite the demands and expectations of her religious workplace. There is, she noted, a "script [she] could follow" but she "deviate[s] from it lots." The religious language used at her place of employment is "not always authentic" to her own experience. At first, Barbara did not know if she could express herself freely regarding the differences between her religious views and those of the Mennonite Brethren church with which the organization that employs her is affiliated. She feared that if she did, she would be "judged or misunderstood or fired." Now she believes that if her "own story is so different from the root story" of the institution that employs her, then she should leave. She does not think her own story *is* so different, however; merely that her spiritual "stumbling is more obvious."[22]

Barbara said she has fully learned to "live with ambiguity." With time, she has accepted that it is "okay not to have answers." She loves what she does, loves her age, loves that she is spiritually aware. And so she is "still here," still employed by a Mennonite Brethren-affiliated organization. She claims that she and the organization "challenge each other" and that she is "still struggling to be authentic on [her spiritual] journey," although there is "much" about her organization's avowed beliefs with which she does not agree. She experiences her work as "sacred" when clients have "Aha! life-altering moments." She takes no credit for such moments, declaring that she "mostly get[s] to stand and watch." She no longer has the "dis-ease" she had at her previous evangelical Christian employer, and has learned to be "okay with who" she is. She has "freedom" despite the religious "script" her employer expects her to follow: no one is "hounding" her to conform. She is "free to be who she is," although she recognizes that not all her co-workers have the same freedom.[23]

Barbara's story reflects some of the difficulties that church-affiliated employers and their employees have experienced in navigating the changes in North American spirituality in the post-1945 period. Sociologist Robert Wuthnow argues that, in the late twentieth century, spirituality shifted from a "spirituality of dwelling" centred in religious institutions to a "spirituality of seeking" that moved beyond organizational loci. More recently, spirituality has changed to a "spirituality of practice" that emphasizes "devotional and social disciplines."[24]

Sociologist Nancy Ammerman discusses this same process, emphasizing "the agency of the religious actor."[25] Ammerman observes, "No single organizational or belief context can explain any person's actions. Whatever internal gyroscopes are guiding individual behavior, they are surely calibrated anew in each of the social settings that call forth religious behavior."[26] Rather than adherence to a set list of religious tenets, religious actors (and those who study them) participate in a continual and context-dependent renegotiation of their religious identities. "The question, then, is not whether the person is religious or how religious they are. The question is rather how religious rhetorics and practices are enacted and how they are situated in various organizational contexts."[27] Church hierarchies – and workplaces affiliated with such institutions – may find such redefinition of the grounds for religiosity to be a challenge to their authority.

As an example of the redefinition of religiosity as a life-long journey rather than a time-specific decision, Ammerman quotes a Jewish rabbi who advises: "There are 613 commandments; find one and begin."[28] She notes that, "rather than assuming that lifelong and total commitments are the only real ones," such a definition "asks simply how and under what circumstances persons enact religious behavior and how that behavior supports the goals of religious organizations and tunes individual sensibilities in religious directions."[29] This definition of religious commitment conflicts with some evangelical Christian churches' understandings of religious identity as the consequence of a salvific "crisis conversion" experience. These definitions become critically important when they are used by a religious workplace as a requirement for employment. If religious identity is not an outcome but a process, then what minimum stage must a person on such a spiritual journey have reached to be hired? What rate of onward progress must be achieved to ensure continued employment? And there is a hidden danger. Religious employers that encourage (or require) reflection on the spiritual component(s) of the job run the risk of their employees reaching religious conclusions that are unexpected or potentially threatening to the organization's espoused religious understandings or religious identity. In her interview, Barbara touches on exactly these questions and concerns.

A further complication arises. Workers, as a result of the religious affiliation of their workplace, may ascribe certain beliefs to and hold certain expectations of their employers. The employers themselves may be complicit in this process through their production and promotion of an organizational "statement of faith" or "mission statement." Ammerman expands the definition of "religious organization" or religious institution beyond "an entity with a name and a constitution and a building on the corner" to include "a shifting collection of persons, engaged in a complex set of actions and rhetorics, actions that are supported by and indeed define the collectivity they inhabit."[30] If, as Ammerman asserts, such collectivities are arenas where "practices of trust and bonding take place,"[31] then what of the damage that accrues when trust is misplaced and bonds are severed? Workers who engage in the kind of religious examination encouraged by their employers and reach unorthodox conclusions, or who identify with the religious mission statements of their employers and are terminated from their jobs, suffer in unique ways. Not only are they subject to the economic and social consequences of job loss, but they may also deal with disappointment with their religious community (of which their employer was a part) and may question their own religious identity.

Dan's story illustrates this problem. Dan was employed as a pastor by a number of Mennonite Brethren churches before the board of an organization affiliated with both MBs and GCs asked him to serve as their leader. Three times he rejected their job offer. He recalled that the search committee then told him that "the Holy Spirit wouldn't release his name." Dan said he "thought and prayed" about the job, and engaged in a one-and-a-half-year-long dialogue with the search committee. The job description was tailored to his "idea of leadership" and he respected that the organization was "one of the few places where the General Conference Mennonite-Mennonite Brethren Conference marriage was working," particularly as "the history of those two groups was not gracious to each other in theology and practice." He finally accepted the job, and it was a "wonderful challenge."[32]

Dan served as the organization's leader for four years. He recalls that "three and a half of [those years] were great," although he found some aspects of the work disturbing, including the "politics." Some of his suggestions on the future of the organization were "not well received." He describes the consequence as a "difficult and shocking and 'corporate' [i.e., non-Christian] end" to his employment, initiated by the organization's board of directors. The process that led to his firing, he said, was "disillusioning. It was not how a community of Christians makes decisions and treats leaders." The termination was the "most wounding" experience "ever."[33]

Following his termination, Dan's theology underwent a "huge shift," he said. Friends took him and his wife to Italy. He described a morning there when he "saw the vineyards and realized God was assaulting [his] heart with beauty, a softening which enabled healing." He is "now done with fear-based Christianity, finished with a faith more defined by fear of what others think." He declared that he "won't go back to that kind of faith or life or leadership." He is "done with working with passive-aggressive ways of dealing with one another and with issues." The core of his theology is "passionate" regarding an understanding of salvation as a personal encounter with a "loving God, and God's redemptive presence on earth as God redeems it." This redefinition of religious belief results, he said, in a "very different motive for engagement with the poor" and in a "redemption or reclamation" of the arts. He recalls having been "motivated by guilt and the observation of living in the first world." Now, his focus is on "God's redemptive purpose."[34]

Dan's dismissal is, of course, not a unique example of how sincere efforts by employees to integrate their religious beliefs with their work experiences can result in serious consequences. Indiana's Goshen College was closed by the (Old) Mennonite Church's Board of Education for the 1923–1924 academic year. The closure was prompted by religious debates in the college between so-called modernists and fundamentalists, and the fears on the part of the church hierarchy that the modernists were gaining the upper hand in defining religiosity. The school re-opened the next year with a new president, although many of the former students had chosen to relocate to Ohio's Bluffton College (also a Mennonite post-secondary institution).[35]

Clara's experience is similar to Dan's, in that her dismissal by her church-affiliated employer was a traumatic experience that resulted in a reassessment of her religious beliefs. Her discussion of this experience, however, was radically different from Dan's. Clara's first job was teaching parenting classes and supervising a high school nursery. She enjoyed the job, which was a new experience for her, she said. She was a "little, old, white Mennonite" in a new city with new ethnicities (African and Latino Americans) and a new culture to which to adapt. She believed that "God called" her to this job and these students, as the "needs of their hearts were great." The job encompassed a variety of roles, including counsellor, mother, disciplinarian, teacher, and social worker. This variety meant she could "feel [her] self as God's hands and feet in the community."[36]

Clara was offered a job as a school principal in a different location. One-and-a-half weeks before she planned to move, the sale of her house fell through. Since the housing market was very bad, her new employer would not hold the job pending her house sale. She stated that the opportunity was thus "thrown away," and found the circumstances "extremely devastating." Part of this devastation was tied to her religious interpretation of the job offer. She felt that the job was "what God wanted her to do" and that she was good at it. Instead, "God slammed the door in [her] face and [her] fingers were caught." She had to rethink: where should she go? What should she do? She needed a job. She asked to be hired back by her previous employer; they did rehire her, but for a different job that she did not enjoy. She asked God, "What are you talking about? This is not right!" It turned out, she explained, that it "was right," that she eventually came to enjoy the job, and that she "saw the great way God was using her gifts that [she] had not considered."[37]

Clara was invited to apply for an administrative job in a Mennonite Brethren church-affiliated institution. She worked there for two years, and was surprised to find that the board of directors of the institution "suddenly, within one month" became unhappy with her performance. She said she did not understand how or why. She was "devastated" when she was asked to resign. She had thought that "God was using [her], that [she] was doing work for the church."

She did not understand "why God would let this happen." The initial shock, she observed, was so traumatic, that she could not think what to do next. She noted that she had given up excellent retirement benefits at her previous employer in order to take this job. "Why did God let this happen?" she asked. She looked for work, but with the economic recession, she obtained few interviews. Her age and the fact that she was overqualified for many of the positions for which she applied may have been factors as well, she noted.[38]

She got a job with another religious (albeit non-Mennonite) institution, but her employment there did not last long either. This employer, she declared, was "great because they were Christian and [she] could help and work with people with needs." She came to believe that her previous challenges had been "like God preparing [her] for another job," as she now had work skills as a result of living through previous crises. A bout of serious illness required her to leave her job and go on disability. She revised her expectations with this new job search. Whereas earlier she had wanted an executive position with good pay, she now was willing to take whatever was offered her, and was happy even for part-time employment. She began volunteering, then found work as a tutor.

Clara concluded her description of her work experiences with a religious reflection on their meaning. Speaking of her dismissal from an executive position at a Mennonite Brethren institution and her current employment as a tutor, she commented on her surprise at "how something [she] thought was so devastating, ended up being what God wants [her] to do now." She noted that she spent much time in "prayer and meditation and reading and journaling" after her dismissal, relying particularly on Joyce Rupp's writings on God's peace and communion with God.[39] She said she had defined her self by her job and, without it, she did not "know who [she] was or what [her] worth was." As a consequence, she "found other ways to be important to God besides a job." Losing her job, getting sick, and being unemployed were a "whole new learning experience," particularly since she had always thought that the latter was neither "decent nor Christian." She had to go through a grieving process and learn to "look at [her] self through God's eyes." She reflected that she has "no idea what God has next" for her, and is "happier than [she has] ever been." She declared herself amazed and thankful for her work experiences, noting that they "have been and will be resources for others. The goal for faith and life is to shoulder each others' burdens." She plans to retire eventually, but enjoys being busy and helping others.[40]

Later in the interview, Clara returned to the story of her dismissal from her executive position at a Mennonite Brethren-affiliated organization, offering further details. Shortly after her firing, she spoke with her church pastor about what she described as unfair treatment in her termination, and he contacted a Mennonite conflict resolution expert on her behalf. This expert led mediation between Clara and the board of the organization from which she had been released. She observed that the board had a right to release her from employment, but declared that the way they did it "was not Christian, and not how it should be done even if they were not Christian." She said she had never been told why she was dismissed, and had been told she did not need to know why. Mediation provided Clara with "a better feeling for why the board had said that." Mediation also gave her the opportunity to tell her side of the story, an opportunity she had not yet had. As part of the mediation process, Clara wrote a letter to the board explaining what she thought they had done wrong, and asking for an apology, more severance pay, and a letter of reference. The board chair wrote in reply that the board did what they thought they needed to do, and that they could not provide a letter of reference unless she had a job application in process. Clara observed that "obviously" the letter contained no apology and the request for more severance pay was ignored.

Clara asserted that even though she did not like to hear what the board had to say, and continued to believe that her dismissal was not fair, "at least [she] was heard this time." Consequently, she began to be "able to be at peace." She had some resolution, and so her "hatred and anger started to dissolve." The dismissal had been "always a sore place," but she now was able to say hello to the board members involved, although she refused to hug them. The process of mediation, for her, was both "new and good." She felt fortunate that the mediator was a member of her church. She particularly appreciated the Christian approach to mediation. At a non-religious institution, she once had had to go to mediation with a co-worker who had asked the union to prevent Clara from supervising. That instance had been a "non-Christian, non-compassionate approach," as unions view administration as "evil" and want to "make them pay." In contrast to the Christian mediation she had experienced, union mediation had been "not a good experience."[41]

At the conclusion of the interview, Clara repeated her position that Mennonite churches do not "know how to deal with the negative well." It was a final reflection, one arising from her firing. She asserted that the identity of GC and MB congregations as peace churches means that they find conflict difficult, hoping that if it is "brushed under the rug," it will "go away." These churches, she claimed, need "more education" on how to handle situations with employees such as dismissals and reprimands.[42]

What made matters worse for Clara was that she felt that her firing came after she had found that "things were not legal there." This was information she shared after I was packing up the recording equipment, and thus volunteered off tape (she later gave consent for my use of it). She explained that her dismissal from her Mennonite Brethren-affiliated employer came when she attempted to address issues she saw as "not legal." It was this matter that was the "origin of the problem with the board," because she had made changes without asking the board for permission – a step she did not believe to be necessary as executive director of the organization. The problems she sought to resolve were violations of labour codes, including failure to pay overtime and refusal to pay overnight shifts in full. Repair work and provision of first aid kits were "seen as a waste of money." Clara commented that she "would think we must follow labour codes as Christian people," but she believed this view was not widely held in her religious community.[43]

Clara's repetitions of the story of her dismissal by her Mennonite Brethren-affiliated employer are revealing not just in their content but also in their structure. In the first iteration, she speaks of God rather than her employer. In the second, she speaks of labour justice in the context of Mennonite conflict resolution. In the third iteration, she notes the problems of Mennonite employers generally. In the fourth (off-tape) iteration, she is more blunt and critical of her employer. Throughout these repeated stories, she makes an interesting use of religious rhetoric.

Clara was unable at first to state that her Christian employer violated labour law and dismissed her for drawing attention to that fact. Instead, she attributed to God (rather than her employer) all actions leading to her termination and spoke of the spiritual insights she gained as a result. Such a casting of the story doubtless was a consequence of her awareness that I was a fellow Mennonite. To speak openly and critically of her employer, even to a co-religionist, would cast her in an irreligious light. Couching her experience in positive language that emphasized religious lessons learned served to place her firmly within an established and respected Christian religious discursive tradition.[44] Clara's second iteration of her termination was slightly more critical, but still structured within a particular religious discourse. Here, her negative experience was an opportunity to discuss the positive example of Mennonite conflict resolution. Her third telling removed herself from the story, which allowed her to speak more critically, yet still enabled her to separate herself from the religious judgment that such direct speech might invoke in her listener. Clara thus did not complain about her own particular experience of dismissal, but instead critiqued the general phenomenon within her religious community. Finally, in the fourth retelling of her story, all religious glosses were removed. Clara stated clearly that the religious failure was not hers but her employer's.

It would be easy to dismiss these individuals' stories as those of disaffected employees. These people, however, are not "organizational cynics." Organizational cynics believe "that the organization lacks integrity"; "feel contempt for and anger toward" their employer and "experience distress, disgust, and even shame"; and tend "toward negative, and often disparaging, behavior."[45] These four interviewees, however, largely saw themselves, and not their employer, as the problem. Their stories – even Clara's – have undercurrents of spiritual guilt and disappointment, not anger or contempt.

The workers discussed in this chapter deliberately sought workplaces that would allow them to integrate their religious beliefs with their work experiences. Their employers professed to provide just such an opportunity. The workers' expectations were betrayed in various ways, from too narrow definitions of spiritual orthodoxy to the institutions' failures to live up to the religious commitments they themselves made. Keith Graber Miller offers a solution for workers trapped in such circumstances: "When Christians find themselves in work that constrains the expression of their discipleship, for example, or that calls them to contribute to brokenness rather than healing, to strife rather than reconciliation, to exploitation rather than nurture, they should leave that place of work and express their vocation as disciples elsewhere."[46] Graber Miller's injunction is too simplistic, of course, in that it places the onus solely on the worker.[47]

Because all the interviewees discussed in this chapter were involved in Mennonite Brethren church-related institutions, it is fair to ask if their common MB identity was coincidental. Do Mennonite Brethren workers have higher expectations of their workplaces than other Mennonites? Are Mennonite Brethren institutions more demanding of their employees? Mennonite Brethren institutions, as the more evangelical of the Mennonite denominations, may indeed stand out in this respect. The denomination historically has been more evangelical and has placed more social strictures on its members than General Conference Mennonites.[48] These higher expectations of church members may have translated into the workplace.

From a broader perspective, these four stories provide an insight into the limits of a traditional labour relations point of view. There is an inherent contradiction between the religious ethos and the marketplace that is reflected in the stories of these people whose work experiences ferreted out those contradictions. Sharing their stories was a courageous act, as well as an important one, since their willingness to do so grants us an opportunity to explore questions of power, class, and identity in church-affiliated organizations. This oral history project may have given these people a voice for the first time, and their very existence and voice are revealing. The tensions religious organizations engender are indeed "not so easy to live." Only in sharing such stories can an "alternative history" be created – one that presents a counterpoint to the "official" stories of corporate entities and religious institutions.

Workplaces that attempt to prescribe a definition of spirituality or religious commitment for their employees will have an increasingly difficult task as spirituality is redefined in the twenty-first century. "Even where a large majority of employees believe that their work practices are spiritual, they experience the sacred in a variety of ways."[49] As church membership continues to decline and the power of hierarchical religious institutions fades, church-affiliated employers may need to embrace a broader understanding of religiosity.[50]

The stories of these four people employed in Mennonite church-related organizations reveal the ways that people struggle to integrate their identities as workers with their identities as religious people. In religious work environments, such integration seemingly should be simple. Unfortunately, such is not always the case. Organizational psychologist Philip Mirvis asserts that, since the 1980s, employers have become increasingly resistant to workers' efforts to integrate their spirituality with their work experiences. Defining spirituality in part as the establishment of community, he notes, "organizations seem far less hospitable to community making than in the recent past."[51]

> From post-WWII to the early 1980s, the American workplace, corporate and governmental, was a relatively stable and secure setting in which to develop a career, make friends, give and get social support, and participate in purposeful activities larger than one's self. Today's workplace, marked by multiple changes in ownership and large-scale layoffs, more internal movement and individual job hopping, and increasing numbers of people on temporary assignment or working part-time, is riven instead by fear, pressure, and impermanence. What are the prospects, then, of making community and finding spirit amidst these spoils?[52]

Mirvis is speaking of secular employers, but his observations are applicable to religiously affiliated organizations as well.

The four North American Mennonites discussed in this chapter sought employment with co-religionists that presumably would limit the need to engage in the workplace conflict typified by unionized workplaces. They endeavoured to restore or recreate the imagined cooperative religious community of the rural past by retreating to employment by co-religionists in Mennonite Brethren church and para-church organizations. For some, these efforts resulted in personal disappointment. Once the reification of capitalist relations was unmasked (that is, once they discovered that there was no escaping capitalist labour relations), they had no collective means of coping with – much less acting upon – that revelation.

Conclusion

This book has examined an ethno-religious group that often opposed organized labour but nonetheless had a labour history – a history of debate, conflict, and decision regarding unions and union membership. As such, it has been a project in the ending of silence among Mennonites on labour issues. Religious scholars of late have done much to end the silence in public discourse regarding those who are thought not to belong: the so-called "nones" and "dones."[1] There is a need for labour scholars to do the same for those who are not seen as having a labour history at all. Such a focus on non-unionized individuals was called for recently by Jarod Roll: referencing fellow labour historian Herbert Gutman, Roll argues that we must understand the "religious (and secular) dimensions" of the thought of those "who have upheld and defended American capitalism in more modern times."[2]

North American Mennonites in the late twentieth century were largely unsupportive of the case for organized labour made by folk songs like "Talking Union":

> Now, if you want higher wages let me tell you what to do,
> You got to talk to the workers in the shop with you,
> You got to build you a union, got to make it strong.
> But if you all stick together, boys, it won't be long –
> You get shorter hours – better working conditions –
> Vacations with pay – take your kids to the seashore –
>
> It ain't quite this simple, so I better explain
> Just why you got to ride on the union train,

'Cause if you wait for the boss to raise your pay
We'll all be waiting 'til Judgment Day –
We'll all he buried – gone to Heaven –
St Peter'll be the straw boss then –

Now you know you're underpaid but the boss says you ain't
He speeds up the work 'til you're about to faint.
You may be down and out but you ain't beaten,
You can pass out a leaflet and call a meetin'
Talk it over – speak your mind –
Decide to do something about it – [3]

Mennonite religious authorities taught that such views were unchristian: Mennonite employees should not selfishly use power to compel improvements in their working conditions, and employers should not be viewed as exploitative. While early twentieth-century prohibitions against union membership were difficult to enforce and were removed by the 1960s, their legacy persisted. This legacy was reinforced by the farming and small business backgrounds of most Mennonites in Canada and the United States, and by perceptions among the general non-Mennonite public of union greed. Personal work experiences and parental attitudes – more so than theological positions – strongly shaped individual Mennonites' perspectives on unions, as did the economic crisis of the early twenty-first century. Although North American Mennonites avoided union membership to a greater degree than non-Mennonites, their disparate attitudes toward organized labour were not dissimilar. Historian Joe Friesen observes that Mennonite anti-unionism "lies partly in religion and partly in the interests of capital. Mennonite business leaders have, like other business people, historically been opposed to unions."[4]

While church authorities strove to create a unified religious identity for their followers, those in the pews defined their religious selves individually as much as collectively. The religious narratives of the more than one hundred Mennonites interviewed across North America for this project incorporated a limited number of narrative structures. These structures reveal that many urban Mennonites valued intellectual over emotional expositions of faith, resisted popular evangelicalism, and viewed themselves and their faith as countercultural. They saw their religious commitments as more than a way to come to terms with death, but as inspiration for self-transformation.

Nor did they see religious belief as presenting neat explanations for life situations, since some had difficulty reconciling their religious understandings with their material circumstances.

For many Mennonites, the shift from rural to urban settings meant the severing of ties to long-standing structures and rhythms that provided a sense of unified community identity. In the urban world, Mennonites belonged to a variety of communities, often with competing identities. The diversity of religious perspective within a single denomination is doubtless "the norm, rather than the exception," as sociologist Meredith McGuire reminds us.[5] Urban Mennonites then, as revealed in these oral histories, were caught in the tension between the individual and the community that characterizes life in industrial and post-industrial economies. One result of this tension is that they defined their religious identity in very individual ways, as revealed by their narratives of religious belief.

At times of labour crisis, as in California in the 1960s and Manitoba in the 1970s, these individualized religious narratives and disparate attitudes toward unions proved problematic. The United Farm Workers' protests regarding wages and working conditions for migrant harvesters touched an ethical nerve for some Mennonites. Others viewed the situation from their class position as growers or their ethnic identity as Hispanic Mennonites. Their employers' political and financial interests hampered those employed in Mennonite church-related organizations from taking a definitive stance on the issue. The result was the creation of a Mennonite collective memory of Cesar Chavez that rests largely on reticence, and in so doing reveals the structure of power relations in North American Mennonite society and the endless struggle for authority in a community's self-definition.

In Manitoba, the labour militancy of the 1970s and the election of an NDP government led to a crisis for some Mennonites. Here, denominational differences rather than racial differences prevented more than a minority of Mennonites from taking an active stance. The government's temporary provision of a conscience clause allowed Mennonite leaders and a few Mennonite laypeople to voice religious objections to unions and opt out of membership. The arguments made in defence of their stance, however, were grounded as much in individual rights as Mennonite theology. With the repeal of the conscience clause, some Mennonites turned to non-Mennonite alternatives to unions, such as the CLAC. Others sought employment with co-religionists as the preventative solution to any potential labour conflict.

For some, the choice of working for fellow Mennonites was no solution, but merely introduced new problems. The challenge of integrating their identities as workers with their identities as religious people, of finding a sense of community in the workplace, could not be so easily resolved. The values of the marketplace too often overruled the values of a religious ethos, and these Mennonite workers were left to face the fallout of the contradiction between the two. Their courage in sharing their stories reveals that issues of power, class, and identity are omnipresent in industrial and post-industrial societies, and that religion is not always the unifying force it sometimes is claimed or hoped to be.

Oral histories such as those studied here hold great promise for understanding religion in the post-1945 era. Sociologist Wade Clark Roof notes that the post-1960 disenchantment with institutions that many North Americans exhibit results in "new opportunities for researchers to explore the elementary forms of the religious. 'That I'm Presbyterian doesn't mean much to me,' as one person told us, 'I'm just trying to figure things out in my life.' Comments like that take us back to square 1 as far as research methods are concerned."[6] The life history method would seem to be a viable solution to the dilemma Roof outlines. Oral historian Tracy K'Meyer, for example, holds that a focus on individual stories is the best way to examine religious experience and its meaning, since "in-depth interviews convey the perspectives of diverse narrators, avoiding generalizations and stereotypes about belief."[7] She cautions, however, that researchers also must "accept the ambiguity of the language of faith and that the narrators' most private beliefs are sometimes inexpressible and unknowable."[8]

Ambiguous and unknowable though it may be, it is clear that religion has not yet been rendered irrelevant. The scholarly debate over secularization in Europe is being supplanted by discussion of religious individualization.[9] Hubert Knoblauch, using fellow sociologist Thomas Luckmann's theory of invisible religion and its emphasis on the "experience of transcendences," notes that "alternative forms of religion" are, in fact, flourishing in Europe.[10] Knoblauch and Luckmann argue that what has taken place in the West in general, and Europe in particular, is "the shrinking of transcendence" – that is, the disappearance of great transcendences (such as "dreams, ecstasy, meditation"[11]) and the proliferation of "minimal" transcendences such as "self-fulfillment."[12] Similarly, in the United States, sociologist

Roman Williams observes that religion may be "less apparent at times, but is by no means absent. It continues to show up unexpectedly," including in "everyday settings that are not overtly religious," such as the workplace.[13]

European secularization theory has meant that twentieth-century religion is under-studied, and the few studies that have been written focus on the traditional themes of religious institutions and leaders.[14] Religious belief came to be equated with agreement to "propositional truths," an intellectual choice made independently of "authority, tradition, or society. What matters about religion from this perspective are its ideas and not its things, practices, or presences."[15] Robert Orsi comments, "This is not necessarily how Americans actually are religious, of course."[16] An oral history approach to religion, however, provides greater access to understanding how people are religious, including "the private nature and meaning of religious belief, the interconnections between belief and public action, and the place of religion in broader historical narratives."[17]

In line with sociologist Herbert Gans's concept of "symbolic religiosity,"[18] lived experience shaped Mennonites' attitudes and actions regarding unions, at the same time as Mennonites used religious scripts and symbols to construct narratives that allowed them to place their individualized decision making in this area within a broader ethno-religious tradition, (re)shaping Mennonite collective memory in the process. While these conclusions may hold for many Christian traditions in North America, there are aspects of North American Mennonites' experiences that distinguish them from their Christian neighbours. For example, historical pietist emphases within Mennonitism have pushed against evangelical Christian influences in North American society and within Mennonite (particularly Mennonite Brethren) churches. As a result, separation has been a more common response than engagement:[19] separation from labour unions (that seek to engage and transform capitalism) and, for some, separation from non-Mennonite employers. In the latter case, such separation was perceived to resolve industrial conflict (but only for the individual) as the shared ethno-religious identity of employee and employer was presumed to trump class identity. Mennonites who nonetheless encountered conflict with their Mennonite employers thus experienced frustration, disappointment, and disillusion not only in their work lives but in their religious lives as well. North American Mennonites have used religious rhetoric to embrace individualism in their work lives, accepting the neoliberal reification of existing capitalist relations.[20]

Given this reification of capitalism, it might be time that Mennonites abandon the notion of "a calling" to work. Recently, religion professor Keith Graber Miller has endeavoured to redefine "calling" for Mennonites: "Calling is best understood simply as following Christ: Our true vocation, no matter what our particular work, is Christian discipleship."[21] "When Christians find themselves in work that constrains the expression of their discipleship ... or that calls them to contribute to brokenness rather than healing, to strife rather than reconciliation, to exploitation rather than nurture, they should leave that place of work and express their vocation as disciples elsewhere."[22] In a post-2008 North American labour market with high unemployment rates, the idea that one can choose a job to reduce or eliminate labour conflict seems naive. Nor can Mennonites rely on their co-religionists to avoid labour conflict – they never could.[23] Mennonites must acknowledge their late-twentieth-century shift in emphasis from the community to the individual, and realize that church leaders – just as much as those in the pews – are responsible for that shift. They must address questions of power within the Mennonite community, which are rooted in both race and class, and recognize that eliding those differences by a refusal to remember or come to terms with history does not actually serve to erase them.

Offering advice to his children, lawyer and novelist John Mortimer suggested that they ask people about themselves: "All that is needed to open the floodgates is a look of rapt attention and an opening request which can be as unsubtle as, 'Do please tell me the story of your life.' Ten to one, no one has ever asked them this and they've been longing to tell it. All this will be of great assistance to you if you're thinking of going in for the business of writing; at least it will convince you that there is no such thing as an ordinary life."[24] This "unsubtle" request is the initial phase of Alexander von Plato's four-stage oral history method that was used for this project.[25] Such a process is of far more value than as the mere generation of source material for a book, of course. Oral history has the potential to bring about reconciliation for both individuals and communities by providing opportunities for people to be heard at length without judgment – a prospect that is all too rare outside the oral history interview context – and by bringing individuals into conversation with each other through books like this one. In speaking with the more than one hundred Canadians and Americans interviewed for this project, one is indeed convinced that these people's lives cannot be dismissed as ordinary, and that their stories reveal much about the complexity of integrating religious identity with work experience in the modern world. It is to be hoped that people – not only scholars – will have many more such unordinary conversations about faith and work. Only in so doing will we begin to map the "inner space" of belief and its intersection with economic life with any accuracy.[26]

The simple telling of such stories is, by itself, insufficient, however. Religion scholar Marsha Hewitt observes,

> Stories have a way of making the hearers feel good, and can even offer the illusion that the telling of the story in itself is enough to change the world. It isn't. Narratives provide a safe, comfortable, but illusory retreat from the very dangerous, unpleasant activity of struggling against the injustices perpetrated by institutions that support us and with which we deeply identify. Narratives do not provide a safe space for telling the stories of injustice in the absence of structures that ensure a sustained and ongoing safety beyond the narrative space. No institution or community that exists in this world is free of politics, and it is politics that infuses the difficult realities of power and authority, whether we like it or not. One of the most difficult realizations for most Christians is that religion is political – political because it is practiced in the world, between people, not beyond it.[27]

The sharing of stories that have not been heard, and that are uncomfortable to hear, is only the first step, then. Mennonites and non-Mennonites alike will need to move from the role of listener to that of activist. Do we have the courage to leave our "safe, comfortable, but illusory retreat"?

Notes

ACKNOWLEDGMENTS

1 Srigley, "Stories of Strife?"
2 Ibid., 2.
3 Wong, "Conversations for the Real World," 251.

INTRODUCTION

1 In North America in 1990, there were 94,265 MC members, 62,806 GCs, and 43,452 MBs. Loewen and Nolt, *Seeking Places of Peace*, 339, appendix A.
2 Ibid., 43.
3 Bender and Stauffer Hostetler, "Mennonite Church (MC)"; Kaufman and Poettcker, "General Conference Mennonite Church (GCM)"; Lohrenz and Janz, "Canadian Conference of Mennonite Brethren Churches."
4 Mennonite Church, "Resolution on Unionism," 20th Session, 24–6 August 1937, Turner, Oregon, in Peachey, *Mennonite Statements on Peace and Social Concerns*, 105. This discussion of official church positions on union membership draws on my article "Communism and Labor Unions."
5 Isaiah 9:6, Matthew 26:61–3, Matthew 5:38–45, John 18:36, Romans 12:17–21, 2 Corinthians 10:4, Ephesians 4:31–2, James 5:6.
6 2 Corinthians 6:14–16, King James Version.
7 Mennonite Church, "Industrial Relations," 22nd Session, 26 August 1941, Wellman, Indiana, in Peachey, 102–3, 105–6.
8 Mennonite Church, "Organized Labor," Study Conference, 24–7 June 1951, Laurelville Mennonite Camp, Pennsylvania, in Peachey, *Mennonite Statements on Peace and Social Concerns*, 106–7.

9 Redekop, "Labor Unions."
10 Mennonite Brethren Church, "The Christian and Labor Unions," 51st Session, 23–6 August 1969, Vancouver, British Columbia, in Peachey, *Mennonite Statements on Peace and Social Concerns,* 104–5.
11 General Conference Mennonite Church and Mennonite Church, "Justice and the Christian Witness (General Conference Mennonite Church, Mennonite Church, 1983)."
12 See the statistical discussion of this issue in chapter 2.
13 Thiessen, *Manufacturing Mennonites.* The book explores the class-based redefinitions of Mennonite identity that occurred in three Mennonite-owned workplaces in Manitoba after 1945: blue-collar workers, business owners and managers, and religious intellectuals (pastors, theologians, and university professors) contested competing ethno-religious identity claims in response to changing political, economic, and social circumstances in Manitoba.
14 Portelli, "What Makes Oral History Different," 50.
15 This group is known as Kanadier Mennonites and their descendants.
16 Hoover, "Lost Causes," 150.
17 Burke, *Varieties of Cultural History*, 181.
18 Jardine, "Whigs and Stories," 127.
19 See, for example, Loewen, *Family, Church, and Market* and *Diaspora in the Countryside.*
20 Analysis of North American historical statistics of union support is provided in chapter 2.
21 The Almanac Singers, "Talking Union," *Talking Union and Other Union Songs,* Smithsonian Folkways Records, 1941.
22 Portelli, "What Makes Oral History Different," 54. Emphasis mine.
23 Copies of recorded interviews were provided to interview participants who requested them. Copies also will be deposited in a Mennonite community archive (the Mennonite Heritage Centre in Winnipeg, Manitoba).
24 Shopes, "Commentary: Sharing Authority," 104.
25 Ibid.
26 For description and analysis of these events, see Sorkin, *Too Big to Fail*; Johan A. Lybeck, *A Global History of the Financial Crash of 2007–10*; Friedman, *What Caused the Financial Crisis*; James B. Stewart, "Eight Days: The Battle to Save the American Financial System," *New Yorker* (21 September 2009): 58–81; Harman, *Zombie Capitalism.*
27 See, for example, the readers' comments on Joann Muller's *Forbes* article, "If GM Collapses, Don't Blame the Union" (5 December 2008), http://www.forbes.com/2008/12/04/detroit-labor-uaw-biz-manufacturing-cz_jm_1205union.html.

28 Portelli, "What Makes Oral History Different," 54.

29 Von Plato, "Contemporary Witnesses and the Historical Profession."

30 Of course, comparisons to other interviews were always made without naming or otherwise identifying interview participants.

31 In Ohio, these included the *Findlay Courier*; the *Delphos Herald*; Bluffton University's student newspaper, *The Witmarsum*; and Bluffton University's magazine, *Bluffton*. In Indiana, ads were placed with the *Goshen News*; the Goshen College *Record*; and the Goshen College *Bulletin*. Ads were placed in California publications that included the *Reedley Exponent*; the *Fresno Bee*; and the California State University (Fresno) student newspaper, *The Collegian*. Ads were sent to the *Waterloo Record*; Conrad Grebel College's newsletter, *Grebel Now*; the *Winnipeg Free Press*; the University of Manitoba student paper, *The Manitoban*; and the University of Winnipeg student paper, *The Uniter*. In British Columbia, newspapers contacted included the *Vancouver Sun*; the *Vancouver Province*; the *Vancouver Courier*; the *Abbotsford Times*; the *Abbotsford News*; and Columbia Bible College's alumni newsletter, *Columbia Cornerstone*.

32 Periodicals included *The Canadian Mennonite, Mennonite Brethren Herald, The Mennonite,* and *Christian Leader.* Notices were placed in the bulletins of churches affiliated with the Canadian Conference of Mennonite Brethren Churches, the United States Conference of Mennonite Brethren, Mennonite Church Canada, and Mennonite Church USA. Announcements also were sent to the regional offices of Mennonite Central Committee Canada and Mennonite Central Committee USA, and to Mennonite colleges and universities.

33 "Oral history interviews are historical documents that are preserved and made accessible to future researchers and members of the public … In keeping with the goal of long term preservation and access, oral historians should use the best recording equipment available within the limits of their financial resources." Oral History Association, *Principles and Best Practices,* http://www.oralhistory.org/about/principles-and-practices/ (accessed October 2009).

34 These five were the (Old) Mennonite Church, the General Conference, the Mennonite Brethren, the Brethren in Christ, and the Evangelical Mennonite Church.

35 As the research progressed and I uncovered Mennonite responses to the 1960s United Farm Workers movement, I did interview a few growers. These people were better described as small business owners than traditional farmers, however.

36 Loewen and Nolt, *Seeking Places of Peace*, 234.

37 Since the late 1970s, Mennonites in Winnipeg, for example, were much more likely than non-Mennonites to be white-collar workers: four times as many Mennonites as non-Mennonites were business owners, and more than twice as many were professionals. Rempel, "Mennonites Better Represented in the 'Status' Jobs," 25–6.

38 Labour history has been invigorated over the last generation through the study of the cultural dimensions of work and the intersection of race, gender, ethnicity, and linguistics with worker identity. E.P. Thompson and Clifford Geertz, for example, have insisted on the importance of culture in understanding workers' lives. Ruth Frager, Joy Parr, Joan Sangster, and Christopher Dummitt have emphasized gender issues, notions of masculinity, and the roles of women. The significance of immigrant status, race, and identity are noted in the works of David Roediger, Franca Iacovetta, Nancy Foner, Kathleen Conzen, and Dirk Hoerder, among others. The scholarship of Herbert Gans, Herbert Gutman, David Harvey, Raymond Williams, and Pierre Bourdieu exemplify the postmodernist focus on power and linguistics in labour history. Most recently, Jefferson Cowie has blended labour history and cultural history to explain the decline or "unmaking" of the working class in the United States in the 1970s. Geertz, *The Interpretation of Cultures*; Thompson, *The Making of the English Working Class* and *Witness against the Beast*; Frager, *Sweatshop Strife*; Frager and Patrias, *Discounted Labour*; Parr, *The Gender of Breadwinners*; Sangster, *Earning Respect*; Dummitt, *The Manly Modern*; Roediger, *Wages of Whiteness*; Iacovetta, Quinlan, and Radforth, "Immigration and Labour"; Iacovetta, *Such Hardworking People*; Iacovetta and Gabaccia, *Women, Gender, and Transnational Lives*; Foner, *In a New Land*; Conzen, Gerber, Morawska, Pozzetta, and Vecoli, "The Invention of Ethnicity"; Hoerder, *Creating Societies* and *Cultures in Contact*; Gans, "Symbolic Ethnicity"; Gutman, *Power and Culture* and *Work, Culture, and Society in Industrializing America*; Harvey, *The Condition of Postmodernity*; Williams, *Keywords*; Bourdieu, *Language and Symbolic Power*; Cowie, *Stayin' Alive*.

39 Christie and Gauvreau, *A Full-Orbed Christianity* and *Cultures of Citizenship in Postwar Canada*; Gauvreau, *The Evangelical Century*; Westfall, *Religion/Culture*; Hall, *Lived Religion in America*.

40 Butler, "Jack-in-the-Box Faith," 1378. A rare examination of the relationship between the first of these two is the collection of articles that appears in a special issue of *Religion and American Culture*. The editors observe that scholarly examinations of the history of class and of religion have proceeded along independent lines. The result, Hackett, Maffly-Kipp,

Moore, and Woodcock Tentler assert, has been the development of "largely separate fields." "Forum: American Religion and Class," 2.

41 Ibid.

42 Weber, *The Protestant Ethic and the Spirit of Capitalism.*

43 Marks, "Challenging Binaries," 118.

44 Ibid.

45 See, for example, Forsey, *Trade Unions in Canada*; Heron, *The Canadian Labour Movement*; Montgomery, *Workers' Control in America*; Fink, *Workingmen's Democracy.*

46 Examples include Gutman, "Protestantism and the American Labor Movement"; Fones-Wolf, *Trade Union Gospel*; Murphy, *Ten Hours Labor*; Fraser, *The Social Uplifters*; Guglielmo, *Living the Revolution.*

47 An early exception, and a model of innovative work in this area, is Thompson, *Witness against the Beast.* Robert Swierenga argues that it is not only scholars of urban labour history who have ignored religion; historians of agriculture and rural life have done so as well. Robert P. Swierenga, "The Little White Church," 422. Exceptions to this neglect include Loewen, *Family, Church, and Market.*

48 Joseph McCartin observes that "despite abundant evidence suggesting the importance of religious influence to the lives, work, and struggles of North American workers, labor and working-class historians have barely begun to probe and illuminate this rich history" – a view echoed by Lynne Marks and William R. Sutton. McCartin, "The Force of Faith," 1; Marks, "Challenging Binaries," 108; Sutton, "Tied to the Whipping Post," 251–6. Helpful efforts in this area include works by Lynne Marks, Robert Orsi, and Franca Iacovetta. Marks, *Revivals and Roller Rinks*; Orsi, *Thank You, St. Jude*; Orsi, *The Madonna of 115th Street*; Iacovetta, *Such Hardworking People.* But too often, such efforts are limited in scope. In a special issue of the journal *Labor,* for example, only one article addresses work and religion outside the narrow context of political or union activism. Polland, "Working for the Sabbath."

49 Examples include Rawlyk, *The Canadian Protestant Experience*; Zeman, *Baptists in Canada*; Rawlyk, *Ravished by the Spirit*; and Van Die, *An Evangelical Mind.*

50 Examples of the former are Westfall, *Two Worlds*, and Valverde, *The Age of Light, Soap, and Water*. The literature on lived religion is much more recent, and includes Hall, *Lived Religion in America*; McGuire, *Lived Religion*; Orsi, *Between Heaven and Earth*; Roof, *A Generation of Seekers*; Wuthnow, *After Heaven*; and Wuthnow, *Growing Up Religious.*

51 See Baker, "Should Mennonite Teachers Strike?"; Hughes, "Should They … ?"; Klassen Neufeld, "Should They … ?"; Houser, "Should They … ?"; Kroeker, "Mennonites and Unions"; Kroeker, "We Think It Was a Good Move"; Sutherland and Van Weelden, "To Strike or Not to Strike"; T. Martin, "Ontario Teachers and the Moral Obligation to Strike"; Schultz-Janzen, "To Strike or Not to Strike"; Thiessen, "Committed to Christ or Conformed to This World?"; Thiessen, "Communism and Labor Unions."

52 Thiessen, "Committed to Christ or Conformed to This World?"

53 Mennonite Historical Society of British Columbia, Mennonite Central Committee collection, 160.3, Peace and Service correspondence, Box 1 File 52.2, undated reply to 11 July 1974 telegram from Doug Snyder, MCC Ontario, to Vernon Reimer, Director of MCC British Columbia; Henry Penner, Labour Study Committee chair, "Report to Peace Committee Re: Public meeting with Mennonite workers and professionals, Vancouver Mennonite Churches," n.d. [late 1964]; letter from Peace Committee BC to area churches, 20 May 1964.

54 These events are discussed in considerably more detail in chapters 3, 4, and 5 of this book.

55 Demerath, "The Varieties of Sacred Experience," 4.

CHAPTER ONE

1 Everett Thomas, city councillor and editor of *The Mennonite*, interview by author, Goshen, Indiana, 12 November 2009.

2 James Yoder, social worker, interview by author, Goshen, Indiana, 16 November 2009.

3 Loewen, *Diaspora in the Countryside*, ix.

4 "Mennonites" is the term I use to refer collectively to a variety of different ethno-religious communities. These include the Mennonite Brethren (MBs), the former Mennonite Church (which will be referred to as the (Old) Mennonite Church), and the former General Conference Mennonites (GCs). The (Old) Mennonites and the GCs united in 2000 to form Mennonite Church USA and Mennonite Church Canada. This naming system follows the usage common in the literature on Mennonites.

5 Harkin, "Feeling and Thinking in Memory and Forgetting," 278.

6 Ibid.

7 Klempner here cites Laub and Felman, *Testimony*. Klempner, "Navigating Life Review Interviews with Survivors of Trauma," 80–1.

8 Ed Penner, dentist, interview by author, Surrey, British Columbia, 12 December 2009.

9 Linda Houshower, nurse and co-owner of natural foods store, interview by author, Bluffton, Indiana, 5 November 2009.

10 Ibid.

11 Proudfoot and Shaver, "Attribution Theory and the Psychology of Religion," 318.

12 "Fred," pseudonym for anonymous interview participant, interview by author.

13 Ibid.

14 Marianne Coleman, nursing home caregiver and former press operator/teacher/musician/physics technician/artist, interview by author, Kitchener, Ontario, 17 October 2009.

15 Coleman's father was Frank H. Epp, founding editor of *The Canadian Mennonite* and *Mennonite Reporter* and author of the first two volumes of the *Mennonites in Canada* series. Epp also served on the boards of a variety of Mennonite church and para-church organizations. See Ens, "Epp, Frank H. (1929–1986)."

16 Marianne Coleman, interview by author.

17 Marlyce Friesen, doctor, interview by author, Abbotsford, British Columbia, 5 December 2009.

18 Dave Klassen, truck driver, farmer, and mechanic, interview by author, Abbotsford, British Columbia, 5 December 2009.

19 Boschman was pastor of Central Heights Church, a Mennonite Brethren church in Abbotsford. Nikkel, "This Century's Journey of Evangelism for Canadian Mennonite Brethren," 228–43; Klix and Klager, "Central Heights Church (Abbotsford, British Columbia, Canada)."

20 Dave Klassen, interview by author.

21 Erwin Cornelsen, woodworker and former pastor, interview by author, Vancouver, British Columbia, 9 December 2009.

22 I certainly found this to be the case when I interviewed Mennonite immigrants to Manitoba. See Thiessen, "Faith and Factory," chapter 2.

23 Allan Dueck, principal of Bethany Christian Schools, interview by author, Goshen, Indiana, 18 November 2009.

24 Roger Miller, sales manager for international hydraulic leveling system manufacturer, interview by author, Goshen, Indiana, 21 November 2009.

25 Brian Hunsberger, former development director, Kitchener House of Friendship, interview by author, Waterloo, Ontario, 15 October 2009.

26 Cox, *The Secular City*.

27 Barb Draper, teacher, interview by author, Waterloo, Ontario, 18 October 2009.

28 "Harold," pseudonym for anonymous interview participant, interview by author.

29 "To speak of one's journey is to emphasize changing conceptions and experiences of faith rather than a once-for-all-time grasp of religious truth." Wuthnow, *Growing Up Religious*, xxxiii. See also Wuthnow, *Sharing the Journey*, 223–7; Roof, *Spiritual Marketplace*, 101–3.

30 Wuthnow, *Sharing the Journey*, 293.

31 Ibid., 295.

32 Ibid., 313.

33 Ammerman, "Studying Everyday Religion: Challenges for the Future," in Ammerman, *Everyday Religion*, 226.

34 Ibid.

35 Ibid., 7.

36 Roof, "Religion and Narrative," 298.

37 Wuthnow, *Growing Up Religious*, xi.

38 As Tracy E. K'Meyer observes, "some of the most interesting results come when personal narratives are used to investigate the private aspects of individual belief." K'Meyer, "'I Just Felt Called ... ,'" 728.

39 "Oral sources tell us not just what people did, but what they wanted to do, what they believed they were doing, and what they now think they did." Portelli, "What Makes Oral History Different," in *The Death of Luigi Trastulli and Other Stories*, 50.

CHAPTER TWO

1 For details of these changing church pronouncements, see Thiessen, "Communism and Labor Unions," 17–28.

2 Loewen and Nolt, *Seeking Places of Peace*, 248.

3 Jeff Boehr, assistant campus pastor for church relations, Bluffton University, used this phrase. Interview by author, Bluffton, Ohio, 27 October 2009.

4 Richards, *Union-Free America*, 83.

5 Stromquist, "Review of Richards' *Union-Free America*," 149.

6 Lipset and Meltz, *The Paradox of American Unionism*.

7 The 1972 and 1989 Mennonite Church Member Profiles (CMPs) were conducted among members of five Mennonite denominations in the United States and Canada: the (Old) Mennonite Church, the General Conference Mennonites, Mennonite Brethren, Brethren in Christ, and Evangelical Mennonite. See Kauffman and Harder, *Anabaptists Four Centuries Later*, and Kauffman and Driedger, *The Mennonite Mosaic*, 92.

8 The CMPs did not distinguish between the two types of organizations, listing as examples the "American or Canadian Medical Association, Phi Beta Kappa, Teacher's Associations, etc." Teachers' associations are usually

considered labour unions, but are not included in the CMPs' union statistics. Since teaching long was considered a religious calling by many Mennonites, it is perhaps not surprising that the church-commissioned CMPs did not group membership in teachers' associations under the category of union membership. Summary of 1972 and 1989 CMP results provided by Bruno Dyck, Asper School of Business, University of Manitoba.

The 2006 Church Membership Profile was conducted only in the United States and did not include questions about union membership or attitudes to unions. Summary of 2006 CMP results provided by Conrad Kanagy, Elizabethtown College.

9 Statistics Canada, Series E17, "Union membership in Canada, in total, as a percentage of non-agricultural workers, 1911 to 1975"; Statistics Canada, "The Labour Force Survey," Labour Statistics Division, and "Union Membership in Canada – 2007," Strategic Policy, Analysis, and Workplace Information Directorate, Labour Program, Human Resources and Social Development Canada, http://www.hrsdc.gc.ca/eng/lp/wid/union_membership.shtml (accessed 29 November 2010); Akyeampong, "A statistical portrait of the trade union movement," 46, Table 1; Galarneau, "Unionized workers," 45, Table 1.

10 Union membership (as a percentage of non-agricultural employment) peaked at 35.4 percent in 1945. As a percent of paid employment, it peaked at 34.8 percent in 1954. By 2003, union membership as a percentage of paid employment was only 12.4. Mayer, "Union Membership Trends in the United States," 12, Appendix A Table A1.

11 Lipset, "Trade Union Exceptionalism," 116.

12 See Conway's scathing review essay, "Canada and the US: What Makes Us Different?" Other negative reviews of Lipset's *Continental Divide* include John Myles in *European Sociological Review* 7, no. 2 (September 1991): 179–81; Rudy Fenwick in *Social Forces* 70, no. 1 (September 1991): 250–2; and William Mishler in *The Journal of Politics* 53, no. 1 (February 1991): 272–4. See also Baer, Grabb, and Johnston, "The Values of Canadians and Americans: A Rejoinder," and Curtis, Brown, Lambert, and Kay, "Affiliating with Voluntary Associations."

13 These surveys include the iPOLL Databank at the Roper Center for Public Opinion Research (University of Connecticut), the American National Election Study, and the Current Population Survey. Panagopoulos and Francia, "The Polls – Trends," 137.

14 In 1952, 47 percent stated that their sympathies were with unions in labour disputes, compared to 52 percent in 2005. Panagopoulos and Francia, "The Polls – Trends," 137, 142 Table 8.

15 Freeman's analysis of Gallup and Harris polls from 1947 through 2005 on approval/disapproval of labour unions reveals that a majority has always

favoured unions. The gap between those approving and those disapproving shrank from 40 percent in 1947 to 20 percent in 1981. By 2005, however, this gap reached 43 percent, although union approval ratings hovered at around 65 percent. Freeman, "Do Workers Still Want Unions?" 7 Figure A. Freeman also includes this information in the updated version of his co-authored work: Freeman and Rogers, *What Workers Want.* According to a poll conducted by Time, CNN, and Yankelovich Partners, 68 percent of Americans thought that American workers still needed labour unions in 1995, while 24 percent thought unions were no longer necessary. Panagopoulos and Francia, "The Polls – Trends," 151 Table 29.

16 Mendelsohn and Nadeau, "The Religious Cleavage and the Media in Canada," 138 Table 1.

17 Chang, "A Structural Model of Race, Gender, Class, and Attitudes toward Labor Unions," 197.

18 Panagopoulos and Francia, "The Polls – Trends," 141–2.

19 See, for example, Greenhouse, "Humbled, the U.A.W. Is Appealing for Support," *New York Times* (5 March 2009): B6; Bob Herbert, "A Race to the Bottom," *New York Times* (22 December 2008): A29; Micheline Maynard, "U.A.W. at Center of Dispute over Bailout," *New York Times* (12 December 2008); Mitt Romney, "Let Detroit Go Bankrupt," *New York Times* (18 November 2008): A35; Kelly McParland, "Stop the Revolution, the CAW Wants to Get Off," *National Post* (19 November 2008).

20 The $70/hour wage was widely reported in the media at the time, often without clarifying that this number combines average wages, benefits, future retirement benefits, and retirement benefits for current retirees. Dave Burdick, "Debunking the $70-an-Hour Auto Worker Gossip," *Huffington Post* (25 November 2008), http://www.huffingtonpost.com/2008/11/25/debunking-the-70anhour-au_n_146448.html (accessed 8 January 2011).

21 David Giesbrecht, former head librarian of Columbia Bible College, interview by author, Abbotsford, British Columbia, 2 December 2009.

22 Carl Yoder, former Sauder employee and former small business owner, interview by author, Goshen, Indiana, 18 November 2009.

23 Theron Schlabach, truck driver and Goshen College history professor, interview by author, Goshen, Indiana, 18 November 2009.

24 Jim Bender, manager of industrial design for high technology company, interview by author, Waterloo, Ontario, 7 October 2009.

25 Tom and Joyce Schumacher, farmers, TNT Farms, interview by author, Pandora, Ohio, 6 November 2009.

26 Vernon Erb, president and chair of Erb Group, interview by author, New Hamburg, Ontario, 14 October 2009.

27 Art Friesen, medical doctor, interview by author, Abbotsford, British Columbia, 5 December 2009.

28 Blaine Millar, addictions counsellor, interview by author, Kitchener, Ontario, 13 October 2009.

29 Statistical surveys of whether or not Mennonites had *non*-religious objections have not been conducted to date, unfortunately.

30 Vogt, "The Impact of Economic and Social Class on Mennonite Theology," 145.

31 See, for example, Sombart, *Why Is There No Socialism in the United States?* and Lipset, "Why No Socialism in the United States?"

32 See Fink, "Looking Backward," 176; Dawley, *Struggles for Justice,* 134.

33 Faue, "Retooling the Class Factory," 111.

34 See, for example, Gutman, *Work, Culture, and Society in Industrializing America* and *Power and Culture*; Roediger, *The Wages of Whiteness*; Kessler-Harris, *Gendering Labor History*; Parr, *The Gender of Breadwinners*; Iacovetta, *Such Hardworking People*; Frager, *Sweatshop Strife*; Marks, *Revivals and Roller Rinks*; Steedman, *Angels of the Workplace*; and Sangster, *Transforming Labour*.

35 See discussion of this challenge in Marks, "Challenging Binaries." Model attempts at such integration include Vecoli, "Prelates and Peasants"; Ammerman and Roof, eds., *Work, Family, and Religion in Contemporary Society* and, from a European perspective, van Voss and van der Linden, eds., *Class and Other Identities*.

36 Thompson, *The Making of the English Working Class*; Gutman, "Protestantism and the American Labor Movement."

37 Marks, *Revivals and Roller Rinks*. See also Palmer's critical review of this book, "Historiographic Hassles," as well as Marks's rejoinder, "Heroes and Hallelujahs."

38 Hearn and Knowles, "Struggling for Recognition."

39 Faue, "Retooling the Class Factory."

40 Taksa, "Retooling the Class Factory," 129–30. Recent work in labour history that incorporates oral history includes Cullum, *Narratives at Work*; Honey, *Black Workers Remember*; Dublin, *When the Mines Closed*; Stepan-Norris and Zeitlin, *Talking Union*; Halpern and Horowitz, *Meatpackers*; Stromquist, *Solidarity and Survival*.

41 2 Corinthians 6:14–16 (King James Version). The New Revised Standard Version replaces the agrarian image "unequally yoked" with the less

evocative "mismatched." The bishops of the Lancaster Mennonite Conference used this same passage in 1941 as the rationale for their opposition to union membership. Mennonite Church Lancaster Conference, "Labor Unions," Board of Bishops Special Meeting, 24 September 1941, Ephrata, Pennsylvania, in Peachey, *Mennonite Statements on Peace and Social Concerns, 1900–1978*, 107.

42 Thiessen, "Communism and Labor Unions."

43 Redekop, "Labor Unions."

44 Mennonite Brethren Church, "The Christian and Labor Unions," 51st Session, 23–6 August 1969, Vancouver, British Columbia, in Peachey, *Mennonite Statements on Peace and Social Concerns, 1900–1978*, 104–5.

45 See Schlabach, *War, Peace, and Social Conscience.*

46 Minutes of meeting on "United Farmworker-Grower Issues," Goshen College, 30 July 1974, Mennonite Church USA archives, Goshen, IN, Guy F. Hershberger collection, Hist Mss 1–171. Also found in IX–7–12 Box 7 File 24.

47 Ibid.

48 Jim Troyer, former school guidance counsellor, interview by author, Manistique, Michigan, 25 October 2009.

49 Ibid.

50 Ibid.

51 Ibid.

52 Ibid.

53 Vernon Erb, interview by author.

54 Dave Klassen, truck driver, farmer, and mechanic, interview by author, Abbotsford, British Columbia, 5 December 2009.

55 Wilbur Roth, former auto worker, interview by author, Kitchener, Ontario, 12 October 2009.

56 Paul Friesen, shelving/equipment clerk at University of Winnipeg Library, interview by author, Winnipeg, Manitoba, 10 March 2010.

57 Ellen Ibele, supply teacher, interview by author, Waterloo, Ontario, 8 October 2009.

58 Barb Draper, teacher, interview by author, Waterloo, Ontario, 18 October 2009.

59 "Do not be yoked together with unbelievers. For what do righteousness and wickedness have in common? Or what fellowship can light have with darkness?" 2 Corinthians 6:14, NIV.

60 Alice Ramseyer, former teacher and missionary, interview by author, Bluffton, Ohio, 5 November 2009. Dan Brown's novel *The Lost Symbol* (New York: Doubleday, 2009) is a work of fiction that sensationalizes Freemasonry.

61 Blaine Millar, interview by author.
62 Barb Draper, interview by author.
63 Art Friesen, interview by author.
64 Anonymous academic worker, interview by author.
65 Barling, Kelloway, and Bremermann, "Preemployment Predictors of Union Attitudes." The study was conducted with a sample of 143 undergraduate university students and 59 high school students in Ontario.
66 Randy Spallinger, engineer at Ford Motor Company, interview by author, Bluffton, Ohio, 6 November 2009.
67 Anonymous academic worker, interview by author.
68 Jonathan Janzen, pastor of Highland Community Church, interview by author, Abbotsford, British Columbia, 30 November 2009.
69 Brian Hunsberger, former development director, Kitchener House of Friendship, interview by author, Waterloo, Ontario, 15 October 2009.
70 David Giesbrecht, interview by author. Others attributed their parents' anti-union attitudes to their experiences in Stalinist Russia. One explained that her father's opposition to unions was because "Dad risked his life [to leave Russia] so he was not wanting communism." Anonymous academic worker, interview by author.
71 Dave Klassen, interview by author.
72 "For the scripture says, 'You shall not muzzle an ox while it is treading out the grain,' and, 'The labourer deserves to be paid.'" 1 Timothy 5:18, NRSV.
73 Tom Bontreger, truck driver and bed-and-breakfast owner, interview by author, Middlebury, Indiana, 20 November 2009.
74 Hans Houshower, professor of anthropology, vice president for advancement at Bluffton University, interview by author, 3 November 2009.
75 Wendy Chappell-Dick, director of MennoFolk, interview by author, Bluffton, Ohio, 3 November 2009.
76 Stefan Epp, University of Manitoba Environmental Conservation Lab research associate, interview by author, Winnipeg, Manitoba, 19 March 2010.
77 Marianne Coleman, nursing home caregiver and former press operator/teacher/musician/physics technician/artist, interview by author, Kitchener, Ontario, 17 October 2009.
78 Ibid.
79 James Yoder, social worker, interview by author, Goshen, Indiana, 16 November 2009.
80 Randy Spallinger, interview by author.
81 Brian Hunsberger, interview by author.
82 Anonymous academic worker, interview by author. Jim Bender expressed similar views, declaring that "of the worthwhile things to advocate, labour is not one of them." He said he preferred to focus his attention on

international human rights, development, health, and welfare, since he felt "more called to the bigger issues." Jim Bender, interview by author.

83 Ruth Roth, elementary school teacher, interview by author, Goshen, Indiana, 21 November 2009.

84 Art Friesen, interview by author.

85 Anonymous academic worker, interview by author.

86 Blaine Millar, interview by author.

87 Vernon Erb, interview by author.

88 Wilbur Bontrager, CEO Jayco, interview by author, Middlebury, Indiana, 11 November 2009.

89 Ed Penner, dentist, interview by author, Surrey, British Columbia, 12 December 2009. See Thiessen, *Manufacturing Mennonites,* for a broader discussion of industrial relations at Palliser.

90 Dave Klassen, interview by author.

91 Steven Webster, former vice-president of human relations at Sauder, adult and graduate education representative at Bluffton University, interview by author, Bluffton, Ohio, 2 November 2009.

92 Anonymous academic worker, interview by author.

93 Valerie Paulley, Riverview Health Centre patient care manager and former chemical technologist, interview by author, Winnipeg, Manitoba, 27 March 2010.

94 Ibid.

95 Lily Hiebert-Rempel, MCC Low German program coordinator, interview by author, Kitchener, Ontario, 15 October 2009.

96 Anonymous academic worker, interview by author.

97 Vernon Erb, interview by author.

98 Henry Peters, former meat-packer, interview by author, Winnipeg, Manitoba, 16 March 2010.

99 See Article 6 of the Schleitheim Confession, available at the *Global Anabaptist Mennonite Encyclopedia Online,* http://www.gameo.org/encyclopedia/contents/S345.html (accessed 8 January 2011).

100 Many Mennonite church members in the past referred to their co-religionists as "brothers and sisters in Christ," a practice less prevalent in the twenty-first century,

101 Paul Friesen, interview by author.

102 Tom Bontreger, interview by author.

103 Lavon Welty, Habitat for Humanity director, interview by author, Lima, Ohio, 5 November 2009.

104 Draper gives the date as 1996, but the Ontario teachers' strike, involving 125,000 educators, occurred in October 1997. Goldfield and Palmer, "Canada's Workers Movement," 167.

105 Barb Draper, interview by author.

106 Greg Ring, senior account executive in private brand sales at Cooper Tire and Rubber, interview by author, Bluffton, Ohio, 29 October 2009.

107 Wilbur Roth, interview by author.

108 Ellen Ibele, interview by author.

109 Ibid.

110 The CLAC is one of many historical examples of Christian involvement in the labour movement – both for and against. See, for example, Rosswurm, "The Catholic Church and Left-Led Unions," and Patrick Pasture, "The Role of Religion in Social and Labour History," in van Voss and van der Linden, *Class and Other Identities*.

111 The CLAC is not affiliated with the Canadian Labour Congress. Christian Labour Association of Canada, "CLAC Tour," 2004, http://www.clac.ca/Flash_Tour.asp (accessed 20 July 2004).

112 For more on Redekop's role in these seminars, see Thiessen, "Winnipeg's Palliser Furniture in the Context of Mennonite Views on Industrial Relations," and Thiessen, *Manufacturing Mennonites*.

113 John Redekop, former Trinity Western University professor of political science, interview by author, Abbotsford, British Columbia, 1 December 2009.

114 Ibid.

115 Ibid.

116 Ibid.

117 Jake H. Dueck, "When a Union Demands First Place," *Mennonite Brethren Herald* 4, no. 11 (19 March 1965): 7.

118 In his account of his experiences, Dueck cites the Bible. "After reading Guy F. Hershberger's article, *The Christian Attitude toward Labour Unions,* I realized for the first time that where a Christian accepts the kind of union obligation that I had accepted, he is unequally yoked with an organization that does not give our Lord and Saviour his rightful place (2 Cor. 6:14). The Lord also spoke to me further from Luke 16:13 that I was endeavouring to serve two masters. Unless I took a positive stand, eventually I would fall and Christ would lose his rightful place in my life as a believer." Jake H. Dueck, "When a Union Demands First Place," *Mennonite Brethren Herald* 4, no. 11 (19 March 1965): 7.

119 John H. Redekop, "Thanks, Brother Dueck!" *Mennonite Brethren Herald* 4, no. 15 (16 April 1965): 2.

120 At least one reader interpreted Redekop's column this way. Responding to both Redekop and the original account by Dueck, Henry Penner suggested that whether Mennonites should be union members or not was a moot point. In a letter to the editor of the *Mennonite Brethren Herald,* he asked rhetorically, "Is the question we are going to answer before God, 'Did you

belong to a labour union?' or 'How did you belong'?" Henry Penner, New Westminster, British Columbia, "Penetration or Isolation," letter to editor, *Mennonite Brethren Herald* 4, no. 20 (21 May 1965): 7.

121 John H. Redekop, "Thanks, Brother Dueck!" 2.

122 John H. Redekop, "Strikes and Strife," *Mennonite Brethren Herald* 15, no. 3 (6 February 1976): 10.

123 John H. Redekop, "Profit not a Bad Word," *Mennonite Brethren Herald* 17, no. 21 (13 October 1978): 10.

124 Ibid.

125 John H. Redekop, "The Work Ethic," *Mennonite Brethren Herald* 18, no. 2 (19 January 1979): 24.

126 John H. Redekop, "Government, Labour, and Ethics," *Mennonite Brethren Herald* 21, no. 16 (27 August 1982): 12.

127 Ibid.

128 John H. Redekop, "Cla$$ War!" *Mennonite Brethren Herald* 8, no. 10 (16 May 1969): 8.

129 Anonymous academic worker, interview by author.

130 Anonymous business manager, interview by author.

131 Vernon Erb, interview by author.

132 See, for example, Yow, "'Do I Like Them Too Much?'" and Ruiz, "Situating Stories."

133 Kanagy, *Road Signs for the Journey*; Conrad Kanagy, personal correspondence with the author, 12 January 2011. Kanagy kindly provided me with a copy of the frequencies of responses to all questions on the 2006 CMP.

134 See, for example, Sangster, *Transforming Labour*.

135 See Resnick, *The Politics of Resentment* and Carty, ed., *Politics, Policy, and Government in British Columbia*.

136 As early as 1945, (Old) Mennonite church leaders were having difficulty enforcing their church conference's stance against union membership among their congregations' members. Mennonite Church USA Archives, Goshen, IN, Hist Mss 1–171, Guy F. Hershberger collection, "Indiana Michigan Survey of Labor Relations," Box 20.

CHAPTER THREE

1 Melvin Enns, general manager, WesPak, interview by author, Dinuba, California, 23 April 2010.

2 For discussion of the tendency of oral historians to ignore awkward interviews, and of the ethical complications of *not* ignoring them, see K'Meyer

and Crothers, "'If I See Some of This in Writing, I'm Going to Shoot You'" and Sheftel and Zembrzycki, "Only Human."

3 At the time the interview was conducted, I was a postdoctoral fellow in history at the University of Winnipeg, on leave from my job as a high school teacher of chemistry, Mennonite history, and social studies at Westgate Mennonite Collegiate.

4 Melvin Enns, interview by author.

5 Ibid.

6 Eugene Enns, board chair, WesPak, interview by author, Dinuba, California, 3 May 2010.

7 Ewy, "The Grape and Raisin Industry"; Krahn, "San Joaquin Valley (California, USA)"; Just and Auernheimer, "California (USA)."

8 Melvin Enns, interview by author; Eugene Enns, interview by author; WesPak, "Our History," http://www.wespaksales.com/about/history.asp (accessed 7 October 2010).

9 For background on the Bracero Program, see Mize and Swords, *Consuming Mexican Labor*; Ngai, *Impossible Subjects*; Calavita, *Inside the State*; Anderson, *The Bracero Program in California*; Daniel, *Bitter Harvest*; Galarza, *Merchants of Labor*; Gilmore and Gilmore, "The Bracero in California." See also the Bracero History Archive, a collection of oral history interviews, images, and documents related to the Bracero Program, http://braceroarchive.org/ (accessed 7 October 2010).

10 Eugene Enns, interview by author.

11 Ibid.

12 The unemployment rate was 15.1 percent in 2009. In the previous two decades, unemployment averaged 12.1 percent. United States Department of Labor, Bureau of Labor Statistics, "Local area unemployment statistics for Fresno CA metropolitan area, 1990 to 2010," http://data.bls.gov/PDQ/servlet/SurveyOutputServlet?series_id=LAUMT06234203&data_tool=XGtable (accessed 7 October 2010).

13 Eugene Enns, interview by author.

14 Recent studies of Chavez include Shaw, *Beyond the Fields* and Garcia, *From the Jaws of Victory*. See also Yates, "The Rise and Fall of the United Farm Workers," which demythologizes Chavez.

15 However, General Conference Mennonites offered assistance to migrant workers as early as 1941. Elmer Ediger, "Migrant Work," typescript, Mennonite Church USA archives, Goshen, IN, MCC West Coast Office, Reedley, CA, 1947–84, IX–54, Migrant V.S. Unit 1957–58, Pronto 2 File 9.

16 "What You Can Do," MCC California, News of the California Migrant Unit, newsletter, September 1952, Mennonite Church USA archives,

Goshen, IN, MCC West Coast Office, Reedley, CA, 1947–84, IX–54, Migrant V.S. Unit 1953, Pronto 2 File 8.

17 Editorial by D.J.G., MCC California, News of the California Migrant Unit, newsletter, September 1952, Mennonite Church USA archives, Goshen, IN, MCC West Coast Office, Reedley, CA, 1947–84, IX–54, Migrant V.S. Unit 1953, Pronto 2 File 8.

18 "Report of the Summer's Work in Stanislaus County, California," MCC California, News of the California Migrant Unit, newsletter, September 1952, Mennonite Church USA archives, Goshen, IN, MCC West Coast Office, Reedley, CA, 1947–84, IX–54, Migrant V.S. Unit 1953, Pronto 2 File 8.

19 Falcón, "Hispanic Mennonites."

20 Penner, "Gaining a Voice," 8.

21 Ibid., 15–17.

22 Vernon L. King, "Evaluation Report of West Fresno Project," page 1, Social Concerns Committee and MCC, September 1969, Mennonite Church USA archives, Goshen, IN, MCC West Coast Office, Reedley, CA, 1947–84, IX–54, Social Concerns Committee, Pronto 4 File 57.

23 Letter from Jake Fransen, Fresno, CA, to [Allen] Linscheid, 6 January 1968, Mennonite Church USA archives, Goshen, IN, MCC West Coast Office, Reedley, CA, 1947–84, IX–54, Social Concerns Committee, Pronto 4 File 57.

24 Letter from Allen Linscheid, MCC West Coast Regional Office, to Edgar Stoesz, VS Director, MCC Akron, 6 February 1968, Mennonite Church USA archives, Goshen, IN, MCC West Coast Office, Reedley, CA, 1947–84, IX–54, Social Concerns Committee, Pronto 4 File 57.

25 Letter from Edgar Stoesz to [Allen] Linscheid, 25 January 1968, Mennonite Church USA archives, Goshen, IN, MCC West Coast Office, Reedley, CA, 1947–84, IX–54, Social Concerns Committee, Pronto 4 File 57.

26 "Grape Workers Get Church Aid; Labor Class Is 6 Months Old," *The Mennonite* 81, no. 16 (19 April 1966): 274–5.

27 Milton K. Staufer, Reedley, CA, "Grape strikers," letter to editor, *The Mennonite* 81, no. 19 (10 May 1966): 324.

28 Robert G. Hunsicker, Souderton, PA, "Sour Grapes," letter to editor, *The Mennonite* 81, no. 22 (31 May 1966): 371.

29 C.G. Boldt, Reedley, CA, "Started by the Migrants," letter to editor, *The Mennonite* 81, no. 23 (7 June 1966): 388.

30 Ibid.

31 James Isaak, Reedley, CA, "State the Grape Facts," letter to editor, *The Mennonite* 81, no. 23 (7 June 1966): 388.

32 Note from editor, *The Mennonite* 81, no. 23 (7 June 1966): 388.

33 United Farm Workers, "Chronology," http://clnet.ucla.edu/research/chavez/chronology/ (accessed 7 October 2010).

34 Loewen and Nolt, *Seeking Places of Peace*, 191.

35 Ted Koontz, "Peace Section Involvement in the Farm Labor Situation," 26 March 1974, Mennonite Church USA archives, Goshen, IN, Mennonite Central Committee, Peace and Social Concerns Committee, IX–7–12, Farm Workers (1974–1975), Box 9 File 28.

36 Lupe de Leon was "the first Hispanic in a prominent place in a Mennonite agency." Flores, "Hispanic Mennonites in North America," 73.

37 For a brief description of how the California farm labour problem contributed to the MCC's creation of the Mennonite Conciliation Service, see Miller, "A History of the Mennonite Conciliation Service, International Conciliation Service, and Christian Peacemaker Teams," 8–9.

38 Ted Koontz, "Peace Section Involvement in the Farm Labor Situation," 26 March 1974.

39 In addition to Phil Hofer, the group included Egon Hofer, Richard Hofer, and Stanley Warkentin, all from the Fresno-Reedley area. It is not known if the Hofers were related to each other.

40 Memo from Ted Koontz, 17 January 1974, Mennonite Church USA archives, Goshen, IN, Mennonite Central Committee, Peace Section Reports IX–7–12, Farm Workers 1973–1976, Series 3 Box 7 Folder 24.

41 Ibid. Jonathan Nathan asserts that there is "no indication that Mennonite farmers were among those who took up arms" and that "this rumor was never substantiated and was almost certainly not true." Clearly, although Nathan consulted the Goshen archives, he did not come across Ted Koontz's memo. Nathan, "*Buena Gente, Jefes Duros*," 12 footnote 30.

42 Ted Koontz, "Peace Section Involvement in the Farm Labor Situation," 26 March 1974.

43 Letter from Lynn Roth, MCC Akron, to Alvin Peters, Reedley, CA, 22 February 1974, Mennonite Church USA archives, Goshen, IN, MCC West Coast Office, Reedley, CA, 1947–84, IX–54, Farm Workers Labor Issues, 1974, Pronto 4 File 20.

44 Brunk was also a well-known tent revivalist, and as such would have appealed to the evangelical nature of the Mennonite Brethren majority in California.

45 Letter from Lynn Roth, MCC Akron, to Alvin Peters, Reedley, CA, 22 February 1974.

46 After the 1974 MCC delegation to California had returned, Koontz delivered a warning to Goshen College professor J.R. Burkholder, who was planning study tours to the region for Goshen students: "I don't feel that

Alvin Peters would be the most helpful farmer to work with directly." Letter from Ted Koontz to J.R. Burkholder, 2 April 1974, Mennonite Church USA archives, Goshen, IN, Mennonite Central Committee, Peace and Social Concerns Committee collection, IX–7–12, Farm Workers (1974–1975), Box 9 File 28.

47 Some Mennonite Brethren believed that MCC emphasized social justice at the expense of evangelism. Letter from [Phil Hofer], Pacific College, Fresno, CA, to Ted Koontz, MCC Peace Section, 26 February 1974, Mennonite Church USA archives, Goshen, IN, Mennonite Central Committee, Peace Section Reports IX–7–12, Farm Workers 1973–1976, Series 3 Box 7 Folder 24.

48 Letter from Paul Toews, Pacific College, to Ted Koontz, MCC Peace Section, 26 February 1974, Mennonite Church USA archives, Goshen, IN, Mennonite Central Committee, Peace Section Reports IX–7–12, Farm Workers 1973–1976, Series 3 Box 7 Folder 24.

49 Letter from Leo L. Miller, First Mennonite Church, Reedley, CA, to Harold Regier, MCC Peace and Social Concerns secretary, 5 March 1974, Mennonite Church USA archives, Goshen, IN, Mennonite Central Committee, Peace Section Reports IX–7–12, Farm Workers 1973–1976, Series 3 Box 7 Folder 24. A copy of this document is also contained in Mennonite Church USA archives, Goshen IN, MCC West Coast Office, Reedley, CA, 1947–84, IX–54, Farm Workers Labor Issues, 1974, Pronto 4 File 20.

50 Letter from Leo L. Miller, First Mennonite Church, Reedley, CA, to Harold Regier, MCC Peace and Social Concerns secretary, 5 March 1974.

51 Letter from Allen Linscheid to William T. Snyder, 4 March 1974, Mennonite Church USA archives, Goshen, IN, MCC West Coast Office, Reedley, CA, 1947–84, IX–54, Farm Workers Labor Issues, 1974, Pronto 4 File 20.

52 "It is my opinion that for you to come at this point, without an invitation by persons asking for your services and to begin discussions with various individuals would very rapidly reflect negatively on all of MCC services … To make an offer of any kind of assistance to one side, at this time, would only be detrimental." Letter from Lynn Roth to Ted Koontz, 25 February 1974, Mennonite Church USA archives, Goshen, IN, Mennonite Central Committee, Peace Section Reports IX–7–12, Farm Workers 1973–1976, Series 3 Box 7 Folder 24. A copy of this document is also contained in Mennonite Church USA archives, Goshen, IN, MCC West Coast Office, Reedley, CA, 1947–84, IX–54, Farm Workers Labor Issues, 1974, Pronto 4 File 20.

53 Ted Koontz, "Peace Section Involvement in the Farm Labor Situation," 26 March 1974.

54 Letter from [Ted] Koontz, MCC Peace Section, to [William] Snyder, MCC executive office, 6 March 1974, Mennonite Church USA archives, Goshen, IN, Mennonite Central Committee, Peace Section Reports IX–7–12, Farm Workers 1973–1976, Series 3 Box 7 Folder 24.

55 In 2010, Lynn Roth worked as executive director of Eastern Mennonite University's Center for Justice and Peacebuilding. In response to my emailed request for his memories of the delegation, he replied that he was "not sure" he was a member "although the record might say something different! I was more the local facilitator." Personal correspondence with the author, 11 October 2010.

56 I asked to interview Phil Hofer, who was still living in California in 2010, about his experiences with this delegation. He declined, explaining that he was "not in fact a member of that mission" but was "a facilitator." He had grown up in central California and thus was asked to facilitate the group's visit, but he "had nothing to do with" the reports by Koontz and others that were generated afterward. Personal correspondence with the author, 29 April 2010.

57 "Mennonites Explore Farm," news release by Ted Koontz, associate executive secretary of MCC Peace Section, 12 April 1974, Mennonite Church USA archives, Goshen, IN, Mennonite Central Committee, Peace Section Reports IX–7–12, Farm Workers 1973–1976, Series 3 Box 7 Folder 24. A copy of this document is also available in Mennonite Church USA archives, Goshen, IN, MCC West Coast Office, Reedley, CA, 1947–84, IX–54, Reedley Monthly, 1969–1975, Pronto 4 File 33, "Farm Labor Issue Explored," *Reedley Monthly* 89, June 1974.

58 Ibid.

59 Ibid.

60 Ibid.

61 Canadian Mennonite periodicals almost completely ignored California's migrant farm worker problems. A search of *The Canadian Mennonite,* the *Mennonite Brethren Herald,* the *Mennonite Reporter,* and the *Mennonite Mirror* uncovered only one article on the subject, written by Phil Hofer in the *Herald* in August 1975. In it, Hofer (who had participated in the 1974 MCC delegation to Fresno-Reedley) discusses the passage of the Agricultural Labor Relations Act in May 1975 that allowed California's farm workers to unionize. Hofer notes that California Mennonites were "surprise[d]" by the "swift and aggressive way" the legislation was passed. While many farmers welcomed the legislation, others worried "that it might result in a union being forced on their permanent workers by temporary workers who do not understand the sense of loyalty and concern

the family farmers have for their workers." Phil Hofer, "California Passes Farm Labor Laws," *Mennonite Brethren Herald* 14, no. 17 (22 August 1975): 24.

62 Lois Barrett Janzen, "The Dialog That Hasn't Begun," *The Mennonite* 89, no. 20 (14 May 1974): 316–17.

63 Harold Regier, "Finding a Role for the Outsider," *The Mennonite* 89, no. 20 (14 May 1974): 328.

64 Ibid.

65 John Swarr, Washington, DC, letter to editor, *The Mennonite* 89, no. 28 (23 July 1974): 462.

66 Froese, "'Is Anabaptism Here a Joke?'"; Froese, *California Mennonites,* 212–30; Hinojosa, *Latino Mennonites,* 136–41. Hinojosa's and Froese's references are, to my knowledge, the only scholarly mentions of these visits, apart from a one-page mention in Miller's "A History of the Mennonite Conciliation Service, International Conciliation Service, and Christian Peacemaker Teams," 8–9, and a single sentence in Schlabach's *War, Peace and Social Conscience*, 475. Neither Kreider and Goossen's *Hungry, Thirsty, A Stranger* nor the four-volume *The Mennonite Central Committee Story,* edited by Dyck with Kreider and Lapp, contains any account. Nor does Falcón's *The Hispanic Mennonite Church in North America*, although prejudice within the Mennonite community is addressed in a general way.

67 Beth Sutter's Labor Study Diary, 1974, Mennonite Church USA archives, Goshen, IN, Guy F. Hershberger collection, Hist. Mss 1–171, California UFW, Box 28 File 2.

68 Ibid.

69 John R. Burkholder, "What Ought Goshen College Be Doing?," appendix to minutes of meeting on "United Farmworker-Grower Issues," Goshen College, 5 August 1974, Mennonite Church USA archives, Goshen, IN, Guy F. Hershberger collection, Hist. Mss 1–171. At this same meeting, MBCM suggested that Mennonite church agencies should establish voluntary service projects "with special concern for agricultural laborers" on the West Coast. They also proposed that a conference on Christian community relations be held in Fresno, sponsored by MCC, the Mennonite Community Association, the Christians in Business Association, and the Mennonite Economic Development Associates. Minutes of meeting on "United Farmworker-Grower Issues," Goshen College, 5 August 1974.

70 See letter from Guy Hershberger to Hertzler regarding Mennonite media coverage of Chavez: letter from Guy Hershberger to Daniel Hertzler, Mennonite Publishing House, Scottdale, PA, 1974, Mennonite Church

USA archives, Goshen, IN, Guy F. Hershberger collection, Hist. Mss1–171, California UFW correspondence, Box 28 File 1.

71 Dan Hertzler, "The Christian and the United Farm Workers: A Case Study in Ethical Decision-Making," 20 January 1975, Mennonite Church USA archives, Goshen, IN, Guy F. Hershberger collection, Hist. Mss1–171, California UFW, Miscellaneous background material etc., Box 28 File 4.

72 See, for example, Philemon 1:8–9a (NIV): "Therefore, although in Christ I could be bold and order you to do what you ought to do, yet I prefer to appeal to you on the basis of love."

73 Letter from William Longenecker to Paul Leatherman, 29 April 1974, Mennonite Central Committee archives, Goshen, IN, Mennonite Central Committee Peace and Social Concerns Committee collection, IX–7–12, Farm Workers (1974–1975), Box 9 File 28.

74 Barger and Reza, *The Farm Labor Movement in the Midwest*, 55, 57, 238.

75 Letter from William Longenecker to Paul Leatherman, 29 April 1974.

76 Joyce Schumacher, farmer, TNT Farms, interview by author, Pandora, Ohio, 6 November 2009.

77 Jeff Boehr, assistant campus pastor for church relations, Bluffton University, interview by author, Bluffton, Ohio, 27 October 2009.

78 George Lehman, chair of Business Studies, Bluffton University, interview by author, Bluffton, Ohio, 27 October 2009.

79 It is not clear whether this man was a relative of Alvin Peters or whether Weaver Sommer misremembered the name and it was actually Alvin Peters himself (as I suspect) who spoke at the debate.

80 Sally Weaver Sommer, vice president and dean of academic affairs, Bluffton University, interview by author, Bluffton, Ohio, 4 November 2009.

81 "TFS's CMC Centennial History, draft 1," 137, Mennonite Church USA archives, Goshen, IN, Theron F. Schlabach, Hist. Mss 1–544, College Mennonite History, 2003, Box 42 File 1.

82 Theron Schlabach, professor emeritus of history, Goshen College, interview by author, Goshen, Indiana, 18 November 2009; "TFS's CMC Centennial History, draft 1," 138.

83 "TFS's CMC Centennial History, draft 1," 138–41. See also Hinojosa, *Latino Mennonites*, 127–30.

CHAPTER FOUR

1 See Portelli, "The Peculiarities of Oral History"; Grele, "On Using Oral History Collections"; Freund, "Oral History as Process-Generated Data";

Strobel, "Becoming a Historian, Being an Activist, and Thinking Archivally."

2 Letter from William T. Snyder, MCC executive secretary, to Mr and Mrs Reuben C. Nikkel, Reedley, CA, 17 July 1974, Mennonite Church USA archives, Goshen, IN, MCC West Coast Office, Reedley, CA, 1947–84, IX–54, Farm Workers Labor Issues, 1974, Pronto 4 File 20.

3 Hinojosa notes, "Siding with the farmworkers would have alienated a small but wealthy segment of Mennonite growers who often gave large donations to the work of church missions and service work through such parachurch organizations as the Mennonite Central Committee (MCC)." Hinojosa, *Latino Mennonites*, 124–5.

4 Letter from J. Winfield Fretz to Cal[vin] Redekop, 8 September 1975, Mennonite Church USA archives, Goshen, IN, MCC Peace and Social Concerns Committee collection, IX–7–12, Farm Workers (1973–1976), Box 7 File 24.

5 Letter from Ken Neufeld, MCC West Coast director, to J. Winfield Fretz, 7 October 1975, Mennonite Church USA archives, Goshen, IN, MCC Peace and Social Concerns Committee collection, IX–7–12, Farm Workers (1973–1976), Box 7 File 24.

6 Letter from Ted Koontz to Paul Leatherman, 19 December 1973, Mennonite Church USA archives, Goshen, IN, MCC Peace and Social Concerns Committee collection, IX–7–12, Farm Workers (1973–1976), Box 7 File 24.

7 Ted Koontz, "Report to the MCC Peace Section on Conversations in California Regarding the Farm Labor Situation," 12–16 March 1974, Mennonite Church USA archives, Goshen, IN, Guy F. Hershberger collection, Hist. Mss.1–171, California UFW correspondence, Box 28 File 1. A copy of this document is also found in Mennonite Church USA archives, Goshen, IN, MCC Peace and Social Concerns Committee collection, IX–7–12, Farm Workers (1973–1976), Box 7 File 24.

8 Ibid.

9 Ibid.

10 Guy F. Hershberger, "Supplement to Ted Koontz Report to the MCC Peace Section," 18 April 1974. This supplement was marked "not for publication." Mennonite Church USA archives, Goshen IN, MCC Peace and Social Concerns Committee collection, IX–7–12, Farm Workers (1973–1976), Box 7 File 24.

11 Ibid.

12 Letter from Harold R. Regier to Leo Miller, Reedley, CA, 1 May 1974, Mennonite Church USA archives, Goshen, IN, MCC Peace and Social

Concerns Committee collection, IX–7–12, Farm Workers (1973–1976), Box 7 File 24.

13 Letter from Harold Regier to Jake Froese (Phoenix, AZ), Phil Hofer (Fresno, CA), and Lynn Roth (Fresno, CA), 1 May 1974, Mennonite Church USA archives, Goshen IN, MCC Peace and Social Concerns Committee collection, IX–7–12, Farm Workers (1973–1976), Box 7 File 24.

14 Letter from Harold Regier to Guy Hershberger, 1 May 1974, Mennonite Church USA archives, Goshen, IN, Guy F. Hershberger collection, Hist. Mss 1–171, California UFW correspondence, Box 28 File 1.

15 Harold Regier, "Report on California Farmer/Worker Issue, Reedley/Fresno and Vicinity Visit, March 12–16, 1974," March 1974, Mennonite Church USA archives, Goshen, IN, Guy F. Hershberger collection, Hist. Mss 1–171, California UFW correspondence, Box 28 File 1. A copy of this document is also found in Mennonite Church USA archives, Goshen IN, MCC Peace and Social Concerns Committee collection, IX–7–12, Farm Workers (1973–1976), Box 7 File 24.

Harold R. Regier, "California Farmer/Worker Issue: Some Reflections," 15 April 1974, Mennonite Church USA archives, Goshen, IN, Guy F. Hershberger collection, Hist. Mss 1–171, California UFW correspondence, Box 28 File 1. A copy of this document is also found in Mennonite Church USA archives, Goshen IN, MCC Peace and Social Concerns Committee collection, IX–7–12, Farm Workers (1973–1976), Box 7 File 24.

16 Harold Regier, "Report on California Farmer/Worker Issue, Reedley/Fresno and Vicinity Visit, March 12–16, 1974," March 1974.

17 Ibid.

18 Ibid.

19 Ibid.

20 Harold R. Regier, "California Farmer/Worker Issue: Some Reflections," 15 April 1974.

21 Ibid.

22 Letter from Ted Koontz to J.R. Burkholder, 2 April 1974, Mennonite Church USA archives, Goshen IN, MCC Peace and Social Concerns Committee collection, IX–7–12, Farm Workers (1974–1975), Box 9 File 28.

23 Ibid.

24 Ibid.

25 Ibid.

26 Ibid.

27 Ibid. Koontz concluded, "I trust you will be discreet about sharing this letter since this is a rather sensitive issue."

28 Letter from J. Richard Burkholder, Goshen College, to Ted Koontz, MCC Akron, 13 April 1974, Mennonite Church USA archives, Goshen, IN, MCC Peace and Social Concerns Committee collection, IX–7–12, Farm Workers (1973–1976), Box 7 File 24.

29 Letter from Guy Hershberger to Daniel Hertzler, Mennonite Publishing House, Scottdale, PA, 19 April 1974, Mennonite Church USA archives, Goshen, IN, Guy F. Hershberger collection, Hist. Mss. 1–171, California UFW correspondence, Box 28 File 1.

30 Letter from Stanley Bohn, Peace and Social Concerns Secretary, to pastors in California, Texas, Ohio, Indiana, Arizona, and to Central and Pacific Districts Peace and Service Committee members, 17 October 1967, Bluffton University Archives, 3–C–d–4, Central District Conference, Peace, Service & Justice Committee, Box 1, Correspondence 1967.

31 Ibid. Bohn also contacted a Connecticut insurance company that held a controlling interest in a California citrus operation that was opposing the UFW: "After checking as carefully as I could I feel UFW is trying to help workers get a fair wage. Is Connecticut Mutual Life aware of the problem and what its funds might be doing to people who are willing to work their way out of poverty if given a chance?" Letter from Stanley Bohn, Chair of Commission on Home Ministries, to Edward Bates, Connecticut Mutual Life Insurance, 27 April 1977, Bluffton University Archives, 3–C–d–4, Central District Conference, Peace, Service & Justice Committee, Box 1, Minutes/Correspondence 1976–1977.

32 See Hinojosa, *Latino Mennonites,* 184–90.

33 Teodoro Chapa Jr, Lupe De Leon Jr, and Naftali Torres Jr, "Task Force Report to the Spanish *Concilio* of the Mennonite Church on the Farmworker Issue in California," July 1974, Mennonite Church USA archives, Goshen, IN, MCC Peace and Social Concerns Committee collection, IX–7–12, Farm Workers (1973–1976), Box 7 File 24.

34 Ibid.

35 Ibid.

36 Ibid.

37 *Guidelines for Today* was an independent Mennonite publication, published in Johnstown, Pennsylvania and founded in 1965. The magazine advocated that Mennonites avoid active public participation in politics and social justice causes. It merged with another independent Mennonite periodical with a similar outlook, *The Sword and Trumpet,* under that magazine's name in 1990. Wenger and Steiner, "Fellowship of Concerned Mennonites"; Burkholder, "Peace."

38 Letter from Lupe De Leon Jr to the editor of *Guidelines for Today,* 14 February 1974, Mennonite Church USA archives, Goshen, IN, MCC Peace and Social Concerns Committee collection, IX–7–12, Farm Workers (1973–1976), Box 7 File 24.

39 Lupe De Leon, Jr, "The Farm Workers' Issue," *Gospel Herald* (18 June 1974): 500–1, Mennonite Church USA archives, Goshen, IN, MCC West Coast Office, Reedley, CA, 1947–84, IX–54, Farm Workers Labor Issues, 1974, Pronto 4 File 20. A copy of this document is also found in Mennonite Church USA archives, Goshen, IN, MCC Peace and Social Concerns Committee collection, IX–7–12, Farm Workers (1973–1976), Box 7 File 24.

40 Letter from Ted Koontz to Lupe De Leon, 3 April 1974, Mennonite Church USA archives, Goshen, IN, MCC Peace and Social Concerns Committee collection, IX–7–12, Farm Workers (1973–1976), Box 7 File 24.

41 Ibid.

42 Memo from Ken Neufeld, MCC Regional Office Reedley, CA, to Paul Longacre, Lynn Roth, and Ted Koontz, 13 September 1974, Mennonite Church USA archives, Goshen, IN, MCC Peace and Social Concerns Committee collection, IX–7–12, Farm Workers (1973–1976), Box 7 File 24.

43 Letter from Lupe De Leon Jr, Mennonite Board of Missions associate secretary, to Ken Neufeld, 26 September 1974, Mennonite Church USA archives, Goshen, IN, MCC Peace and Social Concerns Committee collection, IX–7–12, Farm Workers (1973–1976), Box 7 File 24.

44 Hinojosa, *Latino Mennonites,* 114–15, 135–6.

45 Statement presented to MASA leadership and membership, 22 August 1975, Mennonite Church USA archives, Goshen, IN, MCC Peace and Social Concerns Committee collection, IX–7–12, Farm Workers (1973–1976), Box 7 File 24.

46 Ibid.

47 Nathan instead interviewed acquaintances of his California Mennonite relatives, but "still had trouble finding many who worked in my target time frame and were still alive and interested in talking about it." Nathan, "*Buena Gente, Jefes Duros,*" 3.

48 Although not the subject of this book, readers may be interested in some of the literature on growers' treatment of migrant labour and the history of the UFW. See, for example, Bardacke, *Trampling Out the Vintage*; Garcia, *From the Jaws of Victory*; Adler, McBane, and Winegarden, "Talking Farmwork Blues."

49 Jones and Osterud, "Breaking New Ground," 557. Anthropologist Warren D. Anderson documents some of the difficulties of recording the oral

histories of migrant workers in his own research of more than two decades. See Anderson, "Oral History and Migrant Wage Labor."

50 Steve Penner, pastor, First Mennonite Church of Reedley, interview by author, Reedley, CA, 26 April 2010.

51 Gordon Wiebe, owner, Wiebe Farms, interview by author, Reedley, CA, 28 April 2010.

52 Duane Ruth-Heffelbower, director, Center for Peacemaking and Conflict Studies, Fresno Pacific University, interview by author, Fresno, CA, 1 May 2010.

53 Dennis Fast, senior pastor, Reedley Mennonite Brethren Church, interview by author, Reedley, CA, 4 May 2010.

54 Duane Ruth-Heffelbower, interview by author.

55 Lynn Jost, president, Mennonite Brethren Biblical Seminary, interview by author, Fresno, CA, 11 May 2010.

56 Eugene Enns, board chair, WesPak, interview by author, Dinuba, CA, 3 May 2010.

57 Zemon Davis and Starn, eds., "Introduction," 2.

58 Felipe Hinojosa argues that these events are evidence of the Mennonite churches' efforts to appease wealthy church members at the expense of non-whites. Hinojosa, *Latino Mennonites,* 138–45.

59 Citing an unpublished paper by Jonathan Nathan, Hinojosa states that although "many Mennonite growers were known as 'kind and compassionate' employers they also had the reputation of being 'some of the hardest-driving and miserly employers in California farming.'" Hinojosa, *Latino Mennonites,* 136.

60 Sheftel and Zembrzycki, "Only Human," 204.

61 Vinitzky-Seroussi and Teeger, "Unpacking the Unspoken," 1104.

62 Ibid., 1105, 1117.

63 Ibid., 1117.

64 Layman, "Reticence in Oral History Interviews," 210.

65 Ibid., 216, 227.

66 Portelli, *The Order Has Been Carried Out*, 3.

67 Anna Sheftel and Stacey Zembrzycki observe that "oral historians have the habit of writing most about the interviewees with whom they really connected." Sheftel and Zembrzycki, "Only Human," 200.

68 K'Meyer and Crothers, "'If I See Some of This in Writing, I'm Going to Shoot You.'"

69 For these reasons, and because the interview participants opted not to remain anonymous on their interview consent forms, I have decided that it is not an ethical violation to name the interview participants discussed in

this chapter. Sheftel and Zembrzycki criticize K'Meyer and Crothers for privileging their research agenda over their interviewee's comfort, and for naming the interviewee. Sheftel and Zembrzycki, "Only Human," 213n37.

70 Ibid., 207–8.

71 K'Meyer and Crothers, "'If I See Some of This in Writing, I'm Going to Shoot You,'" 91.

72 Sheftel and Zembrzycki, "Only Human," 209.

73 Hasian and Frank, "Rhetoric, History, and Collective Memory," 98.

74 Ibid., 99.

75 James, *Doña María's Story*, 128.

CHAPTER FIVE

1 James, *Doña María's Story*, 128.

2 Chaired by H.D. Woods from 1964 through 1978, the committee's purpose was to review existing labour legislation. Woods was an economics professor, director of the Industrial Relations Centre at McGill University, and subsequently dean of arts and sciences at McGill.

3 "Highlights of Manitoba's New Labour Relations Act," 15 September 1972, Manitoba Archives, L0045 Labour Department, Assistant Deputy Minister's Files, GR 1990, Box 16, Location B–10–2–20, Notes – The Labour Relations Act, 1972.

4 "Background Information re General Provisions and Trends in Industrial Relations Legislation in Canada, Appendix: Recent Changes in Labour Relations Legislation," June 1971, Manitoba Archives, L0045 Labour Department, Assistant Deputy Minister's Files, GR 1990, Box 16, Location B–10–2–20, Notes – The Labour Relations Act, 1972.

5 Supreme Court Justice Ivan Rand created the Rand Formula (or automatic dues check-off) in arbitration ending the 1945 Windsor Ford strike. It requires payment of union dues by all workers, ensuring that no one receives union benefits without paying for them ("no free rides"). It also granted exemption from union membership and redirection of union dues to charity for those who objected to unions on religious grounds. The Canada Labour Code applied only to workers in industries under federal control, such as (for example) transportation and communications.

6 Amos 3:3.

7 "Plymouth Brethren Object to Proposed Labor Laws," *Winnipeg Free Press*, 13 July 1972, 7.

8 "Government Backs off on Bill," *Winnipeg Free Press*, 18 July 1972, 7.

9 "Union Exemption Granted," *Winnipeg Free Press*, 22 July 1971, 4.

10 Letter to the author from Colin Robinson, Chairperson of the Manitoba Labour Board, Winnipeg, Manitoba, 3 April 2013.

11 "Applications to the Board under Section 68(3) of the Labour Relations Act," [1976], Manitoba Archives, LM 0005 Labour and Manpower, Deputy Minister's Office – Office Files, GR 458, Box 70, Location I-7-6-16, The Labor Relations Act, 1972–1976.

12 Decision of Labour Relations Board in the matter of Chris Vander Nagel, Applicant, and United Steelworkers of America, Certified Bargaining Agent Agreement Holder, and Dominion Bridge Company Limited, Employer, 10 August 1973. Courtesy of Harold Jantz.

13 G[erald] V[anderzande], "Manitoba Labour Board Rejects Charity Clause Application," typescript, n.d. Courtesy of Harold Jantz.

14 Ibid.

15 Letter from David G. Newman of Newman, MacLean to Gerald Vandezande, CJL Foundation, 14 August 1973. Courtesy of Harold Jantz.

16 Letter from Gerald Vandezande to David G. Newman, 27 August 1973. Courtesy of Harold Jantz.

17 Letter from Newman to Vandezande, 30 August 1973. Courtesy of Harold Jantz.

18 Letter from Vandezande to Newman, 18 September 1973. Courtesy of Harold Jantz.

19 Letter from Vandezande to Newman, 6 May 1974. Courtesy of Harold Jantz.

20 Regehr, *Mennonites in Canada, 1939–1970*, 185.

21 Cowie, *Stayin' Alive*, 2, 363; Black and Silver, "Labour in Manitoba: Facing the 1990s," in *Hard Bargains*, 5; Heron, *The Canadian Labour Movement*, 94.

22 Letter from Harold Jantz to Dudley Magnus, *Winnipeg Free Press*, n.d. Courtesy of Harold Jantz.

23 "Testimony of Hilda Friesen and Trudy Barkman, given before the Manitoba Labour Board on April 16, 1974," typescript. Courtesy of Harold Jantz.

24 Letter from Robert Banman, MLA, to A.R. Paulley, Minister of Labour, 28 May 1974. Courtesy of Harold Jantz. "Banman Defends Nurses," *Steinbach Carillon*, 5 June 1974, 1.

25 "Union Opposed; Probe Sought," *Winnipeg Free Press*, 30 May 1974, 17.

26 Ibid.

27 Harold Jantz wrote to an MLA, "I would hope that someone would point out the irony of putting such legislation before the house while blatantly disregarding right in a case such as these [Mennonite] nurses." Letter from Harold Jantz to Robert Banman, MLA, 3 June 1974. Courtesy of Harold Jantz.

28 "Nurses Centre of Rights Debate," *Winnipeg Free Press*, 6 June 1974, 38. Courtesy of Harold Jantz.

29 CJL offered to allow two or three Mennonites to sit as observers on their board: "We all welcome closer contact and cooperation with MCC with regard to basic policy questions." Letter from Gerald Vandezande to Larry Kehler, editor of *The Mennonite,* 15 January 1976. Courtesy of Harold Jantz.

30 MCC Manitoba, Peace and Social Concerns Committee meeting minutes, 13 April 1976. Courtesy of Harold Jantz.

31 Letter from Harold Jantz to Robert Banman, MLA, 3 June 1974. Courtesy of Harold Jantz.

32 Letter from John H. Redekop to Arthur Driedger, 5 April 1976. Courtesy of Harold Jantz.

33 For a detailed description of these seminars, see chapter 5 of Thiessen, *Manufacturing Mennonites*.

34 Letter from Arthur Driedger to John H. Redekop, 22 December 1975. Courtesy of Harold Jantz.

35 "A Christian Response to Labor-Management Confrontation," advertisement, n.d. Courtesy of Harold Jantz.

36 Letter from Larry Kehler, editor of *The Mennonite,* to Peter H. Peters, Diedrich J. Gerbrandt, and Harold Jantz, 4 December 1974. Courtesy of Harold Jantz.

37 Letter from Harold Jantz to friends of the *Mennonite Brethren Herald,* 18 December 1974. Courtesy of Harold Jantz.

38 Letter from A.R. Paulley, minister of labour, to Peter H. Peters, chair of MCC Manitoba, 27 January 1975. Courtesy of Harold Jantz.

39 Harold Jantz, "Labour Board Rejects Conscientious Objector," *Mennonite Mirror* 4, no. 2 (November 1974): 11.

40 Ibid., 11–12.

41 Dudley Magnus, "The Labor Scene: A Conscientious (Union) Objector," *Winnipeg Free Press*, 29 March 1975, 30.

42 Ibid.

43 Scott Edmonds, "Religious Belief Valid Reason to Stay Out of Union, Court," *Winnipeg Free Press*, 6 January 1976, 1.

44 "The Right to Stay Out," *Winnipeg Free Press*, 8 January 1976, 31.

45 Scott Edmonds, "Religion-Union Case Studied; May Appeal," *Winnipeg Free Press*, 7 January 1976, 1.

46 After his dismissal from McGavin Toastmaster, Funk found work as a teacher at Brightstone Hutterite Colony. Ibid.

47 Letter from Gerald Vandezande to Rev. Arie Van Eek, 12 January 1976. Courtesy of Harold Jantz.

48 "The Right to Stay Out," *Winnipeg Free Press*, 8 January 1976, 31.

49 Harold Jantz, "Henry Funk Ruling Has Upset Government, Unions," letter to the editor, *Winnipeg Free Press*, 15 January 1976, 24.

50 Ibid.

51 Ibid.

52 Letter from Gerald Vandezande, executive director CJL Foundation, to Harold Jantz and Larry Kehler, 26 April 1976. Courtesy of Harold Jantz.

53 Letter from David G. Newman of Newman, MacLean to Gerald Vandezande, 20 April 1976. Courtesy of Harold Jantz.

54 Letter from H.H. Barkman to Harold Jantz, 27 April 1976. Courtesy of Harold Jantz.

55 Letter from Harold Jantz to H.H. Barkman, 9 June 1976. Courtesy of Harold Jantz.

56 Ibid.

57 "Applications to the Board under Section 68(3) of the Labour Relations Act," [1976], Manitoba Archives, LM 0005 Labour and Manpower, Deputy Minister's Office – Office Files, GR 458, Box 70, Location I–7–6–16, The Labor Relations Act, 1972–1976.

58 Ruling of Manitoba Labour Board re Gertrude Miriam Friesen, applicant, Swan River Valley Nurses' Association, certified bargaining agent – respondent, Swan River Valley Hospital District No. 1, employer, 30 April 1976, Manitoba Archives, LM 0005 Labour and Manpower, Deputy Minister's Office – Office Files, GR 458, Box 70, Location I–7–6–16, The Labor Relations Act, 1972–1976.

59 Friesen arranged to send the equivalent of union dues to the Swan River branch of the Red Cross. She had been employed for ten years as a casual worker but was required to join the union only when she became a permanent part-time worker, thus prompting her Labour Board application. "Nurse Gets Union Exemption," *Winnipeg Free Press*, 26 May 1976, 3; "Nurse Granted Union Exemption," *Steinbach Carillon News*, 26 May 1976. Courtesy of Harold Jantz.

60 When Friesen received a bill from David Newman for $505.75 for his services, she wrote Jantz, asking if MCC would help pay. Letter from Gertrude Friesen to Harold Jantz, 9 May 1976. Courtesy of Harold Jantz.

61 Letter from J.M.P. Korpesho, Labour Board Office, to Gordon Henry Dyck, Winnipeg, re ruling of Manitoba Labour Board re Gordon Henry Dyck, applicant, United Steelworkers of America Local 8283, certified bargaining agent and agreement holder, International Harvester Canada, employer, 27 May 1976, Manitoba Archives, LM 0005 Labour and

Manpower, Deputy Minister's Office – Office Files, GR 458, Box 70, Location I–7–6–16, The Labor Relations Act, 1972–1976.

62 "Nurse Granted Union Exemption," *Steinbach Carillon News*, 26 May 1976. Courtesy of Harold Jantz.

63 Gertrude Friesen, personal account of her labour board hearing, manuscript, 9 May 1976. Courtesy of Harold Jantz.

64 Ibid.

65 Ibid.

66 Letter from Gertrude Friesen to Harold Jantz, 8 June 1976. Courtesy of Harold Jantz.

67 Letter from Gerald Vandezande to Rev. Arie Van Eek, 12 January 1976.

68 Letter from Gerald Vandezande to MCC Peace and Social Concerns Committee, 15 December 1975. Courtesy of Harold Jantz.

69 "Submission of the Manitoba Labour-Management Review Committee to the Minister of Labour re Possible Changes in Manitoba's Labour Legislation," 20 April 1976, Manitoba Archives, LM 0005 Labour and Manpower, Deputy Minister's Office – Office Files, GR 458, Box 70, Location I–7–6–16, The Labor Relations Act, 1972–1976.

70 Memo from A.R. Paulley to Premier Edward Schreyer and all cabinet ministers, 30 March 1976, Manitoba Archives, LM 0005 Labour and Manpower, Deputy Minister's Office – Office Files, GR 458, Box 70, Location I–7–6–16, The Labor Relations Act, 1972–1976.

71 Ibid.

72 "Union Objectors Get Gov't Concession," *Winnipeg Tribune*, 11 June 1976. Courtesy of Harold Jantz.

73 Mennonite Brethren News Service, "Amendment Weakens Conscience Clause," 4 June 1976. Courtesy of Harold Jantz.

74 Ibid.

75 Letter from Arthur Driedger, executive director MCC Manitoba, to Hardy G. Enns, 21 July 1976. Courtesy of Harold Jantz. The churches spent $1,395 to place the ads; the equivalent expenditure in 2013 dollars would be $5,600. Bank of Canada, *Inflation Calculator*, http://www.bankofcanada.ca/rates/related/inflation-calculator/, using Statistics Canada, *Consumer Price Indexes for Canada, Monthly, 1914–2006* (V41690973 series).

76 The ad was published in the *Winnipeg Free Press*, 8 June 1976, 8, and the *Winnipeg Tribune*, 9 June 1976, 7.

77 "Statement of Concern Regarding Proposed Repeal of Section 68(3), Manitoba Labour Relations Act," *Winnipeg Tribune*, 9 June 1976, 7. Courtesy of Harold Jantz.

78 "Conscience Clause Disputed," *Winnipeg Free Press*, 7 June 1976, 2.
79 Paul Stanway, "Proposed Labor Act Changes Spark Objections," *Winnipeg Free Press*, 8 June 1976. Courtesy of Harold Jantz.
80 Untitled news release, Winnipeg Civil Liberties Association (WCLA), n.d. Courtesy of Harold Jantz. WCLA president Norman Naylor, pastor of First Unitarian Universalist Church of Winnipeg, performed the first same gender marriage in Canada.
81 Arlene Bilinkoff, "Under the Dome," *Winnipeg Free Press*, 8 June 1976, 17.
82 Manitoba Department of Labour, "Summary of Legislative Changes Recommended by Interested Parties re Review of Manitoba's Labour Legislation," January 1975, Manitoba Archives, LM 0005 Labour and Manpower, Deputy Minister's Office – Office Files, GR 458, Box 70, Location I–7–6–16, The Labor Relations Act, 1972–1976.
83 Bilinkoff, "Under the Dome," 17. Christophe later became president of United Food and Commercial Workers Local 832.
84 Stanway, "Proposed Labor Act."
85 MCC Manitoba Peace and Social Concerns Committee, "Draft Statement: Conscientious Objectors in Labour Unions," n.d. [17 December 1974], 1–2. Courtesy of Harold Jantz.
86 Ibid., 4.
87 Ibid., 4–6.
88 Ibid., 9.
89 Ibid., 12.
90 Mennonite Central Committee (Manitoba), "Statement Regarding Conscientious Objectors and Labour Unions," Manitoba Archives, LM 0005 Labour and Manpower, Deputy Minister's Office – Office Files, GR 458, Box 70, Location I–7–6–16, The Labor Relations Act, 1972–1976
91 Ibid.
92 Bilinkoff, "Under the Dome," 17.
93 "Conscience Clause Disputed," *Winnipeg Free Press*, 7 June 1976, 2.
94 "Human Rights Questions Loom over Labor Changes," *Winnipeg Tribune*, 7 June 1976. Courtesy of Harold Jantz.
95 Ibid. While the *Tribune* report suggests Jantz and Green disagreed with each other, the *Free Press* claimed that Green "believed the objection [to union membership] had merit." Bilinkoff, "Under the Dome," 17.
96 "An Abridgement of Freedom," *Winnipeg Free Press*, 9 June 1976, 49, reprinted as "An Abridgement of Freedom," *Steinbach Carillon*, 16 June 1976, 1:4.
97 Ibid.

98 Paul Stanway, "'Conscience' Union Exemption Intact as Govt. Backtracks," *Winnipeg Free Press*, 11 June 1976, 3.

99 John D. Stoesz, pastor of the Winkler Mennonite Brethren Church, letter to editor, *Winnipeg Free Press*, 30 August 1975, 39. Stoesz was pastor to some of the nurses in question.

100 Ibid.

101 Kenneth P. Regier, Q.C., "What Kind of Example Do We Have from NDP on Human Rights?" letter to the editor, *Mennonite Mirror* 6, no. 1 (October 1976): 23.

102 Ibid.

103 Herb Schulz, assistant to the premier, "Conscientious Objections: The Government View," letter to the editor, *Mennonite Mirror* 6, no. 1 (October 1976): 22.

104 See footnote 5 for a definition of the Rand Formula.

105 Schulz, "Conscientious Objections: The Government View," 22–3.

106 Roy Vogt, "Our Word," *Mennonite Mirror* 6, no. 1 (October 1976): 21.

107 Ibid.

108 Roy Vogt, "Strikes Symbolize Union Power but You Wield Power Too!" *Mennonite Mirror* 4, no. 8 (May 1975): 7.

109 Vogt cited the Sermon on the Mount on resisting evil and American (Old) Mennonite theologian Guy Hershberger's *The Way of the Cross in Human Relations* in support. Ibid.

110 Ibid., 8.

111 Ibid.

112 Ibid.

113 "Summary of Amendments to the Labour Relations Act," 16 September 1976, Manitoba Archives, LM 0005 Labour and Manpower, Deputy Minister's Office – Office Files, GR 458, Box 70, Location I-7-6-16, The Labor Relations Act, 1972–1976.

114 A.R. Paulley, "Notes for Opening Statement, Second Reading of a Bill to Amend the Labour Relations Act," June 1976, Manitoba Archives, LM 0005 Labour and Manpower, Deputy Minister's Office – Office Files, GR 458, Box 70, Location I-7-6-16, The Labor Relations Act, 1972–1976.

115 Memo from R.H. Tallin, legislative counsel, to A.R. Paulley, minister of labour, 17 May 1976, Manitoba Archives, LM 0005 Labour and Manpower, Deputy Minister's Office – Office Files, GR 458, Box 70, Location I-7-6-16, The Labor Relations Act, 1972–1976.

116 See footnote 5 of this chapter for a definition of the Rand Formula.

117 Harold Jantz, former editor of *Mennonite Brethren Herald*, interview by author, Winnipeg, Manitoba, 20 November 2012.

118 Letter from Harold Jantz to Gerald Vandezande, 21 July 1976. Courtesy of Harold Jantz.
119 Letter from Harold Jantz to Ed Vanderkloet, 21 July 1976. Courtesy of Harold Jantz.
120 Harold Jantz, interview by author.
121 Ibid.
122 Ibid. Jantz also attributed the loss of interest in labour issues, particularly for Mennonites, to reduced venues for public debate: Mennonite "church papers have less space." When he had been editor, the *Mennonite Brethren Herald* was published weekly; as a monthly publication in the twenty-first century, "it has about half the space or maybe slightly more ... to carry the stories ... that it had when I was there." And church leadership has taken a stronger editorial role since the 1970s: "we've forced a certain focus on our papers that wasn't there when I was editor ... We were interested in a wider range of issues."
123 Peter H. Peters, former chair of Mennonite Central Committee Manitoba, interview by author, Winnipeg, Manitoba, 25 November 2014.
124 Part of the reason for the change in his stance, Peters noted, was his dismissal from employment as principal of Mennonite Brethren Collegiate Institute for his support of the theory of evolution. This action led to his decision to leave the MBs for the GCs.
125 Larry Kehler, former editor of *The Canadian Mennonite,* interview by author, Winnipeg, Manitoba, 3 December 2014.
126 Polishuk, "Secrets, Lies, and Misremembering," 52.
127 See the discussion of this and similar challenges in Yow, "'Do I Like Them Too Much?'" 73–8.
128 Kehler was appointed general secretary of the Conference of Mennonites in Canada in 1981. Mennonite Heritage Centre, fonds description for Conference of Mennonites in Canada – General Board – Executive secretary files, http://www.mennonitechurch.ca/programs/archives/holdings/organizations/CMC_Series/CMC.A.03.htm.
129 Fewer than two dozen applications under Section 68(3) were filed (including by non-Mennonites); the Manitoba Mennonite population in 1971 was 59,555. Friesen, *Building Communities*, 118 Table 15.

CHAPTER SIX

1 The Mennonite Community Movement of the 1940s and 1950s in the United States advocated just such an approach to employment. See Schlabach, *War, Peace and Social Conscience*, 165–216.

2 "Anna," pseudonym for anonymous interview participant.
3 Ibid.
4 Ibid.
5 Ibid.
6 Ibid.
7 Ibid.
8 Ibid.
9 Ibid.
10 Some scholars distinguish between religion and spirituality, equating the former with institutions and the latter with nonhierarchical approaches. See, for example, Grant, O'Neil, and Stephens, "Neosecularization and Craft versus Professional Religious Authority in a Nonreligious Organization."
11 See, for example, Weber, *The Protestant Ethic and the Spirit of Capitalism*; Redekop and Bender, *Who Am I? What Am I?*; Marshall, *A Kind of Life Imposed on Man*; Coombs and Nemeck, *Called by God*; Volf, *Work in the Spirit*.
12 Graber Miller, *Living Faith*, 13.
13 Ibid., 44–5.
14 *Our Daily Bread* is a Christian religious daily devotional guide, produced by Radio Bible Class (RBC) Ministries since 1956.
15 "Barbara," pseudonym for anonymous interview participant.
16 Ibid.
17 Ibid.
18 Arterburn and Felton, *Toxic Faith*.
19 "Barbara," pseudonym for anonymous interview participant.
20 Ibid.
21 Ibid.
22 Ibid.
23 Ibid.
24 Wuthnow, *After Heaven*.
25 Ammerman, "Organized Religion in a Voluntaristic Society," 203.
26 Ibid., 204.
27 Ibid., 205.
28 Ibid., 206.
29 Ibid.
30 Ibid., 208.
31 Ibid., 209.
32 "Dan," pseudonym for anonymous interview participant.
33 Ibid.

34 Ibid.
35 Umble, "Goshen College (Goshen, Indiana, USA)"; Juhnke, *Vision, Doctrine, War*, 265–9.
36 "Clara," pseudonym for anonymous interview participant.
37 Ibid.
38 Ibid.
39 Joyce Rupp is an author of popular Christian books.
40 "Clara," pseudonym for anonymous interview participant.
41 Ibid.
42 Ibid.
43 Ibid.
44 See, for example, Orsi, *Between Heaven and Earth*, and Opp, *The Lord for the Body*.
45 Dean, Brandes, and Dharwadkar, "Organizational Cynicism," 345–6.
46 Graber Miller, "Transforming Vocation," 46.
47 In fairness, Graber Miller is not speaking of religious employers in this quotation. The problem of religious employers who do not live up to their own religious claims is not addressed.
48 Loewen and Nolt, *Seeking Places of Peace*, 43; Bender and Stauffer Hostetler, "Mennonite Church (MC)"; Kaufman and Poettcker, "General Conference Mennonite Church (GCM)"; Lohrenz and Janz, "Canadian Conference of Mennonite Brethren Churches."
49 Grant, O'Neil, and Stephens, "Spirituality in the Workplace," 266.
50 The potential for religious hierarchy to fade as churches decline in membership may be overstated here. The power of evangelical Christian para-church organizations, such as Campus Crusade for Christ, does not appear to be diminishing any time soon, and these organizations are in many ways more authoritarian.
51 Mirvis, "'Soul Work' in Organizations," 198.
52 Ibid.

CONCLUSION

1 The "nones" are those who do not identify with any religion; the "dones" are those who identify as Christian but are "done" with church participation. See, for example, Pew Research Center, "'Nones' on the Rise"; Schultz, "The Rise of the Dones"; Packard and Hope, *Church Refugees*.
2 Roll, "The Christian Spirit beyond the Gilded Age," 28.
3 The Almanac Singers, "Talking Union," *Talking Union and Other Union Songs*, Smithsonian Folkways Records, 1941.

4 Joe Friesen, "'It's not That the Tories Are Closer to God," 184.
5 McGuire, *Lived Religion*, 186.
6 Roof, "Religion and Narrative," 307.
7 K'Meyer, "'I Just Felt Called ... ,'" 733.
8 Ibid.
9 Secularization theory, popular in the late twentieth century, argues that levels of religiosity are declining. More recently, sociologists have argued that it is not religiosity but religious *authority* that is in decline (a process known as neosecularization). D. Martin, *On Secularization*; Wilson, *Religion in Secular Society*; Stark, "Secularization, R.I.P."; Lechner, "The Case against Secularization"; Hadden, "Toward Desacralizing Secularization Theory"; Dobbelaere, "Bryan Wilson's Contributions to the Study of Secularization"; Chaves, "Secularization as Declining Religious Authority"; Yamane, "Secularization on Trial"; Swatos and Christiano, "Secularization Theory"; Grant, O'Neil, and Stephens, "Neosecularization and Craft versus Professional Religious Authority in a Nonreligious Organization"; Pollack, "Religiousness Inside and Outside the Church in Selected Post-Communist Countries in Central and Eastern Europe."
10 Knoblauch, "Europe and Invisible Religion," 270–1. Knoblauch explains Luckmann's distinction between small, intermediate, and great transcendences of experience: small ones involve space and time, such as the assumption that objects from which we turn away will still be there when we turn back; intermediate ones "cannot be experienced directly" such as one's "inner life"; great ones are not experienced directly but also are "not part of the ordinary reality of everyday life," such as "dreams, ecstasy, meditation" (269).
11 Ibid.
12 Ibid.
13 Roman Williams, "Space for God," 258.
14 K'Meyer, "'I Just Felt Called ... ,'" 724–5.
15 Orsi, *Between Heaven and Earth*, 18.
16 Ibid.
17 K'Meyer, "'I Just Felt Called ... ,'" 726.
18 Gans, "Symbolic Ethnicity and Symbolic Religiosity."
19 Lindsay and Smith, "Accounting by Faith."
20 Nadesan, "The Discourses of Corporate Spiritualism and Evangelical Capitalism."
21 Graber Miller, *Living Faith*, 78.
22 Ibid., 81–2.
23 See, for example, the history of intra-Mennonite class conflict in nineteenth-century Russia in Urry, *None but Saints*.

24 Mortimer, *Where There's a Will*, 47.
25 This process is described in more detail in this book's introduction. Von Plato, "Contemporary Witnesses and the Historical Profession."
26 Demerath, "The Varieties of Sacred Experience," 4.
27 Hewitt, "Observer Response," 102–3.

Bibliography

PRIMARY SOURCES

Government Documents

Government of Canada
Statistics Canada, Labour Statistics Division
Government of Manitoba
Labour Department, Assistant Deputy Minister's Files
Labour Department, Deputy Minister's Files
Government of the United States
Department of Labor, Bureau of Labor Statistics

Manuscripts: Public and Church Archives

Bluffton University Archives (Bluffton, Ohio)
Central District Conference, Peace, Service & Justice Committee collection, 3–C–d–4
Mennonite Church USA Archives (Goshen, Indiana)
Guy F. Hershberger collection, Hist. Mss 1–171
MCC Peace Section Reports, IX–7–12
MCC Peace and Social Concerns Committee collection, IX–7–12
MCC West Coast Office collection, IX–54
Theron F. Schlabach collection, Hist. Mss 1–544
Mennonite Historical Society of British Columbia (Abbotsford, British Columbia)
Mennonite Central Committee collection, 160.3

Private collections

Harold Jantz (Winnipeg, Manitoba)

Interviews

Anonymous interviews are not listed.
Occupation listed is at the time of the interview. All interviews were conducted by the author.

Bender, Jim. Manager of industrial design for a high technology company. Waterloo, Ontario, 7 October 2009
Boehr, Jeff. Assistant campus pastor for church relations at Bluffton University. Bluffton, Ohio, 27 October 2009
Bohn, Charles (Chuck). Manager of Reedley Lumber. Reedley, California, 30 April 2010
Bontrager, Wilbur. Chief executive officer of Jayco (manufacturer of recreational vehicles and motorhomes). Middlebury, Indiana, 11 November 2009
Bontreger, Ruby. Bed-and-breakfast owner. Middlebury, Indiana, 20 November 2009
Bontreger, Thomas (Tom). Truck driver and bed-and-breakfast owner. Middlebury, Indiana, 20 November 2009
Braun, William (Bill). Pastor of College Community Church in Clovis, California. Fresno, California, 23 April 2010
Brown, Darcie. Photographer. Abbotsford, British Columbia, 3 December 2009
Brubaker, Donald. Former social work professor. Bluffton, Ohio, 26 October 2009
Burkholder, J. Lawrence. Former professor and college president. Goshen, Indiana, 13 November 2009
Burkholder, Myrna. Remedial education consultant. Goshen, Indiana, 13 November 2009
Chappell, Barbara. Health clinic worker. Bluffton, Ohio, 27 October 2009
Chappell, Terry. Medical doctor. Bluffton, Ohio, 30 October 2009
Chappell-Dick, Wendy. Self-employed and director of MennoFolk. Bluffton, Ohio, 3 November 2009
Coleman, Marianne. Nursing home caregiver. Kitchener, Ontario, 17 October 2009
Cornelsen, Erwin. Woodworker and former pastor. Vancouver, British Columbia, 9 December 2009

Dirks, Teresa (Terry). Teacher. Winnipeg, Manitoba, 14 September 2009

Draper, Barb. Teacher. Waterloo, Ontario, 18 October 2009

Dueck, Allan. Principal of Bethany Christian Schools. Goshen, Indiana, 18 November 2009

Eichorn, Barbara. Administrative assistant. Goshen, Indiana, 20 November 2009

Eidse, Kenton. Employment counsellor. Winnipeg, Manitoba, 13 March 2010

Enns, Eugene. Board chair of WesPak (fruit grower and distributor). Dinuba, California, 3 May 2010

Enns, Melvin. General manager of WesPak (fruit grower and distributor). Dinuba, California, 23 April 2010

Epp, Stefan. Research associate with the University of Manitoba Environmental Conservation Lab. Winnipeg, Manitoba, 19 March 2010

Erb, Vernon. President and chair of the Erb Group (commercial trucking). New Hamburg, Ontario, 14 October 2009

Fast, Dennis. Senior pastor of Reedley Mennonite Brethren Church. Reedley, California, 4 May 2010

Friesen, Art. Medical doctor. Abbotsford, British Columbia, 5 December 2009

Friesen, Marlyce. Medical doctor. Abbotsford, British Columbia, 5 December 2009

Friesen, Paul. Shelving and equipment clerk at University of Winnipeg Library. Winnipeg, Manitoba, 10 March 2010

Giesbrecht, David. Former head librarian of Columbia Bible College. Abbotsford, British Columbia, 2 December 2009

Giesbrecht, Ted. Lawyer. Kitchener, Ontario, 8 October 2009

Giesbrecht, Theodora (Dora). Former bookkeeper and business manager. Winnipeg, Manitoba, 14 September 2009

Gingerich, James. Medical doctor. Goshen, Indiana, 19 November 2009

Graber Miller, Keith. Professor of Bible, religion, and philosophy at Goshen College. Goshen, Indiana, 18 November 2009

Harnish, Steve. Professor of mathematics at Bluffton University. Bluffton, Ohio, 23 October 2009

Heidebrecht Thiessen, Karen. Pastor of Level Ground Community Church. Abbotsford. British Columbia, 4 December 2009

Hiebert-Rempel, Lily. Mennonite Central Committee Low German program coordinator. Kitchener, Ontario, 15 October 2009

Houshower, Hans. Professor of anthropology and vice president for advancement at Bluffton University. Bluffton, Ohio, 3 November 2009

Houshower, Linda. Nurse and co-owner of natural foods store. Bluffton, Ohio, 5 November 2009

Hunsberger, Brian. Former development director of Kitchener House of Friendship. Waterloo, Ontario, 15 October 2009

Ibele, Ellen. Supply teacher. Waterloo, Ontario, 8 October 2009

Isaak, Elsie. Former university instructor and program director. Surrey, British Columbia, 11 December 2009

Isaak, John. Former university instructor and program director. Surrey, British Columbia, 11 December 2009

Jantz, Harold. Former editor of *Mennonite Brethren Herald*. Winnipeg, Manitoba, 20 November 2012

Janzen, Jonathan. Pastor of Highland Community Church. Abbotsford, British Columbia, 30 November 2009

Jost, Lynn. President of Mennonite Brethren Biblical Seminary. Fresno, California, 11 May 2010

Kehler, Larry. Former editor of *The Canadian Mennonite*. Winnipeg, Manitoba, 3 December 2014

Kingsley, Mitchell. Lawyer and village council member. Bluffton, Ohio, 26 October 2009

Kingsley, Phillip. Former psychology professor. Bluffton, Ohio, 28 October 2009

Kirkton, James. Principal of Goshen High School. Goshen, Indiana, 20 November 2009

Klassen, David (Dave). Truck driver, farmer, and mechanic. Abbotsford, British Columbia, 5 December 2009

Langhofer, Dennis. Dean of the School of Business, Fresno Pacific University. Fresno, California, 4 May 2010

Lederach, Lisa. Elementary school principal. Goshen, Indiana, 16 November 2009

Lehman, George. Chair of Business Studies at Bluffton University. Bluffton, Ohio, 27 October 2009

Mast, Gerald. Communications professor at Bluffton University. Bluffton, Ohio, 4 November 2009

Millar, Blaine. Addictions counsellor. Kitchener, Ontario, 13 October 2009

Miller, Roger. Hydraulic levelling systems sales. Goshen, Indiana, 21 November 2009

Nafziger, Lowell. Former co-owner, Leatherman Supply. Goshen, Indiana, 19 November 2009

Neufeld Weaver, Laurel. Professor of social work at Bluffton University. Bluffton, Ohio, 23 October 2009

Paulley, Valerie. Riverview Health Centre patient care manager and former chemical technologist. Winnipeg, Manitoba, 27 March 2010

Penner, Ed. Dentist. Surrey, British Columbia, 12 December 2009

Penner, Stephen (Steve). Pastor of First Mennonite Church of Reedley. Reedley, California, 26 April 2010.

Peters, Henry. Former meat-packer. Winnipeg, Manitoba, 16 March 2010

Peters, Peter H. Former chair of Mennonite Central Committee Manitoba. Winnipeg, Manitoba, 25 November 2014

Purves, Christine. Former professor of music at Bluffton University. Bluffton, Ohio, 28 October 2009

Ramseyer, Alice. Former teacher and missionary. Bluffton, Ohio, 5 November 2009

Ramseyer, Robert. Former missionary and professor. Bluffton, Ohio, 5 November 2009

Redekop, John. Former professor of political science at Trinity Western University. Abbotsford, British Columbia, 1 December 2009

Rich, Phillip (Phil). Owner of Ford dealership. Archbold, Ohio, 4 November 2009

Ring, Greg. Senior account executive in private brand sales at Cooper Tire and Rubber. Bluffton, Ohio, 29 October 2009

Rogalsky, John. Alternative education school principal. Reedley, California, 30 April 2010

Roth, John. Professor of history at Goshen College and editor of *Mennonite Quarterly Review*. Goshen, Indiana, 21 November 2009

Roth, Ruth. Elementary school teacher. Goshen, Indiana, 21 November 2009

Roth, Wilbur. Former auto worker. Kitchener, Ontario, 12 October 2009

Ruth-Heffelbower, Duane. Director of the Center for Peacemaking and Conflict Studies at Fresno Pacific University. Fresno, California, 1 May 2010

Schlabach, Theron. Former professor of history at Goshen College. Goshen, Indiana, 18 November 2009

Schumacher, Joyce. Owner of TNT Farms. Pandora, Ohio, 6 November 2009

Schumacher, Tom. Owner of TNT Farms. Pandora, Ohio, 6 November 2009

Showalter, Anna. Student. Goshen, Indiana, 17 November 2009

Sommers Rich, Elaine. Former professor at Bluffton University. Bluffton, Ohio, 29 October 2009

Spallinger, Randall (Randy). Engineer at Ford Motor Company. Bluffton, Ohio, 6 November 2009

Stednick, Emily. Mennonite Central Committee worker. Fresno, California, 7 May 2010

Thiessen, Steve. Chief executive officer of Communitas Supportive Care Society. Abbotsford, British Columbia, 3 December 2009

Thomas, Everett. City councillor and editor of *The Mennonite*. Goshen, Indiana, 12 November 2009

Troyer, Anna. Wife of James Troyer. Manistique, Michigan, 25 October 2009

Troyer, James (Jim). Former school guidance counsellor. Manistique, Michigan, 25 October 2009

Weaver Sommer, Sally. Vice-president and dean of academic affairs at Bluffton University. Bluffton, Ohio, 4 November 2009

Webster, Steven. Adult and graduate education representative at Bluffton University. Bluffton, Ohio, 2 November 2009

Welty, Lavon. Manager of Habitat for Humanity. Lima, Ohio, 5 November 2009

Wiebe, Gordon. Owner of Wiebe Farms. Reedley, California, 28 April 2010

Yoder, Carl. Former Sauder employee and former small business owner. Goshen, Indiana, 18 November 2009

Yoder, James. Social worker. Goshen, Indiana, 16 November 2009

Yoder, Richard. Former factory worker. Goshen, Indiana, 19 November 2009

Zickafoose, Jordan. Mennonite Central Committee worker. Fresno, California, 7 May 2010

Newspapers and Periodicals

The Canadian Mennonite

Forbes

Huffington Post

The Mennonite

Mennonite Brethren Herald

Mennonite Mirror

Mennonite Reporter

National Post

New York Times

The New Yorker

Statistics Canada *Perspectives*

Steinbach Carillon

Winnipeg Free Press

Winnipeg Tribune

SECONDARY SOURCES

Adler, Lynn, Margo McBane, and Mary Winegarden. "Talking Farmwork Blues: An Account of the Early Years of California Farm Labor." KPFA Berkeley Pacifica Radio, PRA Archive AZ0373, 4 December 1979

Akyeampong, Ernest B. "A Statistical Portrait of the Trade Union Movement." Statistics Canada *Perspectives* (Winter 1997): 45–54

Ammerman, Nancy T., "Organized Religion in a Voluntaristic Society." *Sociology of Religion* 58, no. 3 (1997): 203–15

– ed. *Everyday Religion: Observing Modern Religious Lives.* New York: Oxford University Press, 2007

– and Wade Clark Roof, eds. *Work, Family, and Religion in Contemporary Society.* New York: Routledge, 1995

Anderson, Henry Pope. *The Bracero Program in California.* New York: Arno Press, 1976

Anderson, Warren D. "Oral History and Migrant Wage Labor: Sources of Narrative Distortion." *The Oral History Review* 28, no. 2 (Summer–Autumn 2001): 1–20

Arterburn, Stephen, and Jack Felton. *Toxic Faith: Experiencing Healing from Painful Spiritual Abuse.* Colorado Springs, CO: Shaw Books, 2001

Baer, Douglas, Edward Grabb, and William Johnston. "The Values of Canadians and Americans: A Rejoinder." *Social Forces* 69, no. 1 (September 1990): 273–7

Baker, Robert J. "Should Mennonite Teachers Strike?" *Festival Quarterly* (August–October 1982): 8

Bardacke, Frank. *Trampling Out the Vintage: Cesar Chavez and the Two Souls of the United Farm Workers.* London: Verso, 2011

Barger, W.K., and Ernesto M. Reza. *The Farm Labor Movement in the Midwest: Social Change and Adaptation among Migrant Farmworkers.* Austin: University of Texas Press, 1994

Barling, Julian, E. Kevin Kelloway, and Eric H. Bremermann. "Preemployment Predictors of Union Attitudes: The Role of Family Socialization and Work Beliefs." *Journal of Applied Psychology* 76, no. 5 (1991): 725–31

Bender, Harold S., and Beulah Stauffer Hostetler. "Mennonite Church (MC)." *Global Anabaptist Mennonite Encyclopedia Online* (January 2013). http://www.gameo.org/encyclopedia/contents/M4661oME.html (accessed 7 October 2015)

Black, Errol, and Jim Silver, eds. *Hard Bargains: The Manitoba Labour Movement Confronts the 1990s.* Winnipeg: Manitoba Labour Education Centre, n.d.

Bourdieu, Pierre. *Language and Symbolic Power.* Cambridge, MA: Harvard University Press, 1991

Bracero History Archive. http://braceroarchive.org/ (accessed 7 October 2015)

Burke, Peter. *Varieties of Cultural History.* Ithaca: Cornell University Press, 1997

Burkholder, John R. "Peace." *Global Anabaptist Mennonite Encyclopedia Online,* 1989. http://www.gameo.org/encyclopedia/contents/P4ME.html (accessed 14 September 2010)

Butler, Jon. "Jack-in-the-Box Faith: The Religion Problem in Modern American History." *The Journal of American History* 90, no. 4 (March 2004): 1357–78

Calavita, Kitty. *Inside the State: The Bracero Program, Immigration, and the I.N.S.* New York: Routledge, 1992

Carty, R.K., ed. *Politics, Policy, and Government in British Columbia.* Vancouver: University of British Columbia Press, 1996

Chang, Tracy F.H. "A Structural Model of Race, Gender, Class, and Attitudes toward Labor Unions." *The Social Science Journal* 40 (2003): 189–200

Chaves, Mark. "Secularization as Declining Religious Authority." *Social Forces* 72, no. 3 (March 1994): 749–74

Christian Labour Association of Canada. http://www.clac.ca/ (accessed 7 October 2015)

Christie, Nancy, and Michael Gauvreau, eds. *Cultures of Citizenship in Postwar Canada, 1940–1955.* Montreal: McGill-Queen's University Press, 2003

– *A Full-Orbed Christianity: The Protestant Churches and Social Welfare in Canada, 1900–1940.* Montreal: McGill-Queen's University Press, 1996

Conway, J.F. "Canada and the US: What Makes Us Different? A Response to Seymour Martin Lipset." *Labour/Le Travail* 28 (Fall 1991): 311–21

Conzen, Kathleen Neils, David A. Gerber, Ewa Morawska, George E. Pozzetta, and Rudolph J. Vecoli. "The Invention of Ethnicity: A Perspective from the USA." *Journal of American Ethnic History* 12, no. 1 (Fall 1992): 3–41

Coombs, Marie Theresa, and Francis Kelly Nemeck. *Called by God: A Theology of Vocation and Lifelong Commitment.* Eugene, OR: Wipf and Stock, 2001

Cowie, Jefferson. *Stayin' Alive: The 1970s and the Last Days of the Working Class.* New York: The New Press, 2010

Cox, Harvey. *The Secular City: Secularization and Urbanization in Theological Perspective*. New York: Macmillan, 1965

Cullum, Linda K. *Narratives at Work: Women, Men, Unionization, and the Fashioning of Identities*. St John's, NL: Institute of Social and Economic Research, 2003

Curtis, James E., Steven D. Brown, Ronald D. Lambert, and Barry J. Kay. "Affiliating with Voluntary Associations: Canadian-American Comparisons." *The Canadian Journal of Sociology* 14, no. 2 (Spring 1989): 143–61

Daniel, Cletus E. *Bitter Harvest: A History of Californian Farmworkers, 1879–1994*. Ithaca: Cornell University Press, 1981

Dawley, Alan. *Struggles for Justice: Social Responsibility and the Liberal State*. Cambridge and London: Belknap Press, 1991

Dean, James W., Jr, Pamela Brandes, and Ravi Dharwadkar. "Organizational Cynicism." *Academy of Management Review* 23, no. 2 (April 1998): 341–52

Demerath, N.J., III. "The Varieties of Sacred Experience: Finding the Sacred in a Secular Grove." *Journal for the Scientific Study of Religion* 39, no. 1 (March 2000): 1–11

Dobbelaere, Karel. "Bryan Wilson's Contributions to the Study of Secularization." *Social Compass* 53, no. 2 (June 2006): 141–6

Dublin, Thomas. *When the Mines Closed: Stories of Struggles in Hard Times*. Ithaca: Cornell University Press, 1998

Dummitt, Christopher. *The Manly Modern: Masculinity in Postwar Canada*. Vancouver: University of British Columbia Press, 2007

Dyck, Cornelius J., ed., with Robert S. Kreider and John A. Lapp. *The Mennonite Central Committee Story*. 4 volumes. Scottdale, PA: Herald Press, 1980–81

Ens, Adolf. "Epp, Frank H. (1929–1986)." *Global Anabaptist Mennonite Encyclopedia Online*, 1990. http://www.gameo.org/encyclopedia/contents/E661ME.html (accessed 24 May 2011)

Ewy, Arnold C. "The Grape and Raisin Industry." *Mennonite Life* 5, no. 4 (October 1950): 4–9

Falcón, Rafael. *The Hispanic Mennonite Church in North America, 1932–1982*. Translated by Ronald Collins. Scottdale, PA and Kitchener, ON: Herald Press, 1986

– "Hispanic Mennonites." *Global Anabaptist Mennonite Encyclopedia Online*, 1989. http://www.gameo.org/encyclopedia/contents/H58ME.html (accessed 13 October 2010)

Faue, Elizabeth. "Retooling the Class Factory: United States Labour History after Marx, Montgomery, and Postmodernism." *Labour History* 82 (May 2002): 109–19

Fink, Leon. "Looking Backward: Reflections on Workers' Culture and Certain Conceptual Dilemmas within Labor History." In Leon Fink, *In Search of the Working Class: Essays in American Labor History and Political Culture*, 175–200, The Working Class in American History Series. Urbana and Chicago: University of Illinois Press, 1994

– *Workingmen's Democracy: The Knights of Labor and American Politics.* Urbana, Chicago, and London: University of Illinois Press, 1983

Flores, Gilberto. "Hispanic Mennonites in North America." *Mission Focus: Annual Review* 9 (2001). http://www.anabaptistwiki.org/mediawiki/images/e/e3/Vol._9_Flores,_Hispanic_Mennonites_in_North_America.pdf (accessed 13 October 2010)

Foner, Nancy. *In a New Land: A Comparative View of Immigration.* New York: New York University Press, 2005

Fones-Wolf, Ken. *Trade Union Gospel: Christianity and Labor in Industrial Philadelphia, 1865–1915.* Philadelphia: Temple University Press, 1989

Forsey, Eugene. *Trade Unions in Canada, 1812–1902.* Toronto: University of Toronto Press, 1982

Frager, Ruth. *Sweatshop Strife: Class, Ethnicity, and Gender in the Jewish Labour Movement of Toronto, 1900–1939.* Toronto: University of Toronto Press, 1992

– and Carmela Patrias. *Discounted Labour: Women Workers in Canada, 1870–1939.* Toronto: University of Toronto Press, 2005

Fraser, Brian J. *The Social Uplifters: Presbyterian Progressives and the Social Gospel in Canada, 1875–1915.* Waterloo, ON: Wilfrid Laurier University Press, 1988

Freeman, Richard B. "Do Workers Still Want Unions? More Than Ever." Economy Policy Institute Briefing Paper #182 (22 February 2007): 1–13

– and Joel Rogers. *What Workers Want.* Updated edition. Ithaca: ILR Press, 2006

Freund, Alexander. "Oral History as Process-Generated Data." *Historical Social Research/Historische Sozialforschung* 34, no. 1 (2009): 22–48

Friedman, Jeffrey, ed. *What Caused the Financial Crisis.* Philadelphia: University of Pennsylvania Press, 2011

Friesen, Joe. "'It's not That the Tories Are Closer to God, They're Furthest from the Devil': Politics and Mennonites in Winnipeg, 1945–1999." *Journal of Mennonite Studies* 21 (2003): 175–90

Friesen, John J. *Building Communities: The Changing Face of Manitoba Mennonites*. Winnipeg: CMU Press, 2007

Froese, Brian. *California Mennonites*. Baltimore: Johns Hopkins University Press, 2015

– "'Is Anabaptism Here a Joke?' California Mennonite Farmers, Labour Tensions, and Visitors from Eastern States, 1974." Paper presented at Canadian Historical Association annual meeting, University of Saskatchewan, 30 May 2007

Galarneau, Diane. "Unionized Workers." Statistics Canada *Perspectives* (Spring 1996): 43–52

Galarza, Ernesto. *Merchants of Labor: The Mexican Bracero Story: An Account of the Managed Migration of Mexican Farm Workers in California 1942–1960*. San Jose: Rosicrucian Press, 1964

Gans, Herbert. "Symbolic Ethnicity: The Future of Ethnic Groups and Cultures in America." *Ethnic and Racial Studies* 2 (January 1979): 1–20

– "Symbolic Ethnicity and Symbolic Religiosity: Towards a Comparison of Ethnic and Religious Acculturation." *Ethnic and Racial Studies* 17, no. 4 (1994): 577–92

Garcia, Matthew. *From the Jaws of Victory: The Triumph and Tragedy of Cesar Chavez and the Farm Worker Movement*. Berkeley: University of California Press, 2012

Gauvreau, Michael. *The Evangelical Century: College and Creed in English Canada from the Great Revival to the Great Depression*. Montreal: McGill-Queen's University Press, 1991

Geertz, Clifford. *The Interpretation of Cultures: Selected Essays*. New York: Basic Books, 1973

General Conference Mennonite Church and (Old) Mennonite Church. "Justice and the Christian Witness (General Conference Mennonite Church, Mennonite Church, 1983)," *Global Anabaptist Mennonite Encyclopedia Online* (1983). http://www.gameo.org/encyclopedia/contents/J8722.html (accessed 7 October 2015)

Gilmore, N. Ray, and Gladys W. Gilmore. "The Bracero in California." *Pacific Historical Review* 32, no. 3 (1963): 265–82

Goldfield, Michael, and Bryan D. Palmer. "Canada's Workers Movement: Uneven Developments." *Labour/Le Travail* 59 (Spring 2007): 149–78

Graber Miller, Keith. *Living Faith: Embracing God's Callings*. Telford, PA: Cascadia Publishing House, 2012

– "Transforming Vocation: A Mennonite Perspective." *Mennonite Quarterly Review* 83, no. 1 (January 2009): 29–48

Grant, Don, Kathleen M. O'Neil, and Laura S. Stephens. "Neosecularization and Craft versus Professional Religious Authority in a Nonreligious Organization." *Journal for the Scientific Study of Religion* 42, no. 3 (September 2003): 479–87

– "Spirituality in the Workplace: New Empirical Directions in the Study of the Sacred." *Sociology of Religion* 65, no. 3 (Autumn 2004): 265–83

Grele, Ronald. "On Using Oral History Collections: An Introduction." *The Journal of American History* 74, no. 2 (1987): 570–8

Guglielmo, Jennifer. *Living the Revolution: Italian Women's Resistance and Radicalism in New York City, 1880–1945*. Chapel Hill: University of North Carolina Press, 2010

Gutman, Herbert. *Power and Culture*. New York: Pantheon, 1988

– "Protestantism and the American Labor Movement: The Christian Spirit in the Gilded Age." *American Historical Review* 72, no. 1 (October 1966): 74–101

– *Work, Culture, and Society in Industrializing America*. New York: Alfred Knopf, 1976

Hackett, David G., Laurie F. Maffly-Kipp, R. Laurence Moore, and Leslie Woodcock Tentler. "Forum: American Religion and Class." *Religion and American Culture* 15, no. 1 (Winter 2005): 1–29

Hadden, Jeffrey K. "Toward Desacralizing Secularization Theory." *Social Forces* 65, no. 3 (March 1987): 587–611

Hall, David, ed. *Lived Religion in America*. Princeton: Princeton University Press, 1997

Halpern, Rick, and Roger Horowitz. *Meatpackers: An Oral History of Black Packinghouse Workers and Their Struggle for Racial and Economic Equality*. New York: Twayne, 1996

Harkin, Michael E. "Feeling and Thinking in Memory and Forgetting: Toward an Ethnohistory of the Emotions." *Ethnohistory* 50, no. 2 (Spring 2003): 261–84

Harman, Chris. *Zombie Capitalism: Global Crisis and the Relevance of Marx*. Chicago: Haymarket Books, 2010

Harvey, David. *The Condition of Postmodernity: An Enquiry into the Origins of Cultural Change*. New York: Blackwell, 1989

Hasian, Marouf, Jr, and Robert E. Frank. "Rhetoric, History, and Collective Memory: Decoding the Goldhagen Debates." *Western Journal of Communication* 63, no. 1 (Winter 1999): 95–114

Hearn, Mark, and Harry Knowles. "Struggling for Recognition: Reading the Individual in Labour History." *Labour History* 87 (November 2004): 1–10

Heron, Craig. *The Canadian Labour Movement: A Short History.* 2nd ed. Toronto: Lorimer, 1996

Hewitt, Marsha A. "Observer Response." *The Conrad Grebel Review* 17, no. 1 (Winter 1999): 99–103

Hinojosa, Felipe. *Latino Mennonites: Civil Rights, Faith, and Evangelical Culture*. Baltimore: Johns Hopkins University Press, 2014

Hoerder, Dirk. *Creating Societies: Immigrant Lives in Canada.* Montreal: McGill-Queen's University Press, 1999

– *Cultures in Contact: World Migrations in the Second Millennium.* Durham: Duke University Press, 2002

Honey, Michael Keith. *Black Workers Remember: An Oral History of Segregation, Unionism, and the Freedom Struggle.* Berkeley: University of California Press, 2000

Hoover, Kevin D. "Lost Causes." *Journal of the History of Economic Thought* 26, no. 2 (June 2004): 149–64

Houser, Rodney E. "Should They … ?" *Festival Quarterly* (August–October 1982): 9

Hughes, Gerald L. "Should They … ?" *Festival Quarterly* (August–October 1982): 9

Iacovetta, Franca. *Such Hardworking People: Italian Immigrants in Postwar Ontario.* Montreal: McGill-Queen's University Press, 1992

– Michael Quinlan, and Ian Radforth. "Immigration and Labour: Australia and Canada Compared." *Labour/Le Travail* 38 (Fall 1996) and *Labour History* 71 (November 1996): 90–115

– and Donna R. Gabaccia, eds. *Women, Gender, and Transnational Lives: Italy's Workers of the World.* Toronto: University of Toronto Press, 2002

James, Daniel. *Doña María's Story: Life History, Memory, and Political Identity.* Durham: Duke University Press, 2000

Jardine, Nick. "Whigs and Stories: Herbert Butterfield and the Historiography of Science." *History of Science* 41, part 2, no. 132 (June 2003): 125–40

Jones, Lu Ann, and Nancy Grey Osterud. "Breaking New Ground: Oral History and Agricultural History." *The Journal of American History* 76, no. 2 (September 1989): 551–64

Juhnke, James C. *Vision, Doctrine, War: Mennonite Identity and Organization in America, 1890–1930.* Scottdale, PA: Herald Press, 1989

Just, L.R., and Clayton Auernheimer. "California (USA)," *Global Anabaptist Mennonite Encyclopedia Online,* 1990. http://www.gameo.org/encyclopedia/contents/C2461.html (accessed 13 October 2010)

Kanagy, Conrad L. *Road Signs for the Journey: A Profile of Mennonite Church USA.* Scottdale, PA and Waterloo, ON: Herald Press, 2007

Kauffman, J. Howard, and Leland Harder. *Anabaptists Four Centuries Later: A Profile of Five Mennonite and Brethren in Christ Denominations.* Scottdale, PA: Herald Press, 1975

– and Leo Driedger. *The Mennonite Mosaic: Identity and Modernization.* With a foreword by Donald B. Kraybill. Scottdale, PA and Waterloo, ON: Herald Press, 1991

Kaufman, Edmund G., and Henry Poettcker. "General Conference Mennonite Church (GCM)," *Global Anabaptist Mennonite Encyclopedia Online* (November 2009). http://www.gameo.org/encyclopedia/contents/G4647ME.html (accessed 7 October 2015)

Kessler-Harris, Alice. *Gendering Labor History.* Urbana: University of Illinois Press, 2006

Klassen Neufeld, Kathryn. "Should They … ?" *Festival Quarterly* (August–October 1982): 9

Klempner, Mark. "Navigating Life Review Interviews with Survivors of Trauma." *Oral History Review* 27, no. 2 (Summer/Fall 2000): 67–83

Klix, Waylon, and Andrew Klager. "Central Heights Church (Abbotsford, British Columbia, Canada)." *Global Anabaptist Mennonite Encyclopedia Online,* November 2010. http://www.gameo.org/encyclopedia/contents/C45887.html (accessed 14 June 2011)

K'Meyer, Tracy E. "'I Just Felt Called … ': Oral History and the Meaning of Faith in American Religious History." *The Journal of American History* 86, no. 2 (September 1999): 724–33

– and A. Glenn Crothers. "'If I See Some of This in Writing, I'm Going to Shoot You': Reluctant Narrators, Taboo Topics, and the Ethical Dilemmas of the Oral Historian." *Oral History Review* 34, no. 1 (Winter/Spring 2007): 71–93

Knoblauch, Hubert. "Europe and Invisible Religion." *Social Compass* 50 (2003): 267–74

Krabill, Willard S. "Sexuality." *Global Anabaptist Mennonite Encyclopedia Online,* 1989. http://www.gameo.org/encyclopedia/contents/S493ME.html (accessed 10 August 2011)

Krahn, Cornelius. "San Joaquin Valley (California, USA)." *Global Anabaptist Mennonite Encyclopedia Online,* 1959. http://www.gameo.org/encyclopedia/contents/S2496.html (accessed 5 October 2010)

Kreider, Robert S., and Rachel Waltner Goossen. *Hungry, Thirsty, A Stranger: The MCC Experience.* Scottdale, PA and Kitchener, ON: Herald Press, 1988

Kroeker, Wally. "Mennonites and Unions," *The Mennonite* 4, no. 5 (6 February 2001): 4

– "We Think It Was a Good Move," *The Mennonite* 4, no. 5 (6 February 2001): 4

Laub, Dori, and Shoshana Felman. *Testimony: Crises in Witnessing in Literature, Psychoanalysis, and History.* New York: Routledge, 1992

Layman, Lenore. "Reticence in Oral History Interviews." *Oral History Review* 36, no. 2 (Summer/Fall 2009): 207–30

Lechner, Frank J. "The Case against Secularization: A Rebuttal." *Social Forces* 69, no. 4 (June 1991): 1103–19

Lindsay, D. Michael, and Bradley C. Smith. "Accounting by Faith: The Negotiated Logic of Elite Evangelicals' Workplace Decision-Making." *Journal of the American Academy of Religion* 78, no. 3 (September 2010): 721–49

Lipset, Seymour Martin. *Continental Divide.* New York and London: Routledge, 1990

– "Trade Union Exceptionalism: The United States and Canada." *Annals of the American Academy of Political and Social Science* 538 (March 1995): 115–30

– "Why No Socialism in the United States?" In *Sources of Contemporary Radicalism,* edited by Seweryn Bialer and Sophia Sluzer, 31–149. New York: Westview Press, 1977

– and Noah M. Meltz. *The Paradox of American Unionism: Why Americans Like Unions More Than Canadians Do, But Join Much Less.* Ithaca: Cornell University Press, 2004

Loewen, Royden. *Diaspora in the Countryside: Two Mennonite Communities and Mid-Twentieth-Century Rural Disjuncture.* Toronto: University of Toronto Press, 2006

– *Family, Church, and Market: A Mennonite Community in the Old and the New Worlds, 1850–1930.* Toronto: University of Toronto Press, 1993

– and Steven M. Nolt. *Seeking Places of Peace: Global Mennonite History Series: North America.* Intercourse, PA and Kitchener, ON: Good Books and Pandora Press, 2012

Lohrenz, J.H., and Harold Janz. "Canadian Conference of Mennonite Brethren Churches," *Global Anabaptist Mennonite Encyclopedia Online* (November 2012). http://www.gameo.org/encyclopedia/contents/C363ME.html (accessed 7 October 2015)

Lybeck, Johan A. *A Global History of the Financial Crash of 2007–10.* Cambridge: Cambridge University Press, 2011

Marks, Lynne. "Challenging Binaries: Working-Class Women and Lived Religion in English Canada and the United States." *Labor: Studies in Working-Class History of the Americas* 6, no. 1 (Spring 2009): 107–25

– "Heroes and Hallelujahs – Labour History and the Social History of Religion in English Canada: A Response to Bryan Palmer." *Histoire Sociale/Social History* 34, no. 67 (May 2001): 169–86

– *Revivals and Roller Rinks: Religion, Leisure, and Identity in Late-Nineteenth-Century Small-Town Ontario*. Toronto: University of Toronto Press, 1996

Marshall, Paul. *A Kind of Life Imposed on Man: Vocation and Social Order from Tyndale to Locke*. Toronto: University of Toronto Press, 1996

Martin, David. *On Secularization: Towards a Revised General Theory.* London: Ashgate, 2005

Martin, Ted. "Ontario Teachers and the Moral Obligation to Strike: A Partial Response to 'To Strike or Not to Strike.'" *The Conrad Grebel Review* 16, no. 1 (Winter 1998): 23–30

Mayer, Gerald. "Union Membership Trends in the United States." *Federal Publications,* Paper 174, 2004. http://digitalcommons.ilr.cornell.edu/key_workplace/174 (accessed 7 October 2015)

McCartin, Joseph A. "The Force of Faith: An Introduction to the Labor and Religion Special Issue." *Labor: Studies in Working-Class History of the Americas* 6, no.1 (Spring 2009): 1–4

McGuire, Meredith B. *Lived Religion: Faith and Practice in Everyday Life.* New York: Oxford University Press, 2008

Mendelsohn, Matthew, and Richard Nadeau. "The Religious Cleavage and the Media in Canada." *Journal of Political Science* 30, no. 1 (March 1997): 129–46

Miller, Joseph S. "A History of the Mennonite Conciliation Service, International Conciliation Service, and Christian Peacemaker Teams." In *From the Ground Up: Mennonite Contributions to International Peacebuilding*, edited by Cynthia Sampson and John Paul Lederach, 3–29. Oxford: Oxford University Press, 2000

Mirvis, Philip H. "'Soul Work' in Organizations." *Organization Science* 8, no. 2 (March–April 1997): 193–206

Mize, Ronald L., and Alicia C.S. Swords. *Consuming Mexican Labor: From the Bracero Program to* NAFTA. Toronto: University of Toronto Press, 2011

Montgomery, David. *Workers' Control in America: Studies in the History of Work, Technology, and Labor Struggles.* Cambridge: Cambridge University Press, 1979

Mortimer, John. *Where There's a Will.* London: Viking, 2003

Murphy, Theresa Anne. *Ten Hours Labor: Religion, Reform, and Gender in Early New England.* Ithaca: Cornell University Press, 1992

Nadesan, Majia Holmer. "The Discourses of Corporate Spiritualism and Evangelical Capitalism." *Management Communication Quarterly* 13, no. 1 (August 1999): 3–42

Nathan, Jonathan. "*Buena Gente, Jefes Duros*: The Relationship of Mennonite Farmers and the United Farmworkers Union in California." Unpublished undergraduate paper, Bethel College (North Newton, KS), 2008

Ngai, Mae. *Impossible Subjects: Illegal Aliens and the Making of Modern America.* Princeton: Princeton University Press, 2003

Nikkel, James R. "This Century's Journey of Evangelism for Canadian Mennonite Brethren." *Direction* 28, no. 2 (Fall 1999): 228–43

Opp, James. *The Lord for the Body: Religion, Medicine, and Protestant Faith Healing in Canada, 1880–1930.* Montreal: McGill-Queen's University Press, 2005

Orsi, Robert. *Between Heaven and Earth: The Religious Worlds People Make and the Scholars Who Study Them.* Princeton: Princeton University Press, 2006

– *The Madonna of 115th Street: Faith and Community in Italian Harlem, 1880–1950.* New Haven: Yale University Press, 1985

– *Thank You, St. Jude: Women's Devotion to the Patron Saint of Hopeless Causes.* New Haven: Yale University Press, 1996

Packard, Josh, and Ashleigh Hope. *Church Refugees.* Loveland, CO: Group Publishing, 2015

Palmer, Bryan D. "Historiographic Hassles: Class and Gender, Evidence and Interpretation." *Histoire Sociale/Social History* 33, no. 65 (May 2000): 105–44

Panagopoulos, Costas, and Peter L. Francia. "The Polls – Trends: Labor Unions in the United States." *Public Opinion Quarterly* 72, no. 1 (March 2008): 134–60

Parr, Joy. *The Gender of Breadwinners: Women, Men, and Change in Two Industrial Towns, 1880–1950.* Toronto: University of Toronto Press, 1990

Pasture, Patrick. "The Role of Religion in Social and Labour History." In van Voss and van der Linden, *Class and Other Identities*, 101–32.

Peachey, Urbane, ed. *Mennonite Statements on Peace and Social Concerns, 1900–1978.* Akron, PA: Mennonite Central Committee US Peace Section, 1980

Penner, Jordan. "Gaining a Voice: Hispanic Mennonites in America." Unpublished undergraduate paper, Bethel College (North Newton, KS), n.d.

Pew Research Center. "'Nones' on the Rise." 9 October 2012. http://www.pewforum.org/2012/10/09/nones-on-the-rise/ (accessed 5 January 2015)

Polishuk, Sandy. "Secrets, Lies, and Misremembering: Take II." *The Oral History Review* 32, no. 2 (Summer–Autumn 2005): 51–8

Pollack, Detlef. "Religiousness inside and outside the Church in Selected Post-Communist Countries in Central and Eastern Europe." *Social Compass* 50, no. 3 (2003): 321–34

Polland, Annie. "Working for the Sabbath: Sabbath in the Jewish Immigrant Neighborhoods of New York." *Labor* 6, no. 1 (Spring 2009): 33–56

Portelli, Alessandro. *The Order Has Been Carried Out: History, Memory, and Meaning of a Nazi Massacre in Rome*. New York: Palgrave Macmillan, 2003

– "The Peculiarities of Oral History." *History Workshop Journal* 12, no. 1 (1981): 96–107

– "What Makes Oral History Different." In *The Death of Luigi Trastulli and Other Stories: Form and Meaning in Oral History*, 45–58. Albany: State University of New York Press, 1991

Proudfoot, Wayne, and Phillip Shaver. "Attribution Theory and the Psychology of Religion." *Journal for the Scientific Study of Religion* 14, no. 4 (December 1975): 317–30

Rawlyk, George, ed. *The Canadian Protestant Experience, 1760–1990*. Burlington, ON: Welch, 1990

– *Ravished by the Spirit: Religious Revivals, Baptists, and Henry Alline*. Montreal: McGill-Queen's University Press, 1984

Redekop, Calvin, and Urie A. Bender. *Who Am I? What Am I? Searching for Meaning in Your Work*. Grand Rapids, MI: Academie Books, 1988

Redekop, John H. "Labor Unions." *Global Anabaptist Mennonite Encyclopedia Online*, 1989. http://www.gameo.org/encyclopedia/contents/L205ME.html (accessed 21 July 2011)

Regehr, T.D. *Mennonites in Canada, 1939–1970: A People Transformed*. Toronto: University of Toronto Press, 1996

Rempel, Elfrieda. "Mennonites Better Represented in the 'Status' Jobs." *Mennonite Mirror* 10, no. 9 (May 1981): 25–6

Resnick, Philip. *The Politics of Resentment: British Columbia Regionalism and Canadian Unity*. Vancouver: University of British Columbia Press, 2000

Richards, Lawrence. *Union-Free America: Workers and Antiunion Culture*. Champaign: University of Illinois Press, 2008

Roediger, David. *The Wages of Whiteness: Race and the Making of the American Working Class*. London and New York: Verso, 1991

Roll, Jarod. "The Christian Spirit beyond the Gilded Age." *Labor: Studies in Working-Class History of the Americas* 11, no. 2 (Summer 2014): 25–8

Roof, Wade Clark. *A Generation of Seekers: The Spiritual Journeys of the Baby Boom Generation.* New York: Harper Collins, 1993

– "Religion and Narrative: The 1992 RRA Presidential Address." *Review of Religious Research* 34, no. 4 (June 1993): 297–310

– *Spiritual Marketplace: Baby Boomers and the Remaking of American Religion.* Princeton: Princeton University Press, 1999

Rosswurm, Steve. "The Catholic Church and Left-Led Unions: Labor, Priests, Labor Schools, and the ACTU." In *The CIO's Left-Led Unions,* edited by Steve Rosswurm, 119–37. New Brunswick, NJ: Rutgers University Press, 1992

Ruiz, Vicki L. "Situating Stories: The Surprising Consequences of Oral History." *Oral History Review* 25, no. 1–2 (Summer/Fall 1998): 71–80

Sangster, Joan. *Earning Respect: The Lives of Working Women in Small-Town Ontario, 1920–1960.* Toronto: University of Toronto Press, 1995

– *Transforming Labour: Women and Work in Postwar Canada.* Toronto: University of Toronto Press, 2010

Schlabach, Theron F. *War, Peace and Social Conscience: Guy F. Hershberger and Mennonite Ethics.* Scottdale, PA and Waterloo, ON: Herald Press, 2009

Schultz, Thom. "The Rise of the Dones." 12 November 2014. http://holy-soup.com/2014/11/12/the-rise-of-the-dones/ (accessed 7 October 2015)

Schultz-Janzen, Jane. "To Strike or Not to Strike: First-hand Reflection." *The Conrad Grebel Review* 16, no. 1 (Winter 1998): 31–5

Shaw, Randy. *Beyond the Fields: Cesar Chavez, the UFW, and the Struggle for Justice in the 21st Century.* Berkeley: University of California Press, 2008

Sheftel, Anna, and Stacey Zembrzycki. "Only Human: A Reflection on the Ethical and Methodological Challenges of Working with 'Difficult' Stories." *Oral History Review* 37, no. 2 (Summer/Fall 2010): 191–214

Shopes, Linda. "Commentary: Sharing Authority." *The Oral History Review* 30, no. 1 (Winter–Spring 2003): 103–10

Sombart, Werner. *Why Is There No Socialism in the United States?* Translated by Patricia M. Hocking and C.T. Husbands. White Plains, NY: International Arts and Sciences Press, 1976

Sorkin, Andrew Ross. *Too Big to Fail: The Inside Story of How Wall Street and Washington Fought to Save the Financial System – and Themselves.* New York: Penguin, 2009

Srigley, Katrina. "Stories of Strife? Remembering the Great Depression." Special Issue "Remembering Family, Analyzing Home: Oral History and the Family," *Oral History Forum d'histoire orale* 29 (2009): 1–20

Stark, Rodney. "Secularization, R.I.P." *Sociology of Religion* 60, no. 3 (Autumn 1999): 249–73

Steedman, Mercedes. *Angels of the Workplace: Women and the Construction of Gender Relations in the Canadian Clothing Industry, 1890–1940*. Toronto: Oxford University Press, 1997

Stepan-Norris, Judith, and Maurice Zeitlin. *Talking Union*. Urbana: University of Illinois Press, 1996

Stewart, James B. "Eight Days: The Battle to Save the American Financial System." *The New Yorker* (21 September 2009): 58–81

Strobel, Margaret. "Becoming a Historian, Being an Activist, and Thinking Archivally: Documents and Memory as Sources." *Journal of Women's History* 11, no. 1 (Spring 1999): 181–92

Stromquist, Shelton. "Review of Richards' *Union-Free America*." *International Review of Social History* 55, no. 1 (April 2010): 148–50

– *Solidarity and Survival: An Oral History of Iowa Labor in the Twentieth Century*. Iowa City: University of Iowa Press, 1993

Sutherland, John R., and Susan J. Van Weelden. "To Strike or Not to Strike: Job Action in the Context of Justice and Reconciliation." *The Conrad Grebel Review* 16, no. 1 (Winter 1998): 1–21

Sutton, William R. "Tied to the Whipping Post: New Labor History and Evangelical Artisans in the Early Republic." *Labor History* 36, no. 2 (1995): 251–81

Swatos, William H., Jr, and Kevin J. Christiano. "Secularization Theory: The Course of a Concept." *Sociology of Religion* 60, no. 3 (Autumn 1999): 209–28

Swierenga, Robert P. "The Little White Church: Religion in Rural America," *Agricultural History* 71, no. 4 (Autumn 1997): 415–41

Taksa, Lucy. "Retooling the Class Factory: Response 3: Family, Childhood and Identities: Working Class History from a Personalised Perspective." *Labour History* 82 (May 2002): 127–33

Thiessen, Janis. "Committed to Christ or Conformed to This World? Postwar Mennonite Responses to Labour Activism." *Studies in Religion/Sciences Religieuses* 36, no. 2 (June 2007): 317–38

– "Communism and Labor Unions: The Changing Perspectives of Mennonites in Canada and the United States." *Direction* 38, no. 1 (Spring 2009): 17–28

– "Faith and Factory: Russian Mennonite Workers in 20th Century Manitoba." Ph.D. diss., University of New Brunswick, 2006

– *Manufacturing Mennonites: Work and Religion in Post-War Manitoba.* Toronto: University of Toronto Press, 2013

– "Winnipeg's Palliser Furniture in the Context of Mennonite Views on Industrial Relations, 1974–1996." In *Prairie Metropolis: New Essays on Winnipeg Social History,* edited by Esyllt Jones and Gerald Friesen, 200–22. Winnipeg, MB: University of Manitoba Press, 2009

Thompson, E.P. *The Making of the English Working Class.* London: Penguin, 1963

– *Witness against the Beast: William Blake and the Moral Law.* New York: The New Press, 1993

Umble, John S. "Goshen College (Goshen, Indiana, USA)." *Global Anabaptist Mennonite Encyclopedia Online,* 1956. http://www.gameo.org/encyclopedia/contents/G67775.html (accessed 25 February 2011)

Urry, James. *None but Saints: The Transformation of Mennonite Life in Russia, 1789–1889.* New York: Hyperion Press, 1990

Valverde, Mariana. *The Age of Light, Soap, and Water: Moral Reform in English Canada, 1885–1925.* Toronto: McClelland and Stewart, 1991

Van Die, Marguerite. *An Evangelical Mind: Nathanael Burwash and the Methodist Tradition in Canada, 1839–1918.* Montreal: McGill-Queen's University Press, 1989

van Voss, Lex Heerma, and Marcel van der Linden, eds. *Class and Other Identities: Gender, Religion, and Ethnicity in the Writing of European Labour History.* New York: Berghahn Books, 2002

Vecoli, Rudy. "Prelates and Peasants: Italian Immigrants and the Catholic Church." *Journal of Social History* 2, no. 3 (Spring 1969): 217–68

Vinitzky-Seroussi, Vered, and Chana Teeger. "Unpacking the Unspoken: Silence in Collective Memory and Forgetting." *Social Forces* 88, no. 3 (March 2010): 1103–22

Vogt, Roy. "The Impact of Economic and Social Class on Mennonite Theology." In *Mennonite Images: Historical, Cultural, and Literary Essays Dealing with Mennonite Issues,* edited by Harry Loewen, 137–48. Winnipeg, MB: Hyperion Press, 1980

Volf, Miroslav. *Work in the Spirit: Toward a Theology of Work.* Eugene, OR: Wipf and Stock, 2001

von Plato, Alexander. "Contemporary Witnesses and the Historical Profession: Remembrance, Communicative Transmission, and Collective Memory in Qualitative History." *Oral History Forum d'histoire orale* 29 (2009): 1–27

Weber, Max. *The Protestant Ethic and the Spirit of Capitalism.* Translated by Talcott Parsons. New York: Charles Scribner, 1958

Wenger, Linden M., and Sam Steiner. "Fellowship of Concerned Mennonites." *Global Anabaptist Mennonite Encyclopedia Online,*

September 2009. http://www.gameo.org/encyclopedia/contents/F4552.html (accessed 14 September 2010)

WesPak. http://www.wespaksales.com/ (accessed 7 October 2015)

Westfall, William. *Religion/Culture: Comparative Canadian Studies.* Ottawa: Association for Canadian Studies, 1985

– *Two Worlds: The Protestant Culture of Nineteenth-Century Ontario.* Montreal: McGill-Queen's University Press, 1989

Williams, Raymond. *Keywords: A Vocabulary of Culture and Society.* New York: Oxford University Press, 1976

Williams, Roman R. "Space for God: Lived Religion at Work, Home, and Play." *Sociology of Religion* 71, no. 3 (2010): 257–79

Wilson, Bryan. *Religion in Secular Society.* Harmondsworth: Pelican, 1969

Wong, Alan. "Conversations for the Real World: Shared Authority, Self-Reflexivity, and Process in the Oral History Interview." *Journal of Canadian Studies* 43, no. 1 (Winter 2009): 239–58

Wuthnow, Robert. *After Heaven: Spirituality in America since the 1950s.* Berkeley and Los Angeles: University of California Press, 1998

– *Growing Up Religious: Christians and Jews and Their Journeys of Faith*. Boston: Beacon Press, 1999

– *Sharing the Journey: Support Groups and America's New Quest for Community.* New York: The Free Press, 1994

Yamane, David. "Secularization on Trial: In Defense of a Neosecularization Paradigm." *Journal for the Scientific Study of Religion* 36, no. 1 (March 1997): 109–22

Yates, Michael D. "The Rise and Fall of the United Farm Workers." *Monthly Review* 62, no. 1 (May 2010): 51–9

Yow, Valerie. "'Do I Like Them Too Much?': Effects of the Oral History Interview on the Interviewer and Vice-Versa." *Oral History Review* 24, no. 1 (Summer 1997): 55–79

Zeman, Jarold K., ed. *Baptists in Canada: Search for Identity amidst Diversity.* Burlington, ON: Welch, 1980

Zemon Davis, Natalie, and Randolph Starn, eds. "Introduction." *Representations: Special Issue on Memory and Counter-Memory* 26 (Spring 1989): 1–6

Index